Y0-BBD-886

"And God saw every thing that he had made, and behold, it was very good. And the evening and the morning were the sixth day" (Genesis 1:31).

Massanutten Peak Near Harrisonburg, Virginia

Christian Light Social Studies Series

LIVING TOGETHER ON GOD'S EARTH

"I have made the earth and created man upon it" (Isaiah 45:12).

A Christian text on world geography and social studies

Writer: John D. Martin
Study Questions: Etta Martin

Editorial Committee:
Charles L. Heatwole
John D. Risser
Sanford L. Shank

Cover Credits:

Temple ruins:	Erwin C. "Bud" Nielson, Tucson, AZ
Italian market:	©1996, by Blair Seitz. All rights reserved.
Indian fisherman:	Sterling Beachy
Bucket Brigade:	David Miller

CHRISTIAN LIGHT PUBLICATIONS, INC.
Harrisonburg, Virginia 22801-1212

Introduction for Adults 3
Student Introduction 4

I. GOD'S EARTH
This Is God's Earth 5
God's Earth Supplies Our Needs 9
Living Together 17
Learning About Maps 37

II. COMMUNITIES OF BIBLE TIMES
Egypt, Land of the Nile River 45
God Changes Communities in Egypt 50
The Sinai Peninsula, Bridge Between Continents 75
God's Nation in the Desert 79
Palestine, Land of Two Seas .101
Jerusalem, a City Community in Palestine 109
Greece, a Land Between Seas 135
The Two Communities at Corinth 139

III. COMMUNITIES WHERE CHRISTIANS HAVE LIVED
Netherlands, Land From Under the Sea 165
The Story of Amsterdam 173
America, the New World 199
Philadelphia, the City of Brotherly Love 207

IV. USING GOD'S EARTH
Israel, an Old and New Country 237
Using Natural Resources in Israel 245

Glossary 270
Index 282
Scripture Index 288

Copyright ©1974
Christian Light Publications, Inc.
Revised 1978, 1996

ISBN: 0-87813-915-X

Lithographed in U.S.A.

INTRODUCTION FOR ADULTS

The social studies represent a particularly crucial study in the school curriculum. This is because such a study assumes the task of teaching boys and girls a complete spectrum of social values. These values help build a philosophy which influences students throughout life.

If the philosophy of a social studies curriculum is God-centered, each text in the series becomes a powerful tool for molding lives into the likeness of Jesus Christ. On the other hand, if the social values are cleverly distorted, a social studies text can be the most devastating part of the total curriculum and a direct cause for children of Christian parents to be spoiled through "philosophy and vain deceit."

The standard social studies textbooks being published today are humanistic. That is to say, they are man-centered. The philosophy of these texts builds on the assumption that man is innately good, and that through the persistent efforts of modern science, he will eventually solve all of his problems. According to this philosophy, the world is moving toward a utopia where men will have learned to coexist in an uninterrupted peace. The cancer of this demonic philosophy has crept from the classroom into the Christian church, and we have only seen the beginning of the havoc to follow in the form of arrogant individualism, disrespect for Biblical authority and traditional values, and a situation approach to ethics.

The most modern social studies texts now boldly assert the concepts of humanism that were peddled only cautiously in the textbooks of yesterday. Alarmed by these emboldened attacks on the roots of society and Christian faith, Christian Light Publications has been moved by God to the preparation of a social studies curriculum based upon the revealed value system of God's Word.

Living Together on God's Earth is the first in a series of Bible-centered social studies texts published by Christian Light Publications. This first text aims at the third-grade level, but could be used profitably for older students if such use is preferred.

The editors and writers of this new social studies series have labored to build their curriculum upon the solid principles of the Bible. In contrast to other social studies texts, this series assumes the depravity of man since his fall in the Garden of Eden. It develops a system of social values based on God's revealed Word, recognizing the New Testament as God's final revelation to men. The way of salvation through Jesus Christ is presented as the only remedy for man's present deplorable condition both individually and socially. The spread of this Gospel of salvation is presented as the responsibility of the Christian community.

The Christian Light Publications social studies series also recognizes God's hand in history as well as His sovereignty over present developments on the world scene. The series highlights God's blessings upon people who obey and honor Him even when facing persecution and death. In this series the remnant of God's people throughout history is traced as a bright ray in the history of mankind who, as a whole, are plunging ever deeper into the morass of spiritual blindness and depraved humanistic ambitions. The student is encouraged to follow in the train of the faithful followers of God who stand on the unchanging values of His Word in an aimlessly changing world.

Living Together on God's Earth develops a basic understanding of communities. The student first sees his community as one small part of God's earth. He then learns how God works in communities caring for His children. Each section clearly pictures the duty of the Christian in a variety of situations and cultures. Using Israel as an example, the last unit emphasizes the responsibility of people to use wisely the natural resources God has placed in communities. The author draws from the Scriptures God's directives for the use of the land He has given mankind.

There are over 150 direct quotations from the Bible in the body of the text of *Living Together on God's Earth*. The reference for each verse is clearly indicated in the margins.

This textbook includes pictures and illustrations carefully chosen to supplement its Christian emphasis.

An additional feature helpful to both student and teacher is the division of the chapters into lessons—each lesson representing material for two day's work. Thought-provoking questions conclude each section.

We trust that this textbook will help meet the need for a Bible-centered, Christ-honoring social studies program in the elementary school. We send to you *Living Together on God's Earth* with the prayer that God might be praised and that the children we teach may better learn to love our Creator.

Student Introduction

Dear Boys and Girls,

How would you like to live all by yourself? In some ways it might seem like a good idea. But in most ways it would never work. God knew this. That's why He put many people around you. You spend much of your time working, playing, and worshiping God with these people. God planned for you to live together with people this way.

You like to work at home doing jobs for your parents. You can have happy times studying the Bible and praying with others who live in your home. You enjoy singing and working with other boys and girls in church and school. God wants you to live together with others and be happy.

Are the people around you happy all the time? Are you happy all the time? What makes people unhappy? Does God have anything to say about unhappy ways of living together? What about the mean things that happen in our towns and cities? Does God have answers for the troubles people have living together?

Yes, God does know all about the problems people have living with each other. He knows about the troubles people have in towns and cities. God gives the answers for these problems in the Bible.

In this book, you will study what God has to say about living together. You will see how God sometimes changes the plans people make. These changes help people stop and think about God's way.

At the beginning, you will read about the way God wants people in a family to live together. Next, you will read about towns and cities. You will find Bible verses to help you see what God has to say about people living together in these places. You will see the trouble people have when they disobey and do not follow God's way.

This book tells about some of the ways people lived together in Bible times. Perhaps you have read in the Bible about Joseph, Moses, and Paul. Do you know how these people lived together with others around them? In your reading you will find answers for this question and many others. You will also learn about the way some people have lived together since Bible times.

As you study, you will see how God wants you to live with others. Your study will also help you understand how God wants you to use the earth He made for you to enjoy.

Turn to page 270. Beginning here you will find some things to help you study this book. First you see the *glossary*. It tells you what some of the harder words in the book mean. Now turn to page 282. Here is the *index*. It tells you where you can find out about people, places, and things in *Living Together on God's Earth*. The *Scripture Index* is on page 288. It tells you where you can find all the Bible verses in the book.

Use your glossary and index often. They will help you to learn more. Before you use the glossary and index, be sure to read carefully the directions given at the beginning of each part.

God bless you,

John D. Martin

" . . . The earth also is thine: as for the world and the fulness thereof, thou hast founded them" (Psalm 89:11).

Men took this picture of the earth from a spaceship many thousands of miles away from God's earth. This picture shows the earth's ball shape.

Photo: NASA

This Is God's Earth

FLAT OR ROUND?

You live on a very small part of God's earth. God's earth is so large that none of us has seen every part of it.

Many years ago, people thought the earth was flat. Men would not sail their ships very far from land. Sailors were afraid they would drop off the edge of the earth.

Does the earth seem flat to you? The above picture of the earth was taken from a spaceship thousands of miles away from the earth. It shows that the earth is shaped like a ball.

Something shaped like a ball is called a **sphere** (sfir). The earth is a sphere. God created this sphere called the earth. The Bible says, "He hath made the earth by his power." **Jeremiah 10:12a**

God hung the earth in space. "He stretcheth out the north over the empty place, and hangeth the earth upon nothing." **Job 26:7**
The earth is a huge sphere hanging in space.

5

A MODEL OF THE EARTH

We can learn a lot about the sphere we live on by looking at a **globe.** A globe is a model of the real earth. It is a small sphere that turns on a rod.

Look at your classroom globe. You will see that it turns around points at the top and bottom. These points are called **poles.**

God set the earth turning around its poles as your globe does. The Bible says, "The north and the south thou hast created them." The pole at the top of the earth is called the **North Pole.** The other pole is called the **South Pole.**

Psalm 89:12

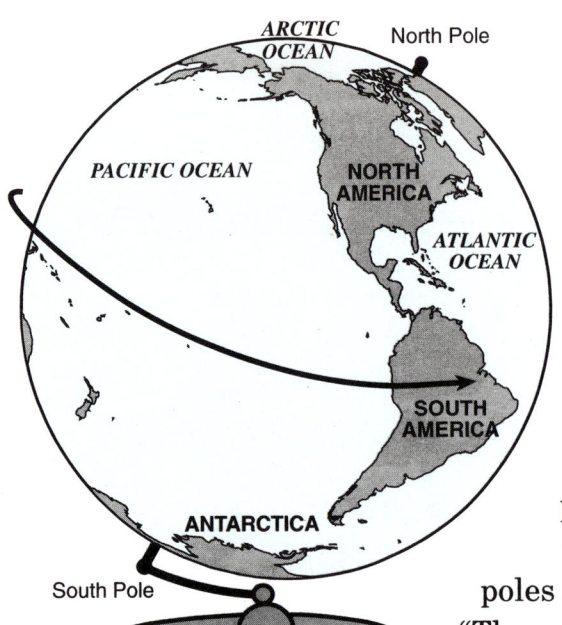

This picture of a globe shows the shape of God's earth. What else can you learn from the globe?

THE EARTH FOR MAN

Psalm 115:16 God made the earth to be a home for people. The Bible tells us, "The heaven, even the heavens, are the LORD's: but the earth hath he given to the children of men."

Genesis 1:2a At first people could not live on the earth. "The earth was without form [shape], and void [empty]." There was no dry land. Water covered everything.

Genesis 1:9 God divided the water from the land. "And God said, Let the waters under the heaven be gathered together unto one place, and let the dry land appear: and it was so." Our earth now has bodies of land and bodies of water.

Use your globe to see where there is water on our earth. The largest bodies of water are called **oceans** (ō´ shənz). Find four oceans on your classroom globe or on the globes pictured on this page and page 7.

You can see many smaller bodies of water on the earth. Some small bodies of water are called **seas.** The

Island　　　　　Ocean　　　　　　　　Continent　　　　　　Sea

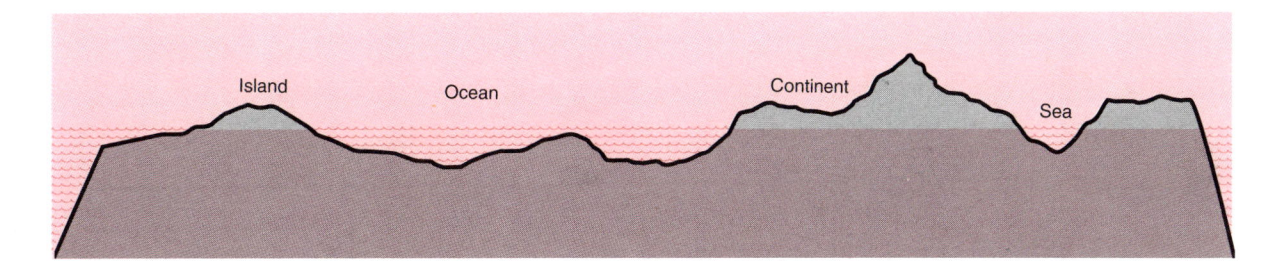

Mediterranean Sea is the largest sea on the earth. Find it on your globe. Most stories in the Bible took place in lands around this sea.

The largest bodies of land on the earth are called **continents** (kän´ tən ənts). Find seven continents on your globe or on the globe pictures on this page and page 6. Say their names. Don't forget the continent at the South Pole.

Did you see smaller bodies of land surrounded by water? These are called **islands** (ī´ ləndz). The largest island on the earth is Greenland. Look for it on your globe near the North Pole.

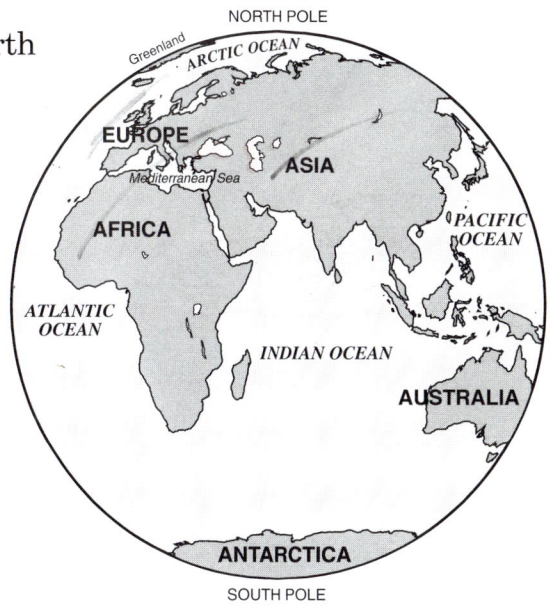

Find five continents and three oceans on this map.

SHOW YOUR KNOWLEDGE

1. Why didn't sailors travel very far from land years ago?
2. Which thing is most like the shape of the earth?
    a. a table
    b. a ball
    c. a hill
3. What new word did we learn to tell about the shape of the earth?
4. God created the earth by His _____ and hung the earth in _____ .
5. What is a model of the earth called?
6. What is the name for the top point of the earth?
7. What is the name for the bottom point of the earth?
8. Why did God make the earth?

9. Write the word that means:
   a. the largest bodies of water
   b. the largest bodies of land
   c. small bodies of water
   d. small bodies of land surrounded by water
10. List four oceans. Use the globe pictures.
11. What is the name of the largest sea on the earth?
12. List the earth's seven continents.

SHARE YOUR KNOWLEDGE

1. In what ways is a globe like the earth? In what ways is it different?
2. On the globe picture, move your finger toward the North Pole. If your finger were a man walking on the earth, we would say, "He is going north." Now move your finger toward the other pole of the globe. If your finger were a man walking, he would be going _____ .
3. Read Isaiah 40:22. What did God tell people long ago about the shape of the earth?
4. What name does the Bible give for the Mediterranean Sea in Joshua 15:12?

Planting fields this way is called strip farming. How does strip farming prevent erosion?

Photo: USDA

God's Earth Supplies Our Needs

God knew that people would need food, clothing, and shelter. He placed water, soil, plants, and other things here to supply our needs. We call them **natural resources** (na´ chə rəl rē´ sōr səz), because God created them. We only use them.

EVERYBODY NEEDS WATER

Water is one of the earth's most important natural resources. Without water, you could live only about seven or eight days. Your body needs almost one-half gallon of water every day.

Plants need water, too. The place where you live would be a **desert** without water.

God's earth has more water than land. But most of the earth's water is in salty oceans or in salty lakes and seas. Salt water is not fit to drink. Plants cannot use it. People, plants, and animals must have lots of **fresh water.**

Many people get fresh water from wells. Some wells dry up when there has been no rain for a while. Finally there is a heavy rain. Water soaks down through the soil to streams under the ground. Dry wells soon have water again. Rains give wells their fresh water.

All of the earth's fresh water comes from rains. Rain waters fields of thirsty plants. Rains fill streams and rivers with fresh water. God sends the rain. "[He] giveth rain upon the earth, and sendeth waters upon the fields." We must trust Him for this important natural resource.

Job 5:10

This picture shows how rain gets to wells under the ground. Can you find the topsoil in the picture?

SOIL FOR CROPS

Soil is another important natural resource. Plants grow in the soil. "And God said, Let the earth bring forth grass, the herb yielding seed, and the fruit tree yielding fruit." God made soil to supply food for all people and animals.

Genesis 1:11a

Good soil is a mixture of many things. Tiny pieces of rock make up much of this mixture. Plants and animals become a part of the soil after they die. "All go unto one place; all are of the dust, and all turn to dust again." This dead material in the soil is called **humus** (hyü´ məs).

Ecclesiastes 3:20

10

Like a sponge, humus holds water near the top of the soil for plants. Humus also stores up important plant foods.

Crops grow best in the top layer of soil called **topsoil**. Topsoil is only about one foot deep in most places.

Sometimes wind, or the water from a heavy rain, carries the topsoil off a piece of land. The carrying away of soil by wind or water is called **erosion** (i ro´ zhən).

When erosion takes topsoil away, it is hard to replace. But much erosion can be prevented. The roots of trees and plants can help to hold the soil. Wise farmers keep their hillsides covered with forests and crops to save the topsoil.

SHOW YOUR KNOWLEDGE

1. Something that God made and placed on the earth for man to use is called a _____ .
2. Both people and _____ need water to live.
3. A place that is too dry to grow crops is called a _____ .
4. The earth has more:
    a. water
    b. land
5. Most of the earth's water is:
    a. salty
    b. fresh water
6. The fresh water in wells comes from _____ which soaks down through the soil.
7. Besides water, what other natural resource do plants need to grow?
8. Good soil is a mixture of tiny pieces of _____ and dead plant and animal material called _____ .
9. List two things humus does.
10. What is the name for the top layer of soil where plants grow best?
11. Name two things that cause erosion.
12. What can farmers do to prevent erosion?

11

SHARE YOUR KNOWLEDGE

1. In what ways have you used water today? How many more uses of water can you think of?
2. Why can't ocean water be used to water the earth's deserts?
3. Read Acts 14:17. List three things God gives us by sending rain.
4. Read Genesis 3:17, 18. Which natural resource did God change by placing a curse on it? Why did He change it? How is it different now?

DIGGING FOR RESOURCES

Men dig deep into the earth to find other natural resources. One natural resource from under the ground is rocks. Some rocks are pure white. Others are different colors.

Men drilled this well into the earth and found a sticky black oil. At first the oil shot into the air. Finally workers were able to make it flow into a pipe. Why did men want this smelly, sticky oil?

Men cut white blocks of stone from this quarry. These stones are used for building.

Job 28:2

Men cut these rocks from the earth in large blocks. These blocks can be used for beautiful buildings.

Some rocks have **metals** in them. Such rocks are called **ores**. "Iron is taken out of the earth, and brass is molten [melted] out of the stone." Men get the metals out by heating the ores in large furnaces.

Iron is one of the most important metals. Men use iron to make a stronger metal called **steel**. Steel is used in building bridges, machines, cars, and many other things we use every day.

Photo: Ryan Photographic Service

Men use these windmills to produce electricity. What natural resource do windmills use?

Photo: Lloyd Hartzler

This picture shows what can happen when people are careless in the woods.

Copper metal comes from copper ore. Men make pennies, electric wire, and many other things from copper.

Men dig wells deep into the earth to get out a sticky, black liquid. This liquid is used to make gasoline and oil. These products keep cars, trucks, buses, trains, and factories running.

Some factories and homes use coal for fuel. Men dig **mines** into the earth to get coal.

USING GOD'S EARTH

God filled the earth with riches for us to use. "O LORD, how manifold [many] are thy works! In wisdom hast thou made them all: the earth is full of thy riches."

Psalm 104:24

Every day we breathe God's air. We use water from His rivers and underground streams. We eat fish from God's lakes, rivers, and oceans.

God's animals give us milk and meat. We use God's soil, water, air, and sunshine to grow the plants we need for food and for making clothing.

We use wood from God's trees to build houses and make furniture. Even the paper in this book was made from wood.

14

From the sticky sap of trees, men make paint, rubber, tar, and many other things. "The trees of the LORD are full of **sap**."

Trees supply us with fruits to eat. The Bible says, "The tree of the field is man's life."

Every natural resource belongs to God. "The earth is the LORD's, and the fulness thereof." How does God want us to use His property?

God trusts us to be His **stewards** (stü´ ərdz). A steward does not own property. He watches over the property of someone else.

A steward must use the owner's property carefully and wisely. "It is required in stewards, that a man be found faithful." The owner is displeased with an unfaithful steward who wastes or ruins his property.

We are stewards of God's earth. God expects us to take good care of His natural resources. Look at the pictures on pages 13 and 14. Which show the work of good stewards? Which show bad **stewardship**?

Psalm 104:16a
Deuteronomy 20:19b
Psalm 24:1a

1 Corinthians 4:2

SHOW YOUR KNOWLEDGE

1. Some natural resources are found under the _____ .
2. Rocks that have metals in them are called _____.
3. How do men get the metals out of ores?
4. Name the metal that is used to make steel.
5. Gasoline and oil are fuels for cars, trains, and factories. Find the name of a fuel that comes from a mine.
6. List three things that can be made from the sap of trees.
7. Every natural resource belongs to _____ and He wants us to be careful _____ of His property.
8. Make two lists on your paper with these headings: Natural Resources, Man-Made. Put these words in the right lists: cars, air, soil, paper, rocks, trees, animals, pennies, furniture, water, coal, clothing, iron, fruits, wire, sunshine, steel, sap, copper, buildings.

SHARE YOUR KNOWLEDGE

1. Can you think of some natural resources that are not listed in number 8 on page 15? Add them to your list.
2. How can we be good stewards of each of these: water, soil, wood, gasoline?
3. Study Psalm 50:10. What natural resource does this verse tell about?
4. Isaiah 44:15 tells ways men can use wood. List three of these ways. Put a check beside one way wood is used unwisely.

"If it be possible, as much as lieth in you, live peaceably with all men" (Romans 12:18).

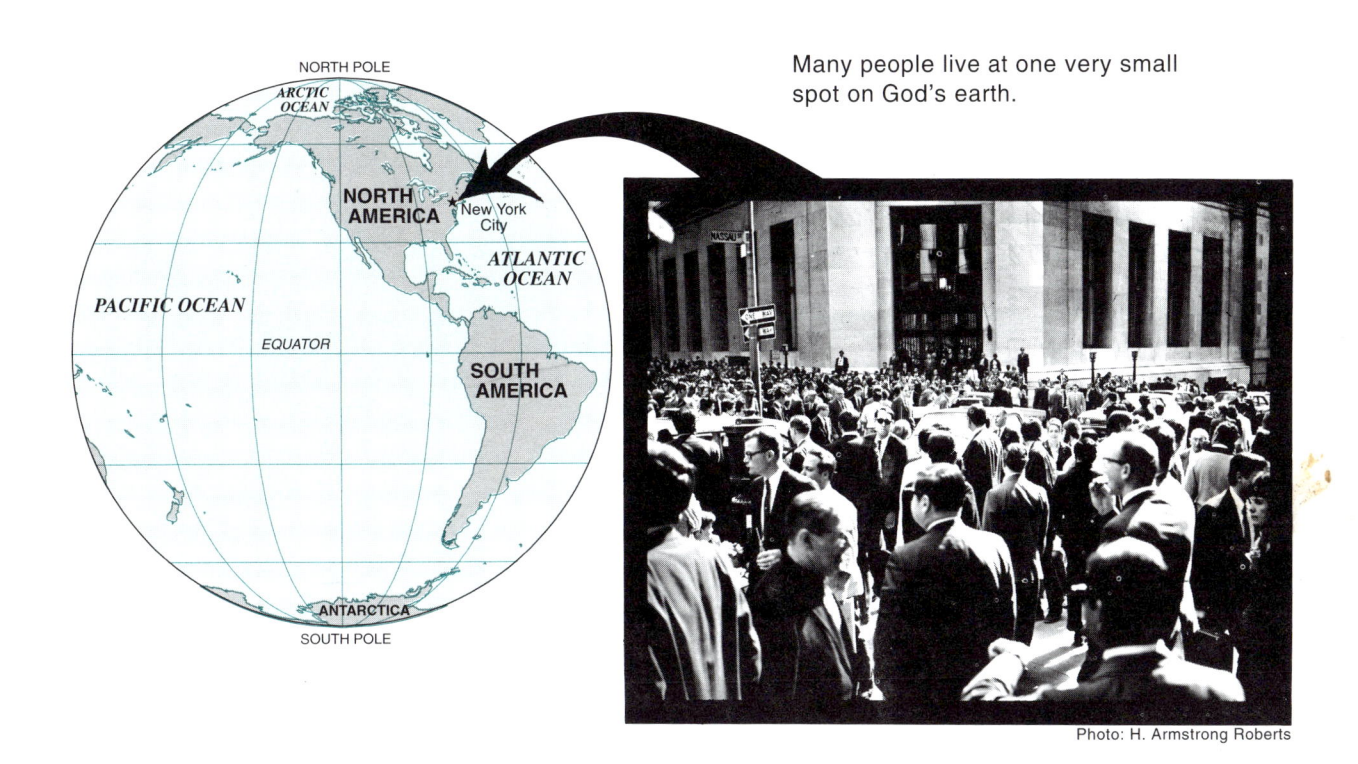

Many people live at one very small spot on God's earth.

Living Together

Many people live on God's earth. Suppose everyone could join hands and stand in a long line. The line would reach around the world over 150 times! God did not plan a lonely world.

In the beginning God created Adam.

And God said, "It is not good that the man should be alone; I will make him an help meet [fit] for him" (Genesis 2:18b).

God created animals to help Adam. He watched as Adam

Genesis 2:18-20

Pets make good friends. How is sharing with a family in worship even better?

Photo: Florence Sharp

named each one. Perhaps the animals made good pets. But they could not think like Adam. They could not share his kind of love.

Genesis 2:21-24

Adam needed someone like himself. God made another person. Adam called her Eve. The name *Eve* means "a person who gives life." Together Adam and Eve gave life to the first children.

Adam no longer was lonely. He could share his love and thoughts with his **family.**

Adam and Eve's family was the first **community.** A community is a group of people living together. Families are the most important communities in the world.

GOD'S PLAN FOR FAMILY COMMUNITIES

God created people so He could share His love and thoughts with them. "This people have I formed [made] for myself."

Isaiah 43:21a

The Marsh family enjoyed sharing with God together in **family worship**.

"God shares with us through His Word," Father Marsh said as he opened his Bible. "Tonight we will study His plan for families. In Genesis 2:24, God tells us how families begin."

18

The Marshes opened their Bibles.

Mother read, "Therefore shall a man leave his father and his mother, and shall cleave [be joined] unto his wife: and they shall be one flesh." **Genesis 2:24**

Father explained, "A family begins when one man and woman get married. They promise to love each other and live together. They leave their homes to begin a new home of their own. God hears their promises," Father went on. "He joins them together for the rest of their lives. They become a new family."

Ruth spoke up. "What about the Len family next door?" she asked. "Today Alice told me her father went off to marry someone else."

Father turned to Matthew 19:6b. "What therefore God hath joined together, let not man put asunder [apart]," he read.

"God joined Mr. and Mrs. Len," Father pointed out. "Mr. Len had no right to break his marriage. He sinned by marrying someone else."

"The Len family had an unhappy home because they did not follow God's plan," added Mother. "The Bible gives God's plan for happy homes in Colossians 3:18-20."

"We'll take turns reading," said Father. "Each of us will explain a part of God's plan."

Mother read, "'Wives, submit yourselves unto your own husbands, as it is fit in the Lord.'" **Colossians 3:18-20**

"Father is the leader in our family," Mother began. "We talk things over together. But God wants me to obey what Father plans." Mother squeezed Father's hand and smiled.

Father read next. "'Husbands, love your wives, and be not bitter against them.'"

"God wants me to plan things which show my love to Mother," Father explained. "Doing this makes Mother's part easier."

James read last. "'Children, obey your parents in all things: for this is well pleasing unto the Lord.'"

"I can see how God's plan works," he said. "Everyone in a family must obey God. Mothers should obey fathers. And children should obey both parents."

"That's right," said Father. "Giving in to others is God's plan for order and happiness in family communities."

SHOW YOUR KNOWLEDGE

1. Why did God create the animals? What two things could the animals not do?
2. Tell what a community is.
3. Why did God create people?
4. We learn about God's plan for families when we read the _____ .

SHARE YOUR KNOWLEDGE

1. In what ways was Eve a helper fit for Adam?
2. How long does God plan for a father and mother to live together?
3. What must each of these do to have a happy home: father, mother, children?

LEARNING GOD'S WAY

Father Marsh had a question. "Ruth, who was your first teacher?" he asked.

Ruth looked puzzled. "Don't you remember?" she replied. "My first teacher was Miss Trace, the first grade teacher at Oak Ridge School."

"Really!" Father's eyes twinkled. "Maybe we should learn more about God's plan from Deuteronomy 6:6, 7."

Quietly everyone read, "And these words, which I command thee this day, shall be in thine heart: and thou shalt teach them diligently unto thy children, and shalt talk of them when thou sittest in thine house, and when thou walkest by the way, and when thou liest down, and when thou risest up."

"You see," said Mother, "Father and I were really your first teachers. God planned for our home to be your first school."

Father added, "Parents are to teach their children to love, worship, and obey God. The children will grow up and many will start new homes. They should pass the teaching on to their children. In this way, God planned for everyone in the world to learn about Him." Father continued, "Now you can see why families are the most important communities. God planned that every person in the world should come from a family. Some families take God's way. Other families try to do as they please. Their children often grow up without learning about God."

LARGE COMMUNITIES

The Marsh family lives in a neighborhood with other families. The Len family is one of their neighbors.

Sometimes the Marsh family says, "This is our community." Their community is a group of family communities living together.

We have heard and known . . . our fathers have told us.

We will not hide them from their children.

God's Plan for Parents
Psalm 78:1-6

. . .They should make them known to their children.

Who should arise and declare them to their children.

The Marsh family lives in a **rural** (rür′ əl) **community.** Most of the people in their community live on farms. Families do not live close together in a rural community.

Rural communities do not have large stores. The Marsh family goes shopping in the city of Greenville. Greenville is an **urban community**. In an urban community, families live very close together.

Rural and urban communities.

You have learned God's plan for happy family communities. God also wants rural and urban communities to be happy. Next, you will learn about His plan for large communities.

SHOW YOUR KNOWLEDGE

1. What is the most important thing for parents to teach their children?
2. In a rural community the families:
    a. do not live close together
    b. live close together
3. In an urban community the families:
    a. do not live close together
    b. live close together

SHARE YOUR KNOWLEDGE

1. Why are families the most important communities in the world?
2. Read Deuteronomy 6:6, 7 again. What must parents do before they can teach their children? In one sentence, tell how much time they should spend teaching.

How do government leaders, school crossing guards, and speed limit signs help make a community a safe place to live?

GOD'S PLAN FOR LARGE COMMUNITIES

The Marsh family was talking about something that happened in Greenville.

"There was a bad accident on Main Street this morning," Father reported. "A driver tried to dash through a red light."

"Why?" asked James.

Father shook his head. "Perhaps he was in a hurry. Some people think they may break rules or **laws** when it doesn't suit them to obey."

"Who makes the laws for Greenville?" James wanted to know.

"Leaders in the city **government** (gə´ vərn mənt) make laws for our community," replied Father. "God gives leaders the right to make rules. He knows laws help communities to have order."

Romans 13:1b

From the Bible Father read, "For there is no power but of God: the powers that be [governments] are ordained of God."

"'Ordained of God' means God sets up the governments," Father explained.

James' eyes opened wide. "Do you mean people are really disobeying God when they disobey government leaders?" he asked.

24

"Exactly!" answered Father. "The Bible says, 'Whosoever therefore resisteth [goes against] the power, resisteth the **ordinance** (ȯrd´ nəns) [order] of God.' **Romans 13:2a**

"In this verse, God commands us to obey government laws," Father pointed out. "God wants us to **respect** government leaders. **Policemen** (pə lēs´ men) are a part of the government. They help to see that laws are obeyed."

Ruth had a question. "What if government leaders make laws against worshiping and obeying God? Must we obey their laws and disobey God?"

"Who can answer Ruth's question?" asked Father.

Everyone thought hard. Finally James spoke up.

"I remember a Bible story about that," he said. "Some leaders tried to keep the disciples from telling about Jesus. But Peter said, 'We ought to obey God rather than men.' Doesn't that mean God's laws come first?" **Acts 5:29b**

"Yes," answered Father. "But God wants us to obey all laws that do not go against Him. Obeying government laws is God's plan for order and happiness in rural and urban communities."

SHOW YOUR KNOWLEDGE

1. Who makes the laws for a community?
2. Who gives the leaders the right to make rules?
3. Why do communities need laws?
4. Who are people really disobeying when they do not obey community laws?
5. What is the work of policemen?
6. When is the only time God allows us to disobey a community law?

SHARE YOUR KNOWLEDGE

1. List three laws people are to obey in your community. What happens when people disobey these laws? What happens when they obey?
2. Does your community have a **mayor**? Ask your parents to tell you his name.

GOOD AND EVIL

After talking with Father, James did more thinking about government. That evening in family worship, he had more questions.

"Why must God set up a government in every community?" he asked. "Couldn't people learn to live together without laws?"

"You can help to find the answer to that question," said Father. "First, let's think about the trouble on Main Street this morning. Tell me why the man did not wait his turn at the street crossing this morning."

"I know," said Ruth. "He was too selfish to wait on other

And as ye would that men should do to you, do ye also to them likewise.
Luke 6:31

If everyone obeyed God's "Golden Rule,"
how would communities be better?

people. A law can help to make people do what is right, even if they don't want to."

"Very good," said Father. "Selfishness is the problem. Now, who can think of another word for selfishness?"

"Sin," Mother replied.

"Yes," said Father. "And the Bible says, 'All have sinned.' That means there is sin in every community." **Romans 3:23a**

Father went on. "The Bible also tells us that 'one sinner destroyeth much good.' Selfishness causes people to steal, lie, and hurt others. Every community needs a government to keep sin from spoiling it." **Ecclesiastes 9:18b**

"The government must force some people to obey," said Mother. "God wants Christians to help another way. He wants Christians to **witness** to sinners about Jesus who can change their hearts. Jesus helps people want to do what is right."

"Christians have a big job," said Father. "In Matthew 5:13, Jesus tells us, 'Ye are the salt of the earth.' Salt helps to keep food from spoiling. Christians must help to save communities from evil by bringing sinners to Jesus." **Matthew 5:13**

SHOW YOUR KNOWLEDGE

1. Why does every community need a government?
2. How does the government get some people to obey?
3. How do Christians help communities in a different way?

SHARE YOUR KNOWLEDGE

1. What word did Jesus use to describe Christians? What does this word tell about the job of Christians in each community?
2. Study Romans 13:3. Who should be afraid of a good government? Who will be praised by a good government?

DIFFERENT COMMUNITIES

One summer Brother Marsh took a long trip to visit other lands. He saw strange ways of doing things in different places. Ways of doing things are called **customs.**

Brother Marsh visited families who had different eating customs. In one country, the people sat on the ground and ate with their fingers.

Brother Marsh saw many different kinds of houses. He decided that the natural resources in a community made a difference in the way people built their houses.

These people used animal skins to make a place to live.

If there were many trees in a community, people used wood to build their houses. Which picture shows a house built in an area where hardly any trees or grass grows?

Brother Marsh noticed that **climate** (klī′ mət) is another thing that makes a difference in the ways people live. Climate is the usual kind of weather in a place over the years.

The people in Japan eat with small sticks called chopsticks. In what other ways are their eating customs different from yours?

These houses are along a river. Why do you think they are built so high off the ground?

Banana trees and many other plants grow where the sun shines hot most of the time.

Many plants cannot grow in the cold place where this man lives. What kind of food does he find to eat?

All places do not have the same climate. The climate is hot in places where the sun shines bright most of the time. In some places the climate is cold.

Where it is hot most of the time, people may live in grass houses. Find the picture of houses built along a river. What is the climate like there? What natural resources make the people decide to build their houses like this?

Climate also helps to decide what people eat. In hot climates, plants grow well. Meat spoils quickly in the hot sun. People in hot climates have a lot of plant foods in their **diet**.

On his trip, Brother Marsh used different ways of getting

A camel is an important means of transportation in a desert. In a city, a bicycle can be an easy way to get around.

29

Each picture shows a person from a different **race.** Brother Marsh saw people like these. What differences do you see?

from place to place. Natural resources helped to decide these customs of **transportation.** If there was much water, people traveled by boat.

Climate also made a difference in how people traveled. Find the picture that shows how people in a cold climate might travel.

Dogsleds are still used for transportation in some places in the Far North.

SHOW YOUR KNOWLEDGE

1. Which two things help to make customs different between communities?
    a. natural resources
    b. races
    c. climate
2. People who live in a forest will probably build their houses of:
    a. stone
    b. animal skins
    c. wood
3. Why do people in hot climates have a lot of plant foods in their diet?
4. Which way of travel would you use if you lived in a desert?
    a. boat
    b. camel
    c. dogsled

SHARE YOUR KNOWLEDGE

1. Study Jeremiah 10:1-3. What word does God use to describe heathen customs? In your glossary find the meaning of the word you found in Jeremiah 10:1-3.
2. List some customs in your community. Are all customs good?

LIVING TOGETHER IN A COMMUNITY

Father Marsh said to the family, "Now you have seen customs in different communities. I have a question. Do people in one community all have the same customs?"

Ruth said, "The Hobson family has a custom we don't have. They stop work in the middle of the morning to have tea and cake. They also have a tea break in the afternoon."

"I know why," said James. "The Hobsons (häb´ sənz) moved to our country from Europe. Jerry Hobson told me everyone has tea breaks over there."

"That's right," said Father. "People move from place to place. They carry customs with them.

These people have a tea break every morning and noon.

These men are helping their neighbor build a barn. What do you think of this custom?

These people from different races all live together in the same community.

31

Each community has a mixture of customs from other places."

"Our community has a mixture of people too," said James. "The Wang Fu (wäng fü´) family moved here from China. The Koshys (kō´ zhēz) came from India. These families belong to different races, don't they?"

"Yes," replied Father. "They look different in some ways. But let's see what the Bible says about races of people."

Acts 17:26a

Father read, "'[God]... hath made of one blood all nations of men for to dwell on all the face of the earth.'

We are thankful for community workers who carry messages to our homes.

"This verse tells us that God made all races very much alike," Father explained. "He did not make any race better than the others."

Mother added, "God knew we would enjoy differences. Different customs and races of people in a community help make life interesting."

"We should always be kind to people of other races," said

How do rescue workers and firefighters help their communities?

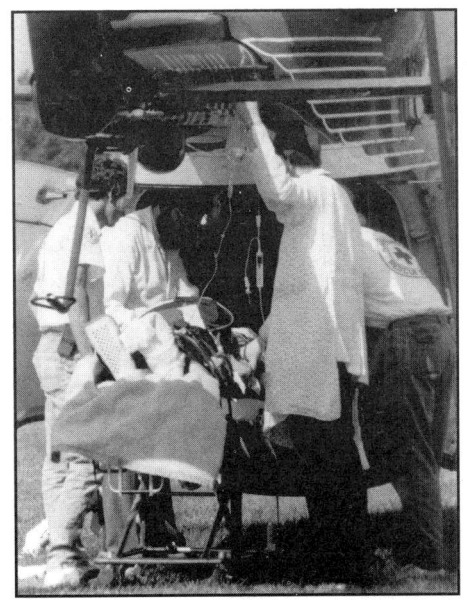

Mother. "We should also respect good customs that are different from ours. But we must watch out for bad customs. In His Word, God says, 'Thou shalt not follow a multitude [group] to do evil.' Christians must never copy evil customs."

Exodus 23:2

Father said, "We must follow the Bible way of living. This means our customs will be different from any evil customs in our community."

WORKING TOGETHER

Brother Marsh is a **dairy farmer**. He grows crops to feed a **herd** of cows. The cows produce milk to sell. A truck comes every day from Greenville to get the milk.

The money Brother Marsh gets for the milk is called his **income.** He uses his income to buy things his family needs from Greenville.

In Greenville most of the people work in **factories.** The people in one factory make clothes. In another factory, people make furniture. Each factory produces something the community needs.

Factory workers get paid wages, or money, for their work. They use their wages to buy food, clothes, and other things they need.

In Greenville and the nearby rural community, workers need to **cooperate.** This means they must work together.

How is the owner of this business honoring God?

Photo: Kevin and Bethany Shank

This boy does an important job for his community.

Photo: Library of Congress

Workers in the rural community help supply food for Greenville. The workers in Greenville supply many goods the rural people need.

However, not all workers do the right kind of work.

Some workers help make things that harm others. They help produce tobacco for people to smoke, or drinks that make people get drunk. Other workers produce bad books, bad pictures, or other evil things. God's people cannot cooperate with such evil workers.

2 Corinthians 6:17 "Wherefore come out from among them, and be ye separate [set apart], saith the Lord, and touch not the unclean thing." Christians must never join up with evil workers in their community. Christians only work at jobs that please God.

Some workers make good things for the whole community, like streets and roads. Everybody uses streets and roads. Who pays to build them? The government does. Where does the government get its money?

Each person in a community pays part of his income to the government. This money is called a **tax.** The government uses tax money to build and repair streets. Government leaders and policemen get their pay from tax money. Tax money pays for streetlights, bridges, fire trucks, and other things everybody uses.

The Bible teaches Christians to help the government in four ways:

Romans 13:6 "Pay ye tribute." Christians should pay taxes.

Titus 3:1 "Obey **magistrates**" (ma´ jə strāts) Christians should obey government leaders.

1 Timothy 2:1, 2 "Prayers [should] . . . be made for all men . . . for all that are in authority." Christians should pray for all leaders.

I Peter 2:17 "Honour the king." Christians should respect their rulers.

This shows one way God wants you to help your government.

34

SHOW YOUR KNOWLEDGE

1. When people move from one place to another, they carry _____ with them.
2. Each community has a mixture of customs and people who belong to different _____ .
3. How does a rural community help an urban community?
4. How does an urban community help a rural community?
5. Where does a government get money?

SHARE YOUR KNOWLEDGE

1. How should we treat people of other races?
2. Why did the Marsh family have some customs that were different from the customs of other people in their community?
3. List ways that government money is used.
4. God wants Christians to help the government in four ways. List them.

CHANGES IN COMMUNITIES

Some communities grow. More and more people move there to find jobs. More houses and stores need to be built. New roads are needed. Building new roads and buildings is called **construction** (kən strək´ shən). Construction changes communities.

Some communities get smaller. People move away when jobs get scarce.

The number of people in a community is called its **population** (pä pyə lā´ shən). The population of a community keeps changing.

People left this community when there were no more jobs.

Photo: Library of Congress

Why do communities need changes like this one?

Proverbs 11:11

God changes communities. He changed Noah's community by sending a flood. God punishes communities that go bad. "By the blessing of the upright the city is exalted: but it is overthrown by the mouth of the wicked."

God does not like to punish. He wants to change communities another way. He sent Jesus to take away the sins of people who believe on Him. Jesus can change a community by changing the people who live there.

In this book you will read about different communities. You will see changes God made. You will see the way God wants His people to live in their communities.

SHOW YOUR KNOWLEDGE

1. Communities _____ when people move there to get jobs. Communities get _____ when people move away because jobs are scarce.
2. Sometimes God _____ communities that go bad. But He would rather change a community by changing the _____ who live there.

SHARE YOUR KNOWLEDGE

1. Read Genesis 19:24, 25. How did God change the city where Lot lived?

Western Hemisphere

Eastern Hemisphere

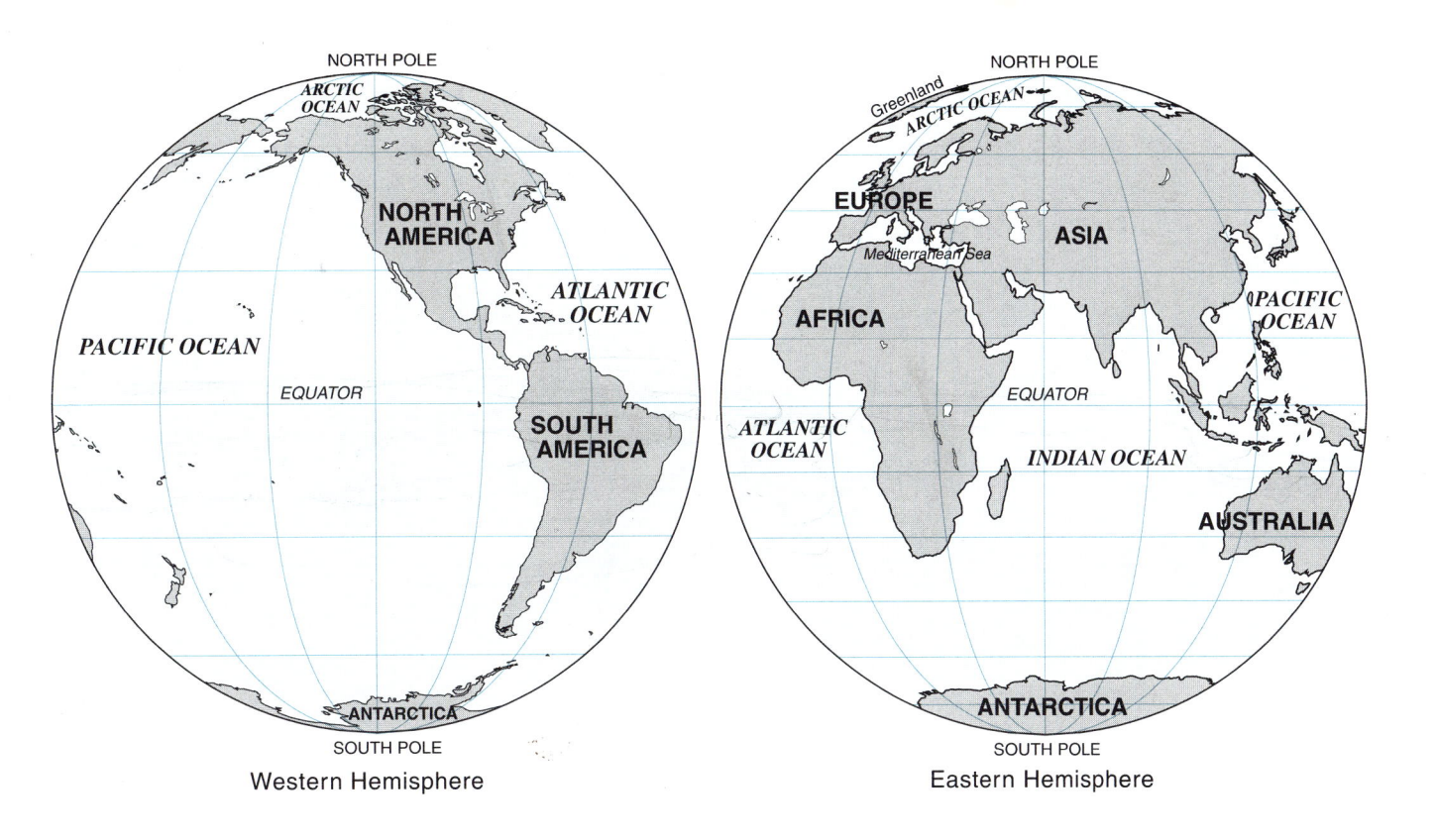

Learning About Maps

GLOBES ARE MAPS

A **map** shows places that can be found on the real earth. A globe is a good map of the earth because it has the same shape. A globe is a small sphere.

Look at the first globe picture at the top of this page. You are looking at one-half of the earth. One-half of a sphere is called a **hemisphere** (he mə sfir´). The left globe picture shows the **Western Hemisphere** of God's earth.

The Western Hemisphere has two continents. Name them. You live on the continent of North America.

Some continents are divided into smaller areas. Each smaller area is called a **country.** Do you live in the country of Canada or the United States? Find your country on the map of North America on page 39.

The globe picture on the right above shows the other half of the earth. This half is called the **Eastern Hemisphere.** Name the five continents you can see. In which hemisphere do you find the Mediterranean Sea?

Look at your classroom globe. Turn it until you can see only the Western Hemisphere. Turn it again until you see only the Eastern Hemisphere.

Sometimes we divide the earth into hemispheres another way. In the first picture on this page you see the north half of the earth around the North Pole. This north half of the earth is called the **Northern Hemisphere.**

Northern Hemisphere

Look at the picture showing the south half of the earth. This half of the earth is called the **Southern Hemisphere**. Name the continent that is found in this hemisphere.

Find a line around your globe that divides the Northern Hemisphere from the Southern Hemisphere. This line is called the **equator** (ē′ kwā tər).

The equator is halfway between the poles. Find the equator on the globe pictures at the top of page 37.

Of course the real earth does not have a line at the equator. The equator is a make-believe circle to help us find places on the earth. We can say, "Europe is north of the equator." This helps us know where to look for it.

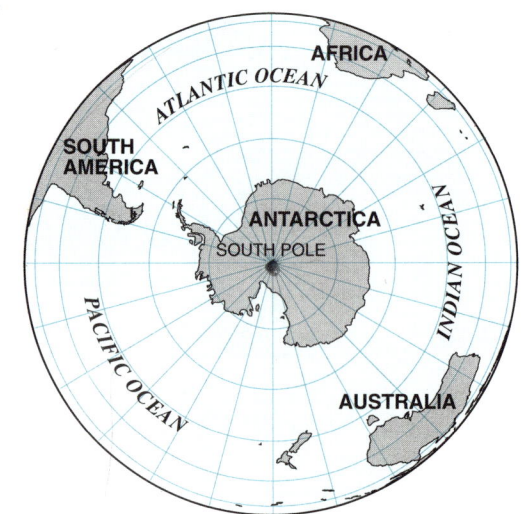

Southern Hemisphere

FLAT MAPS

No matter how you look at a globe, you can see only one-half of the world at one time. But sometimes we need a map that shows the whole world at one look. A flat map can do this. Look at the flat map on the inside front cover of your book.

Flat maps are handy. They can be put into books. You can fold a flat map and carry it in your pocket. But always remember, a flat map is never exactly like the real earth. A flat map is not a sphere.

FINDING DIRECTIONS ON A MAP

On a globe, the North Pole and South Pole can help you find directions. A flat map often doesn't show the poles. Look at the map of North America on this page.

At the bottom left side of the map, you can see a **direction finder.** It can help you find the directions north, south, east, and west.

North is toward the top of most flat maps. South is toward the bottom. When north is toward the top of a map, east is always toward your right. West is always toward your left.

Learn to say, "North at the top. South at the bottom. East on the right. West on the left." Do this until you can remember map directions.

SHOW YOUR KNOWLEDGE

1. Study the map of North America on this page. Answer these questions.
    a. Find your country. What country is to the north?
    b. What country is to the south?
    c. What ocean is to the east?
    d. What ocean is to the west?
2. Study the maps of the Eastern Hemisphere and Western Hemisphere on page 37. Answer these questions.
    a. Which hemisphere has the most water?
    b. Which hemisphere has the most land?

c. Find the continent where you live.

d. Is the place where you live to the north or to the south of the equator?

3. Study the maps of the Northern Hemisphere and Southern Hemisphere on page 38.

    Answer these questions.

    a. Which hemisphere has the most land?

    b. Which hemisphere has the most water?

    c. Which hemisphere has a continent in its center? What is the name of the continent?

    d. Which hemisphere has an ocean in its center? What is the name of the ocean?

4. In what way is a flat map better than a globe?

5. In what way is a globe better than a flat map?

6. Study your classroom globe.

    a. Move your finger toward the north along one of the lines on the globe. Name the point where the line ends in the north.

    b. Move your finger toward the south along one of the lines. Name the point where the line ends in the south.

    c. Move your finger toward the east along the equator. Do you come to a point called "East"? Answer *yes* or *no*.

    d. Move your finger toward the west along the equator. Do you come to a point called "West"? Answer *yes* or *no*.

SHARE YOUR KNOWLEDGE

1. How far is it between the "east" and the "west"?
   Choose the right answer.

       a. The distance around the world.

       b. The distance cannot be measured.

       c. The distance halfway around the world.

USING MAPS

Men have used maps ever since people first began moving about on the earth. The oldest map in the world is scratched on a

This map made from clay is the oldest map in the world. It shows the lands of a rich man.

piece of baked clay. Men found this map in the part of the world where God placed the first people.

Explorers made some of the first maps. They drew simple maps to show places they had discovered. Explorers often had to draw their maps on rough pieces of bark or wood.

Instead of using different colors, explorers often drew their maps with only black pieces of charcoal. On the next page you see a map like the maps explorers sometimes made. In some ways it is like the other maps in this book.

Do you see how the explorer marked his directions, north and south? Can you find the directions east and west?

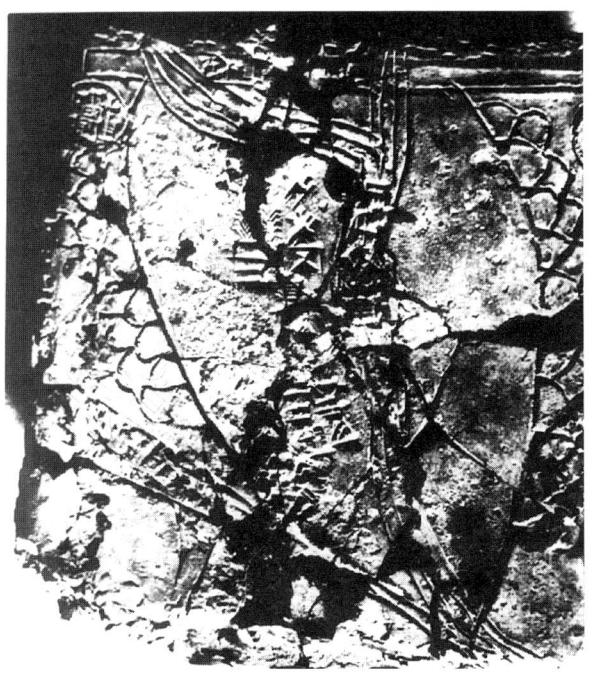

Photo: Harvard University, Semitic Museum

The explorer used a **symbol** (sim´ bəl) to stand for each thing he wanted to remember. What symbol did he use to show where he saw trees? How did he show where the Indian camp was?

At the bottom corner of the map, find the **map legend**. The explorer made this to show what all of his symbols stand for. Use the map legend to learn what each symbol means.

On page 43, you see a map of the United States and Canada. Like the explorer's map, it has symbols. Do you see the wiggly lines on the map? These lines are symbols to show large rivers. Use the map legend to figure out what all of the symbols stand for.

If you live in the United States, find the state where you live. If you live in Canada, find your province. Someone may ask you, "In what part of your country do you live?" Will you say, "I live in the eastern part"? Or will you say, "I live in the western part"?

Can you find a symbol like this ★ in your state or province? The map legend tells you it stands for the **capital** of your state or province. A capital is a city where government leaders meet to make laws. Use the map legend to help you find the capital of your country.

Study the different colors on the map. The colors show

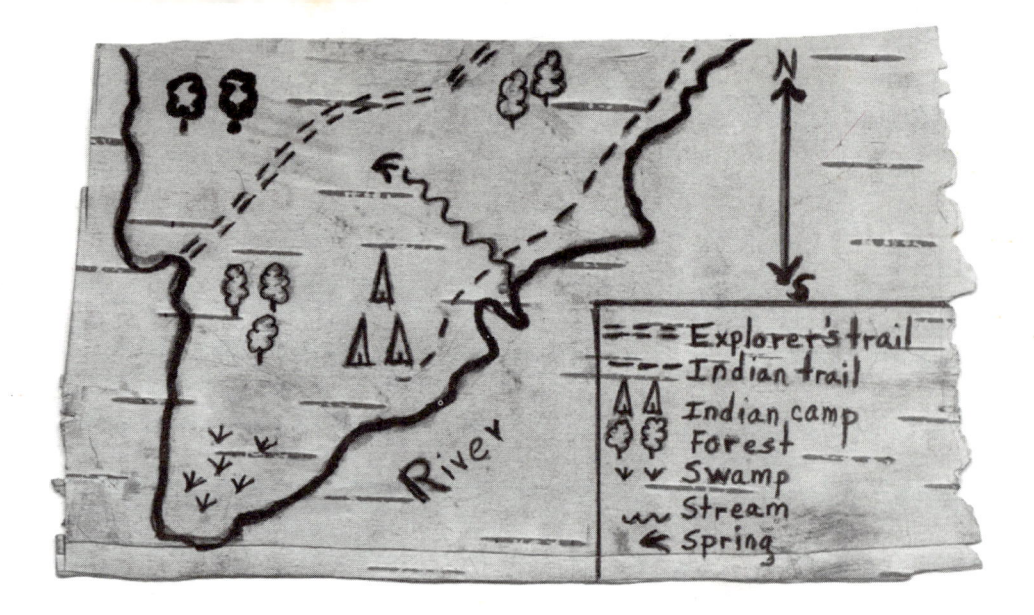

where the land is high or low. The map legend tells you what each color means. Find the mountains in your country. What do the colors tell about the land at the place where you live?

The map can tell you how far apart any two places are. Beside the map legend, find a line called the **scale of miles**. Each inch on this map stands for about 500 miles on the earth.

Use your ruler and the scale of miles to find the distance between the capital of Canada and the capital of the United States. Did you find it to be about 500 miles?

You will be an explorer as you study this book. Maps in this book will help you to learn about other places. Each map has a map legend. Map legends are keys to understanding maps. Always remember to use them.

SHOW YOUR KNOWLEDGE

1. Why did early explorers make maps?
2. Why did an explorer put a map legend on his map?
3. Why is the capital city of a state important?
4. Are the highest mountains of the United States in the east or in the west?
5. How many miles is it between the east **coast** and west coast of the United States?

43

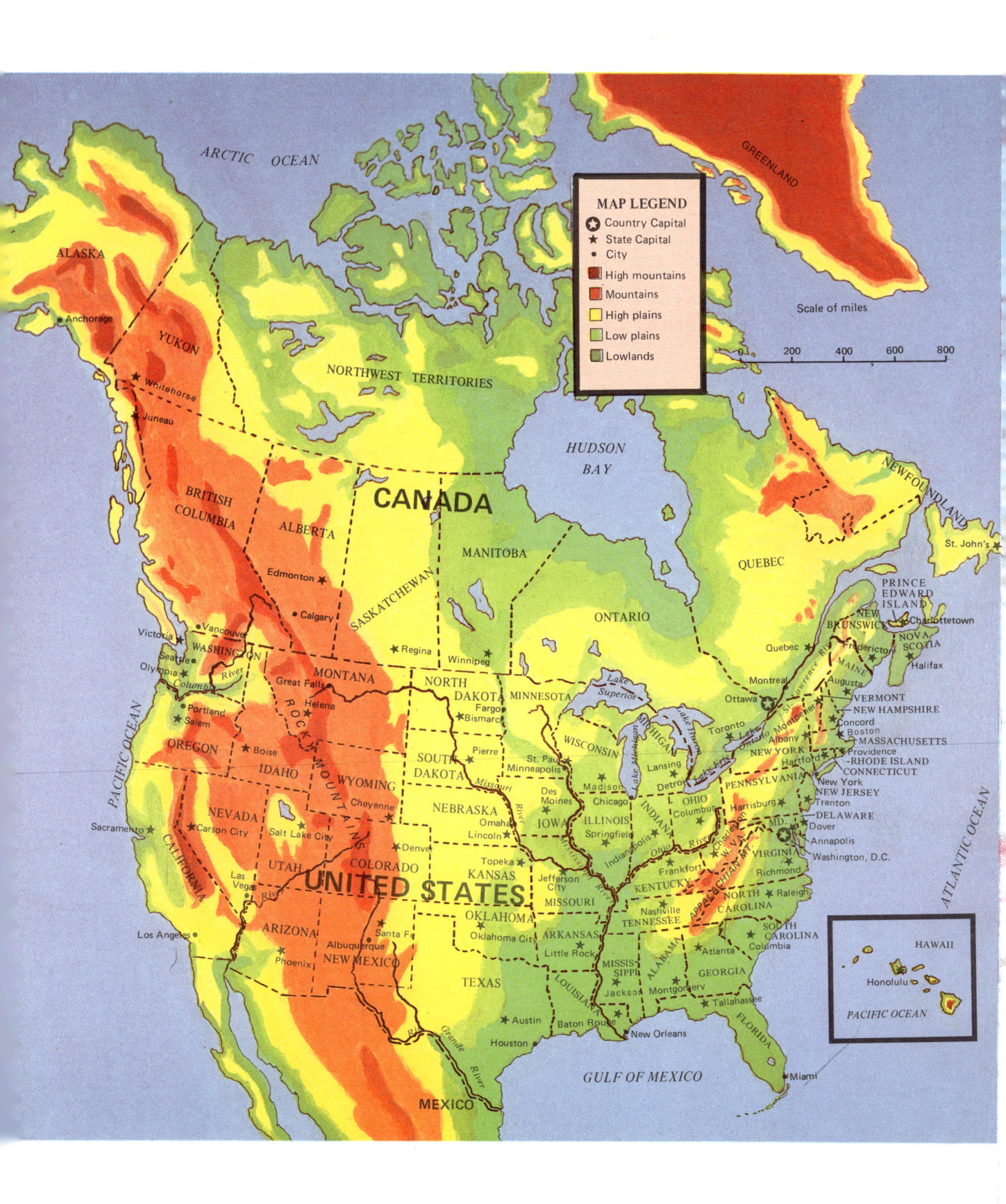

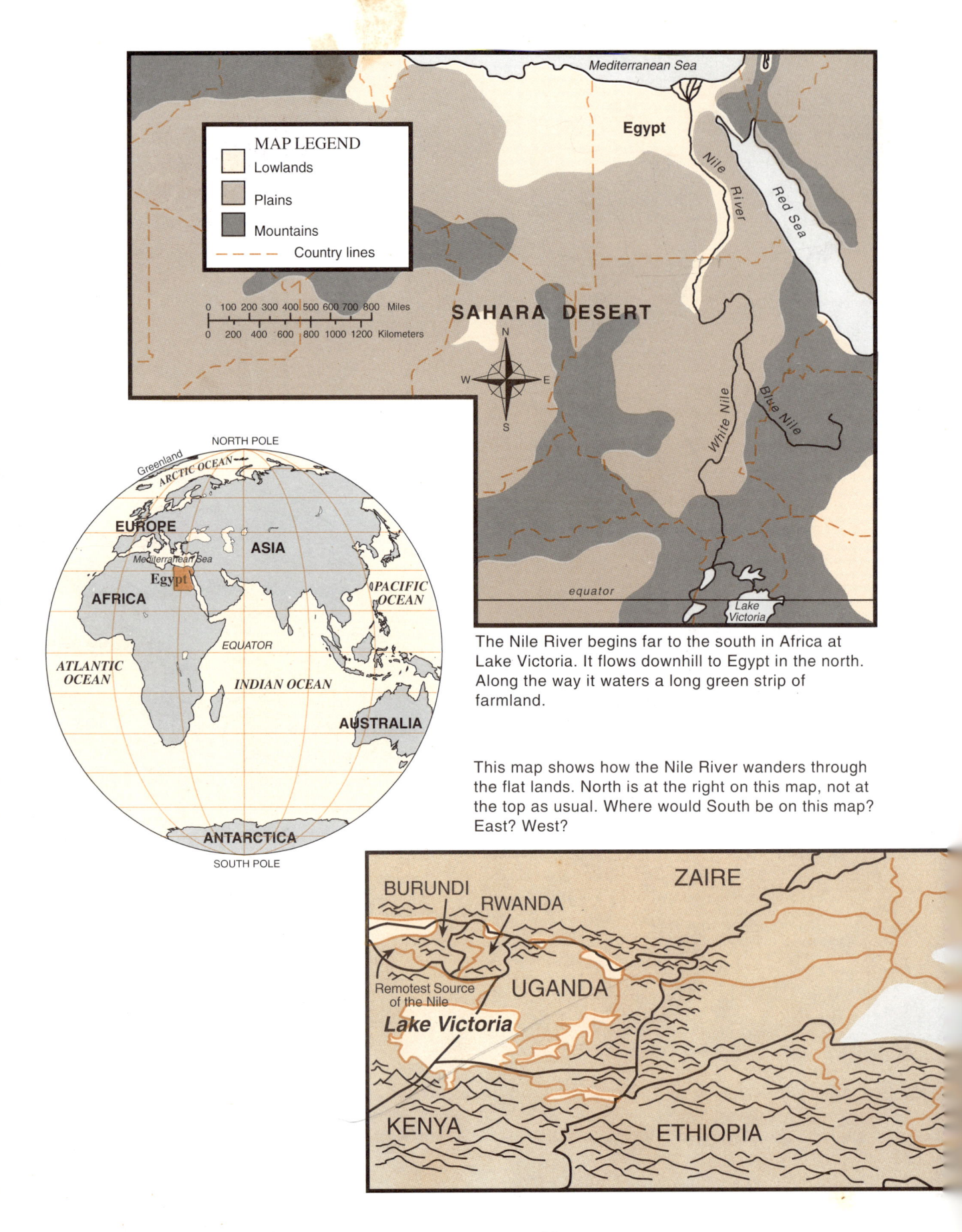

MAP LEGEND
- Lowlands
- Plains
- Mountains
- – – – Country lines

The Nile River begins far to the south in Africa at Lake Victoria. It flows downhill to Egypt in the north. Along the way it waters a long green strip of farmland.

This map shows how the Nile River wanders through the flat lands. North is at the right on this map, not at the top as usual. Where would South be on this map? East? West?

44

"Unto the river of Egypt, and the goings out of it shall be at the sea." (Numbers 34:5b).

Egypt, Land of the Nile River

On the map of Africa, look for the country of Egypt. You will find Egypt in the northern part of this large continent.

Locate Egypt on a globe. You would need to travel almost halfway around the earth to get there. Is Egypt in the Eastern or Western Hemisphere?

North of Egypt is the Mediterranean Sea. East of Egypt is the Red Sea you read about in the Bible. Much of Egypt is in the **Sahara** (sə har´ ə), a desert which stretches to the west across Africa. The Sahara is the largest desert in the world.

Most of the land in Egypt is hot and dry. Some places get only about one inch of rain in a whole year. People in such a thirsty land must live where they can get water.

Most of the people in Egypt live along the Nile River.

The Nile River is the longest river in the world. On the map, find Lake Victoria near the equator where the Nile River begins. The beginning of a river is called its **source.**

From its source, the Nile River flows toward the north.

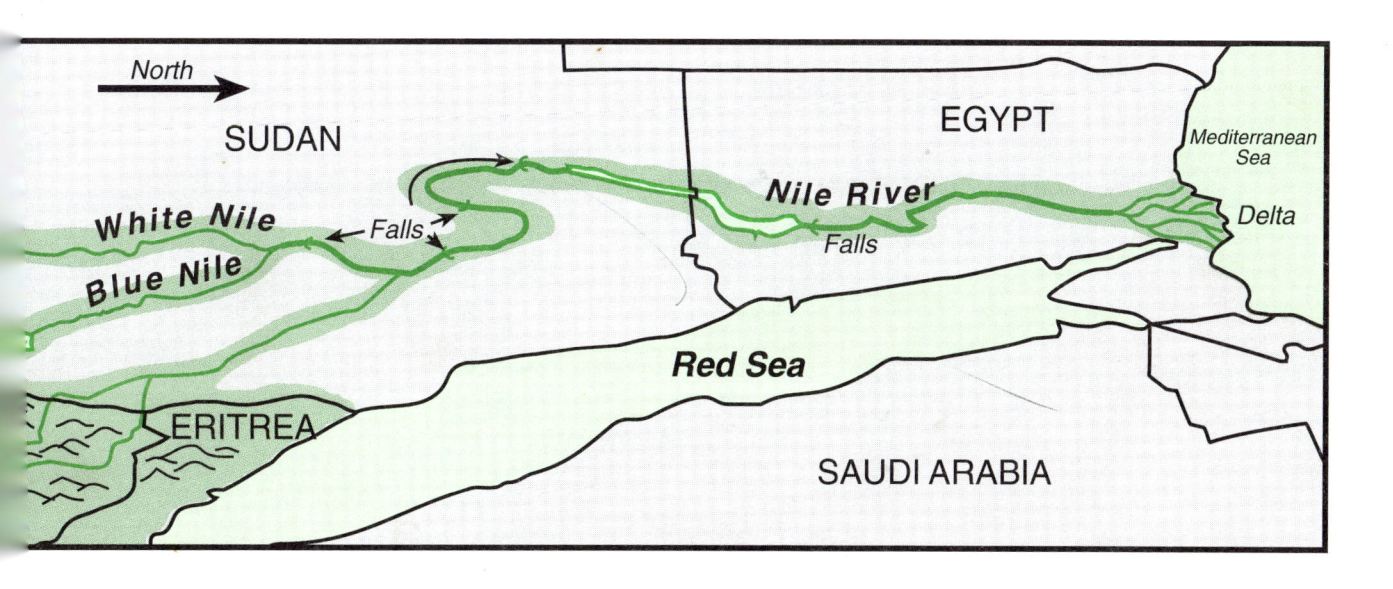

Other rivers empty into the Nile River as it flows downhill to Egypt.

In Egypt, the river wanders through flat lands called **plains.** Most people in Egypt live on these plains along the river where they can get water for drinking, washing, and growing crops.

The waters of the Nile River finally drain into the large Mediterranean Sea. The end of a river is called its **mouth**. Find the mouth of the Nile River on the map.

In the month of June, heavy rains begin to fall in the mountains near the source of the Nile River. Rushing streams carry fine soil called **silt** down the mountainsides. The rains cause the waters in the river to rise. Huge **dams** across the river catch the extra water and store it.

But in Bible times these huge dams had not been built. The rising waters spilled over the riverbanks and flooded the plains of Egypt.

After many weeks, the floodwaters drained back into the river. They left a new layer of black silt on the land. Crops grew well in this wet new topsoil.

The Nile River drops much of its silt at its mouth. Here the river slows down as it meets the calm sea, and the silt settles to the bottom.

Year after year, the silt piles up. It builds up a piece of land called a **delta.** Over the years, a delta keeps growing larger and larger.

On your map, find the delta at the mouth of the Nile River. This delta has some of the best soil in Egypt. With good soil and plenty of water, farmers on the delta can grow large crops.

SHOW YOUR KNOWLEDGE

1. What part of Africa is Egypt in?
    a. southern
    b. northern
2. Egypt is in the _____ Hemisphere.
3. What body of water is north of Egypt?
4. What body of water is east of Egypt?

5. What is the name of the large desert in northern Africa?
6. Why do most of the people in Egypt live along the Nile River?
7. Write the word that means:
    a. the beginning of a stream or river
    b. the end of a river where it enters a larger body of water
    c. a piece of land formed at the mouth of a river where the water drops its silt
    d. a wall built to hold back the water of a stream or river
    e. large, flat stretch of land
    f. small pieces of soil or sand carried by moving water
8. The source of the Nile River is _____ .
9. At the mouth of the Nile River is the _____ .
10. The Nile River flows from:
    a. north to south.
    b. south to north.
11. In Bible times, what two natural resources did the Nile River give the farmers every year?
12. How is a delta formed at the mouth of the Nile River?

SHARE YOUR KNOWLEDGE

1. Would the land in Africa be higher at Lake Victoria or in Egypt at the Mediterranean Sea? Why?

JOSEPH IN EGYPT

In Bible times, countries near Egypt sometimes did not have enough rain to grow crops. In these countries, there would be **famines**, and people would begin to starve.

These starving people knew about the watered lands along the Nile River. They often came to Egypt to buy grain for food. Sometimes they stayed until the famine in their own country was over.

In the Bible are stories about Jacob and his twelve sons. God changed Jacob's name to Israel. His sons were called the children of Israel.

The children of Israel lived in the country called Israel

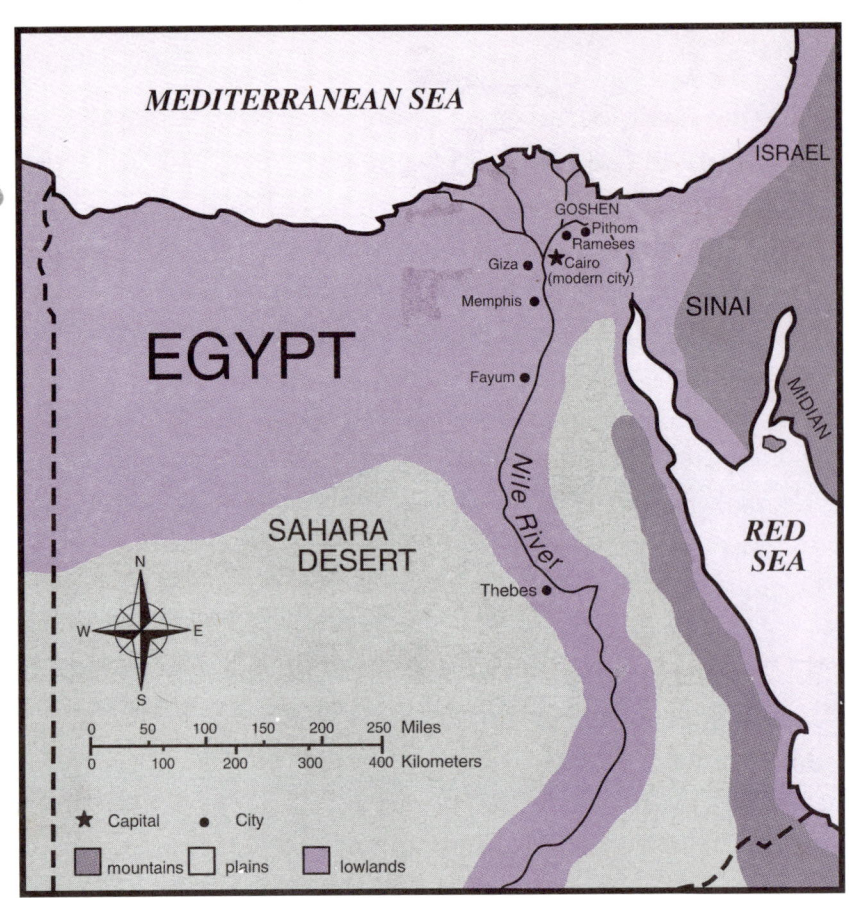

today. Find Israel on the map. In Bible times, it was called the land of Canaan. You can see that Canaan was close to Egypt.

Do you remember how Israel's sons sold their brother Joseph? Traders carried him to Egypt.

God had a plan for Joseph in Egypt. Joseph became a ruler of the whole nation.

For seven years, God made the crops grow well in Egypt. Joseph taught the people how to store the extra grain in storehouses.

Genesis 41:48a "And he gathered up all the food of the seven years, which were in the land of Egypt, and laid up the food in the cities."

For the next seven years, crops would not grow well in Israel or Egypt, not even along the Nile River. Perhaps the waters in the river did not rise to flood the land.

We do not know for sure what caused the great famine. But we do know that Egypt had storehouses filled with grain for food.

The children of Israel went to Egypt to buy food. They found Joseph living there. Joseph told them to move their families to Egypt during the famine. The children of Israel settled on the east side of the delta. This part of the delta was called the land of Goshen.

At last Joseph could see God's plan. He said to his brothers, "God did send me before you to preserve [save] life." God wanted Joseph in Egypt to save his own family from starving.

Genesis 45:5b

The famine lasted for seven years. But the children of Israel stayed in Egypt for 430 years! In this chapter, you will learn about communities in Egypt. The boys you will read about are make-believe. But the story tells how people really lived in Egypt during Bible times. You will see why God could not let His people stay there.

SHOW YOUR KNOWLEDGE

1. Why did people from other countries often go to Egypt?
2. The children of Israel moved from their country called _____ to a part of Egypt called _____ . They lived there for _____ years.
3. What is the land of Canaan called today?
4. What did Joseph teach the people of Egypt?
5. What plan did God have for Joseph in Egypt?

SHARE YOUR KNOWLEDGE

1. Study Genesis 12:10. Who went to Egypt? Why did he go?

"The LORD showed signs and wonders, great and sore, upon Egypt" (Deuteronomy 6:22a).

God Changes Communities in Egypt

"All aboard!" cried the boatmaster.

Amar (ā´ mär) and Themose (thē´ məs) leaped from the shore to the empty wooden boat. Other boys came running from every direction.

The Egyptian master shouted, "Amar and Themose will raise the sail." He tossed a heavy cloth bundle to Themose.

Themose spread the white sailcloth on the bottom of the boat. Amar fastened it to the end of a rope hanging from a tall boatpole. Together the two boys pulled on the other end of the rope. One corner of the sail climbed to the top of the pole.

The boat jerked as the wind caught the sail. Slowly it began to move upstream on the Nile River.

THE HEBREWS IN EGYPT

Amar lived in the land of Goshen on the delta. His family belonged to the children of Israel. Other people called them **Hebrews**.

Almost 430 years had gone by since Joseph and his brothers came to Egypt. That first group of Hebrews had been small. But now the Hebrew group was a large **nation**.

"And the children of Israel were fruitful . . . and the land was filled with them."

Exodus 1:7

The **pharaoh** (fā´ rō) kings of Egypt no longer remembered Joseph. They worried about the Hebrew nation becoming strong. They feared the Hebrews might rise up and fight against the Egyptians.

One pharaoh thought hard work would make the Hebrew nation weak. He made the Hebrews work as **slaves**. He forced them to make bricks and build cities for him.

"And they built for Pharaoh treasure cities, Pithom and Raamses." Find these two cities on the map on page 48.

Exodus 1:11b

Usually Amar had to help make bricks. The work did not bother him. But slave life was hard. Cruel **taskmasters**

These pictures show slaves making bricks in Egypt. Egyptians drew these pictures many years ago. How can you tell which men are the taskmasters? Find the pool where the slaves are dipping out water. What else do you see the slaves doing?

Exodus 1:14a

watched over the work and punished slaves who became tired and slow. "And they made their lives bitter with hard bondage." Amar had often felt their stinging whips on his back.

Amar did not know it, but God was making changes in Egypt. The Hebrews had learned to enjoy life there. But the people of Egypt had evil customs. God did not want the Hebrews to stay.

God saw that the leaders of Egypt had turned against the Hebrews. He knew that their cruel actions would help His plan. God let the Egyptians treat the Hebrews badly. Slave work would make the Hebrews want to leave Egypt.

SHOW YOUR KNOWLEDGE

1. What was another name for the children of Israel?
2. What did the pharaohs of Egypt fear?
3. What work did the Hebrew slaves do for the pharaoh?
4. God wanted the Hebrews to leave Egypt because:
    a. slave life in Egypt was hard.
    b. the Hebrews might learn Egyptian customs.
    c. the land was filled with them.
5. God's changes in Egypt:
    a. made the Hebrew nation strong.
    b. helped the cruel taskmasters.
    c. made the Hebrews dislike the Egyptian communities.

SHARE YOUR KNOWLEDGE

1. Exodus 1:9 says that the Hebrew nation had become:
    a. larger than the nation of Egypt.
    b. smaller than the nation of Egypt.
    c. the same size as the nation of Egypt.
2. Study Exodus 1:12. What happened to the Hebrews when Pharaoh made them work hard? Who do you think caused this to happen?

TRAVELING UP THE NILE

Amar looked out across the river. Soft breezes swept the smell of the river into his face. He forgot about slave life. Today he would have his first boat ride.

The taskmaster had picked Amar and other slave boys to help bring back a load of grain from a farm along the river. What new sights would he see? His slave friend Themose would tell him about things along the river. Themose traveled on the Nile every day.

"There are many boats on the river this morning, aren't there, Themose?" asked Amar.

"Yes," answered Themose. "The Nile is always crowded with boats. The communities along the river use the Nile like a large road," he said. "The land along the river is needed for crops. There is not much space for roads.

"Look at the boats going downstream, Amar." Themose pointed. "You see they have their sails down. Boats can travel north with the movement of the river called the **current**."

"I see," said Amar. "Our boat needs a sail to go upstream.

Going downstream

Going upstream

Boats on the Nile River travel downstream with the river current or upstream with the wind. Which direction does the current flow? Which way does the wind blow in Egypt?

53

The wind pushes our boat against the current."

Themose nodded. "The Nile River flows toward the north," he said. "The wind blows toward the south. The wind pushes sailboats toward the south against the current. Boats travel north with the current. On the Nile, boats do not need oars."

The Egyptians made boats and paper from papyrus plants. Baby Moses' mother may have used papyrus plants for the little ark she made for him.

Photo: Joseph G. Strauch, Jr.

"The small boats look like they are made from grass," said Amar. "Why aren't all of the boats made from wood?" he asked.

"Egypt has hardly any trees," Themose replied. "It costs a lot of money to buy wood from other countries," he said. "Only large boats like ours are made from wood."

Themose pointed to thick bushes of grassy plants along the river.

"Those are **papyrus** (pə pī′ rəs) plants," he said. "Men tie bundles of those reed-like plants together to make cheap, small boats. They cover the papyrus boats with a sticky, black tar called **pitch**. These small boats are light. They can travel faster than large boats."

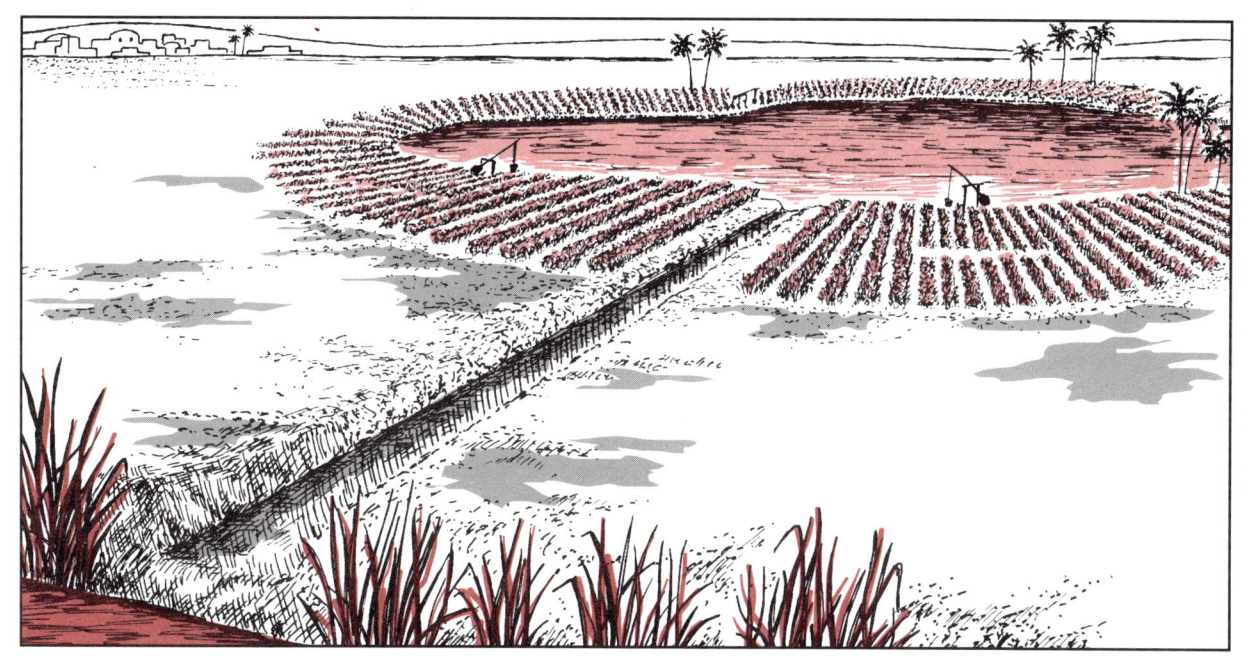

This picture shows how the Egyptians made the oasis at Fayum. What happened when the waters of the Nile River rose high during the flood each year?

WATERING DESERT LAND

Amar's boat stopped at Fayum (fī yüm). Find it on the map on page 48. The land around Fayum was an **oasis** (ō ā´ səs). An oasis is a watered place in a desert. Plants and trees grow at an oasis.

The Egyptians had made the oasis at Fayum. They made a large lake near the Nile River. Then they dug a ditch called a **canal** from the lake to the river.

Each year when the Nile flooded, water ran through the canal and filled the lake.

After the flood, farmers plowed the wet, new soil with sticks pulled by oxen. They scattered seeds on the loose soil by hand. Then the farmers chased goats over the fields. The goats' hoofs helped press the seeds into the soft soil.

After the crops were planted, the fields began to dry off. The farmers dug **irrigation** (ir ə gā´ shən) ditches from the lake to their fields. Irrigation means bringing water to thirsty plants.

The farmers used a **shadoof** (shə düf´) to lift water from the lake up into the irrigation ditches. Look at the picture on the next page.

Some farmers worked the shadoofs to keep the irrigation ditches filled with water. Other farmers walked along the ditches tramping openings in the soft soil with their feet to let the water flow into the fields.

Egyptian farmers grew fields of barley and a kind of

wheat. They also grew such vegetables as beans, cabbages, lettuce, peas, cucumbers, radishes, onions, garlic, and watermelons. The farmers grew **leeks** which look and taste much like onions.

Some of these vegetables were strange to the Hebrew people at first. They were used to eating simple foods such as bread, cheese, and milk. But the Hebrew people soon learned to enjoy the many different vegetables of Egypt.

The sun shines hot in Egypt every day. By irrigating, farmers could grow two or three crops each year. Egypt was a land of plenty.

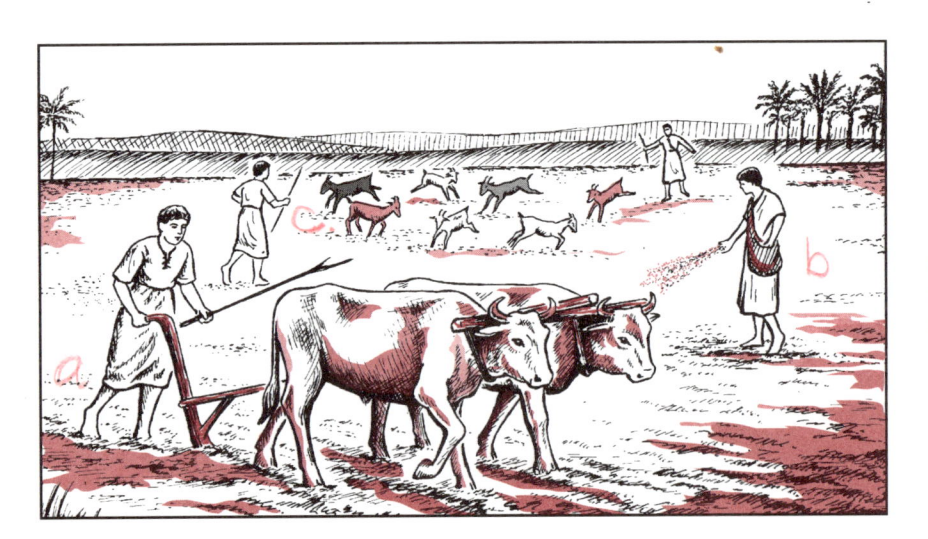

How is each farmer helping with the planting?

The shadoof is a simple tool some people still use for lifting water into irrigation ditches. The weight on one end of the pole makes the bucket of water easier to lift.

SHOW YOUR KNOWLEDGE

1. On the Nile River, a boat with its sail up would be going toward the (north, south).
2. Why didn't the people of Egypt make all of their boats from wood?
3. An Egyptian who wanted to travel quickly down the Nile River would use a:
    a. papyrus and pitch boat.
    b. wooden boat.
4. Number these sentences about the oasis at Fayum in the order in which they happened:
    a. ___ Men made a large lake near the river.
    b. ___ The Nile flooded.
    c. ___ Men dug a canal from the lake to the river.
    d. ___ The lake filled with water.
5. Number these sentences about the Egyptian farming in the order in which they happened:
    a. ___ Farmers scattered seeds on the soil.
    b. ___ Farmers used a shadoof to lift water.
    c. ___ The farmers dug irrigation ditches.
    d. ___ Goats were chased over the fields.
    e. ___ Farmers plowed the soil.
6. What custom did the Hebrews learn from the Egyptians?

SHARE YOUR KNOWLEDGE

1. In what two ways is the Nile River important to the people of Egypt?
2. Study Exodus 2:3. **Bulrushes** could have been (garlic, leek, papyrus) plants.
3. Study Deuteronomy 11:10. Copy the words that tell how the Egyptians irrigated their fields.

GOVERNMENT IN EGYPT

Themose said, "The job of irrigating is too much work for one farmer.

"Long ago, the Egyptians learned to divide the work," he went on to explain. "One group of men made the lake. Another group built the shadoofs. Other groups dug the irrigation ditches. Each worker learned to do his part well. Dividing the work got the job done fast and made it easier for everyone."

Amar asked, "Didn't they have trouble with many workers wanting to do the same job?"

"No," Themose replied. "The farmers had leaders to plan the different jobs. The leaders made rules to keep the work going smoothly. These rules became laws for the farming communities."

Themose had more to say. "You can see how the job of using the Nile River helped Egypt set up a **government.** The government kept order in the communities along the river.

"More people live in Egypt now than at first," Themose went on. "The government is run by many leaders. Pharaoh is the most important leader. He lives in the **palace** at Thebes (thēbz´)."

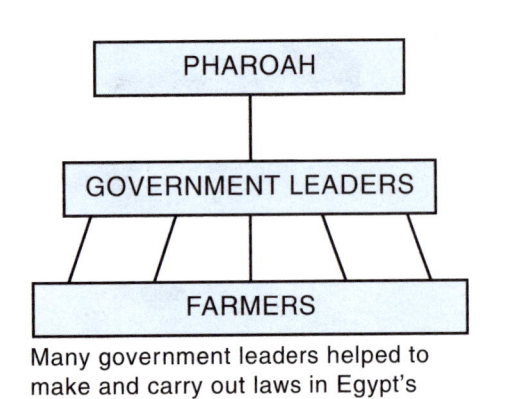

Many government leaders helped to make and carry out laws in Egypt's government.

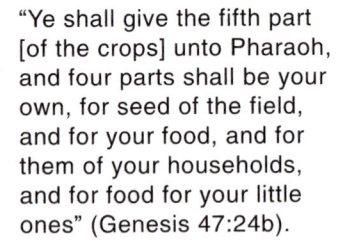

"Ye shall give the fifth part [of the crops] unto Pharaoh, and four parts shall be your own, for seed of the field, and for your food, and for them of your households, and for food for your little ones" (Genesis 47:24b).

Sickle

Flail

"Who pays the government leaders for their work?" asked Amar.

Themose replied, "The farmers pay **taxes** by giving the government part of all their crops."

HARVESTING THE CROPS

At Fayum, the grain was ripe. Amar and Themose saw the farmers cut the golden stalks of wheat and barley with sickles. The men piled the stalks of grain at a place where the ground was flat and hard.

Animals and men knocked the grain from the stalks. Oxen

Farmers in some lands still cut and thresh grain as the Egyptians did many years ago. Why did men put muzzles over the mouths of the oxen?

This man is winnowing grain. Winnowing lets the wind carry dirt and chaff away from the grain.

and goats walked over the piles of grain. A group of farmers beat the piles with **flails.**

Another group of farmers **winnowed** the grain by throwing it into the air. The wind blew the dirt and **chaff** away. After it was winnowed, the clean grain was gathered into bags.

Amar and Themose helped to load the bags of grain onto the boat. Then they began the trip back down the river to the delta where they would store the grain in large storehouses.

Themose pointed to farmers working in other fields along the river. "They are harvesting **flax**," he said. "Flax plants have woody stems. Inside each stem are tiny strings called **fibers.**

"Workers soak the stems in water to rot the woody parts of

These pictures show how the Egyptians made linen from flax.

60

the stems," Themose explained. "Then they remove the white fibers and twist them together to make long threads. Egyptian workers weave the threads into soft white cloth called **linen**."

SHOW YOUR KNOWLEDGE

1. Why did Egyptian farmers divide the work of irrigating crops?
2. What was the work of the government leaders?
3. Who was the most important government leader in Egypt in Bible times?
4. What did the farmers use to pay taxes?
5. Number these sentences about grain harvesting in the order in which they happened:
    a. ___ The men piled the grain on the flat, hard ground.
    b. ___ Farmers winnowed the grain.
    c. ___ Farmers cut the grain with sickles.
    d. ___ Animals walked over the grain, and men beat the grain with flails.
    e. ___ The clean grain was gathered into bags and taken to the storehouse.
6. Number these sentences about linen making in the order in which they happened:
    a. ___ The flax stems were soaked in water.
    b. ___ Workers wove the threads into linen cloth.
    c. ___ Farmers harvested the stalks of flax.
    d. ___ Workers twisted the fibers together to make long threads.
    e. ___ Workers removed the white fibers from the rotted stems.

SHARE YOUR KNOWLEDGE

1. How much grain did Joseph have placed in storehouses? Find the answer in Genesis 41:49.
2. Isaiah 30:24 tells two things men used for winnowing grain in Bible times. Name the two things and tell how each would be used for this job.

EGYPTIAN RECORDS AND PAPER

Amar had a question. "Themose, why did a government leader count every bag of grain we loaded?" he asked.

"He must keep a **record** for the pharaoh," Themose explained. "The leader marked down each bag with his pen. His record will show the pharaoh how much grain was harvested this year.

"That white sheet the leader used for his record was made from papyrus plants," Themose said. "The Egyptians split the papyrus stalks into narrow strips. They lay these strips side by side. On top of these, the men place another layer of strips crosswise. Then they press the two layers together to make a sheet of papyrus."

Papyrus sheets look much like the paper you use in school. Our word *paper* comes from the word *papyrus*.

The Egyptians wrote many records on papyrus sheets. They kept records about their kings. They wrote songs and poetry.

The dry climate of Egypt helped to keep the papyrus records in good shape for thousands of years. Today, these records tell us many things about the way people lived in Egypt many, many years ago.

The Egyptians wrote with symbols called hieroglyphics (hī rə gli´fiks). This hieroglyphic message is carved in stone.

Papyrus plants   Splitting the stems   Placing the strips in layers   Pressing the layers together   Papyrus sheet

62

Photo: Library of Congress

Slaves built these large pyramids for the pharaohs of Egypt. The pharaohs believed these large buildings would keep their bodies safe after they died. But robbers broke into many of the pyramids to steal treasures.

TOMBS IN EGYPT

Amar's boat passed Giza (gē´ zə). Find it along the Nile River on the map on page 48. At Giza, Themose pointed toward three large buildings with pointed tops.

"Those three buildings are called **pyramids** (pir´ ə midz)," he said. "Each one is a tomb where a pharaoh is buried."

Themose explained. "When a pharaoh dies, skillful men **embalm** his body to keep it from decay.

"They soak the body in special liquids for 40 days. Then the men wrap the body with long strips of white linen. This bundle is called a **mummy.** Workers place the mummy in a carved wooden coffin to be buried."

Amar remembered that the body of Jacob had been embalmed. "And Joseph commanded his servants the physicians to embalm his father: and the physicians embalmed Israel. And forty days were fulfilled for him; for so are fulfilled the days of those which are embalmed."

Genesis 50:2, 3a

Joseph believed God would someday lead the Hebrews out of Egypt. He had said to the Hebrews, "God will surely visit you, and bring you out of this land unto the land which he sware to Abraham, to Isaac, and to Jacob . . . ye shall carry up my bones from hence [here]. So Joseph died . . . and they embalmed him, and he was put in a coffin in Egypt."

Genesis 50:24b, 25b, 26

Themose broke into Amar's thoughts. "The Egyptians bury

63

their pharaoh in a room inside a pyramid," he was saying. "Workers bury food, tools, and treasures with him. The Egyptians believe a dead person will need these in a place called 'the land of the dead.'

"It took at least 20 years for 100,000 slaves to build the largest pyramid," said Themose. "The slaves cut large rocks from a **quarry** up the Nile. They dragged the rocks to the river and loaded them on flat-bottomed boats called **barges** and floated them down the river.

"At Giza, the slaves unloaded the rocks and dragged them one by one up the sides of the pyramid. Thousands of slaves died from the hard work."

Some people believe this is the mummy of the pharaoh who made the Hebrews work as slaves. Moses may have talked to this pharaoh about the ten plagues.

SHOW YOUR KNOWLEDGE

1. The records that the government leaders kept for the pharaoh were written on sheets of _____ .
2. Old records are important to us because:
    a. they are written on papyrus.
    b. they help us understand how people lived long ago.
    c. they are written in strange letters and words.
3. Why did the Egyptians bury food and tools with their pharaohs?

SHARE YOUR KNOWLEDGE

1. Our word *paper* came from the word *papyrus* because:
    a. our paper is made from papyrus plants.
    b. all of our paper is made in Egypt.
    c. sheets of paper and papyrus are much alike.
2. Name two Hebrews that were embalmed in Egypt.
3. Study 1 Timothy 6:7. Explain what was wrong with Egyptian burying customs.

The people of Egypt believed they would meet these awful creatures after they died. They were afraid of their gods. The Egyptians did not know about the true God who loves the people who obey Him.

WORSHIP CUSTOMS IN EGYPT

Amar knew that the Egyptians were **heathen**, because they did not worship the only true God. Themose explained their ungodly worship customs to him.

"The Egyptians worship the pharaohs because of their great power," he said. "They also worship the Nile River, because water from the river is the most important natural resource in Egypt.

"If the river doesn't rise to flood the land, the people believe the river god is angry," Themose explained. "The Egyptians believe sacrifices and gifts to the river help to keep their god happy and kind.

"The people of Egypt believe the sun is a god called Ra (rä). They also worship the moon and stars. The Egyptians embalm the

This statue of a pharaoh stands in the doorway of his temple at Thebes in Egypt. The Egyptians made many statues of their pharoahs and worshiped them. But the pharoahs were only people. Often they were very evil, and not holy like the true God.

This Great Sphinx of Egypt stands at Giza. It has the head of a pharoah and the body of a lion. The Egyptians believed the Sphinx had the power to guard tombs and temples. But the Sphinx could not even take care of itself. Some men shot off its nose. This false god had no power at all.

Photo: Library of Congress

bodies of sheep, goats, lions, dogs, birds, cats, fish, snakes, frogs, and flies and worship them."

Themose pointed to a large **image** at Giza. "That image is called a **sphinx**," he said. "A sphinx has the head of a pharaoh and the body of a lion. The Egyptians worship images of their gods and pharaohs."

Amar knew that the Egyptian gods could not help anyone. "They have mouths, but they speak not: eyes have they, but they see not: they have ears, but they hear not: noses have they, but they smell not: they have hands, but they handle not: feet have they, but they walk not: neither speak they through their throat."

Psalm 115:5-7

The gods of Egypt were not holy and perfect. The pharaohs whom the people worshiped often married their own sisters. This custom was unholy and sinful.

The Egyptians had many feasts to honor their gods. They did not thank the true God for their food. Often the people ate too much. Many Egyptians drank lots of wine and became very drunk.

The true God of the Hebrews was holy and perfect. He wanted the Hebrews to be perfect too. He said, "Ye shall therefore be holy, for I am holy." The sinful customs of Egypt displeased God.

Leviticus 11:45b

These men are making bricks with a mold. How can you tell which man is the taskmaster? What do you think the men are building in the background?

STOREHOUSES

Amar's boat stopped at Pithom. Here the Hebrew slaves were building large buildings for the pharaoh. Some of the buildings were storehouses for grain.

Amar helped to unload bags of grain. The slaves dumped the grain through holes in the storehouse roofs. A government leader kept a record of each bag of grain. After the boat was unloaded, Amar said good-bye to Themose and hurried back to his usual job of carrying straw to the brickmakers.

Using their feet, the slaves mixed the straw with mud. They placed this mixture into **molds** to shape the clay into bricks. Then slaves laid the bricks in rows to dry in the hot sun. Sweat poured down their tired backs, but the crack of the master's whip kept them hard at work.

SHOW YOUR KNOWLEDGE

1. Why did the Egyptians worship the pharaohs?
2. Why did the Egyptians worship the Nile River?
3. What does a sphinx look like?

4. (*True* or *False*?) If the Egyptians gave sacrifices and gifts to their gods, the gods would help them.
5. God wanted the Hebrews to be _____ and _____ .

SHARE YOUR KNOWLEDGE

1. The Egyptians probably made the sphinx to show that:
    a. the pharaoh had great power as the lion does.
    b. they didn't really like their leaders.
    c. wild animals could be tamed.
2. Why do you think the pharaoh was having storehouses filled with grain?

The people of Egypt believed these rows of sphinxes could guard a temple at Thebes. But we know they have not moved themselves an inch for thousands of years.

Photo: Library of Congress

GOD PREPARES A LEADER

Amar and his Hebrew friends had no way of seeing God's plan to get them out of Egypt. But years before, God knew the Hebrews would need a leader. He had saved baby Moses from being killed. God helped Moses get the training he would need later when he became a leader.

Moses became the son of the pharaoh's daughter. He grew up in the palace where the pharaoh lived. Moses may have

68

What lessons did God teach Moses in the desert of Midian that he could not have learned in the schools of Egypt?

lived in the palace at Thebes.

In the palace, Moses went to the best schools in Egypt. He learned to read, write, and solve problems. "And Moses was learned in all the wisdom of the Egyptians, and was mighty in words and in deeds." He might have been the next ruler in Egypt. But that was not God's plan.

Acts 7:22

When Moses was 40 years old, he killed one of the Egyptians to help a Hebrew slave. Then he ran away across the desert of **Sinai** (Sī´ nī) to the land of **Midian** (mid´ ē ən). Find these places on the map on page 48. In Midian, Moses tended sheep in the desert. Nobody in Egypt had heard from him for 40 years.

But God knew all about Moses. In the desert, God was teaching Moses to trust Him for food and water. Moses was also learning about desert life. God knew that Moses would need to know these things later.

GOD DELIVERS THE HEBREWS

Early one morning Amar heard his father calling, "Moses is back!"

Amar opened his sleepy eyes. His father was still talking. "Moses and his brother Aaron say that God told them to speak with the pharaoh," he was saying. "They will ask him to let us leave Egypt."

But the pharaoh did not agree to free the Hebrews. He needed slaves to do his hard work. To punish the Hebrews, he made them work even harder.

Moses and Aaron went again to the pharaoh. They said, "Because you did not let the Hebrews go, God will send **plagues** (plāgz)."

Plagues are happenings which make people suffer. God sent ten plagues. The plagues showed the Egyptians that their gods were weak and false. God said, "Against all the gods of Egypt I will execute judgment: I am the LORD." God showed that He was more powerful than any other gods.

Exodus 12:12b

In the first plague, God changed the Nile River to blood.

God commanded the Hebrews to put the blood of the Passover lamb on the tops and on the sides of their doors. The blood of the Passover lamb also pointed to Jesus who came later and shed His blood to save sinners.

Photo: Library of Congress/Matson Photo Service

Blood cannot be used to drink or to irrigate. God proved He was more powerful than the river-god. In the second plague, frogs came out of the river to bother the Egyptians.

Another plague killed cattle, which the Egyptians also worshiped. Hail destroyed their crops.

An east wind brought swarms of **locusts** to eat the crops that were left. A locust is an insect which looks like a grasshopper. The Egyptians worshiped the locust. But instead of helping the Egyptians, the locusts made them suffer.

A plague of darkness proved that God was more powerful than the sun-god, Ra.

Most of the plagues did not hurt God's people on the delta. Only the Egyptians suffered. God proved that the Hebrews were His special people.

After the ninth plague, Moses told the Hebrews to get ready to leave Egypt. He told each family to kill a lamb to eat. God commanded them to place blood from the lamb on the door frames of their houses.

In the night, God passed through the land of Egypt. The oldest son in each Egyptian family died that night. But God passed over each Hebrew house that had blood on the door.

This last plague changed the Pharaoh's mind. He told the Hebrews to hurry out of the land. They gladly left with Moses, their leader. Their leaving was called an **exodus**.

From that time on, the Hebrews remembered the Exodus by having a **Passover** feast. The Passover feast kept them from forgetting the night when God had passed over the houses of His special people and spared their oldest sons.

Exodus 12:26, 27 "And it shall come to pass, when your children shall say unto you, What mean ye by this service? That ye shall say, It is the sacrifice of the LORD's passover, who passed over the houses of the children of Israel in Egypt, when he smote the Egyptians, and delivered our houses."

Years later, at a Passover feast, Amar told the story to his children. Later, they passed the story on to their children. And so the wonderful story about God's changes in Egypt was never forgotten.

WHAT DO WE LEARN FROM EGYPT?

The story of Egypt teaches us that God wants His people to be special people. He does not want His people to copy the sinful customs of the communities where they live. He wants his people to be different.

We also learn from Egypt that God can punish the strongest nation in the world. He can change the heart of the strongest leader. He can make changes to protect His people. God still changes communities to punish sin or to help His people.

SHOW YOUR KNOWLEDGE

1. What did Moses learn in the schools of Egypt?
2. What did God teach Moses in the desert?
3. What did the ten plagues show the Egyptians?
4. The Passover feast helped the Hebrews remember the night when God _____ the houses of His people and _____ .

5. When the Hebrews kept the Passover feast every year:
    a. it saved the lives of their children.
    b. it helped their children learn about God's changes in Egypt.
    c. it taught their children about the good foods of Egypt.
6. The story of Egypt helps us to see that:
    a. God always turns the hearts of leaders against his people.
    b. God is displeased when His people copy sinful community customs.
    c. Christians must always leave sinful communities.

SHARE YOUR KNOWLEDGE

1. Name the second book of the Bible. How does the name tell you what you will find in this book?

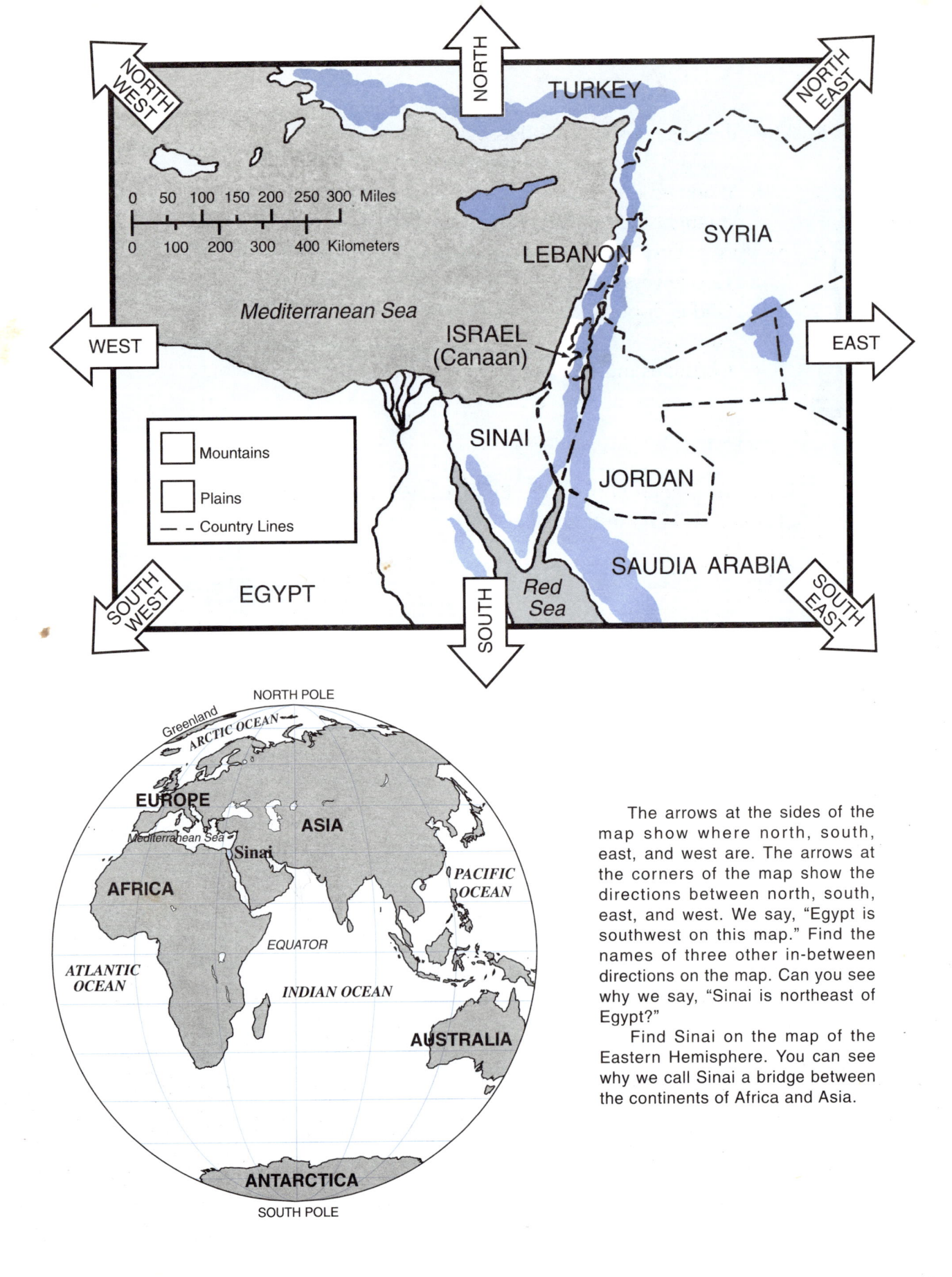

The arrows at the sides of the map show where north, south, east, and west are. The arrows at the corners of the map show the directions between north, south, east, and west. We say, "Egypt is southwest on this map." Find the names of three other in-between directions on the map. Can you see why we say, "Sinai is northeast of Egypt?"

Find Sinai on the map of the Eastern Hemisphere. You can see why we call Sinai a bridge between the continents of Africa and Asia.

"And the children of Israel took their journeys out of the wilderness of Sinai" (Numbers 10:12a).

The Sinai Peninsula, Bridge Between Continents

Study the map on this page. Suppose you wanted to go from Africa to Asia. Find a way you could get there without crossing a large body of water.

You could cross the land of Sinai (sī′ nī). See how this piece of land is like a bridge between Asia and Africa. Now you know why people sometimes call this land a bridge between continents.

For many years, traders from Africa crossed the land of Sinai to sell their goods in Asia. From Asia, traders crossed this land on their way to Africa. The Hebrews crossed this land bridge to get from Egypt back to their homeland of Canaan in Asia.

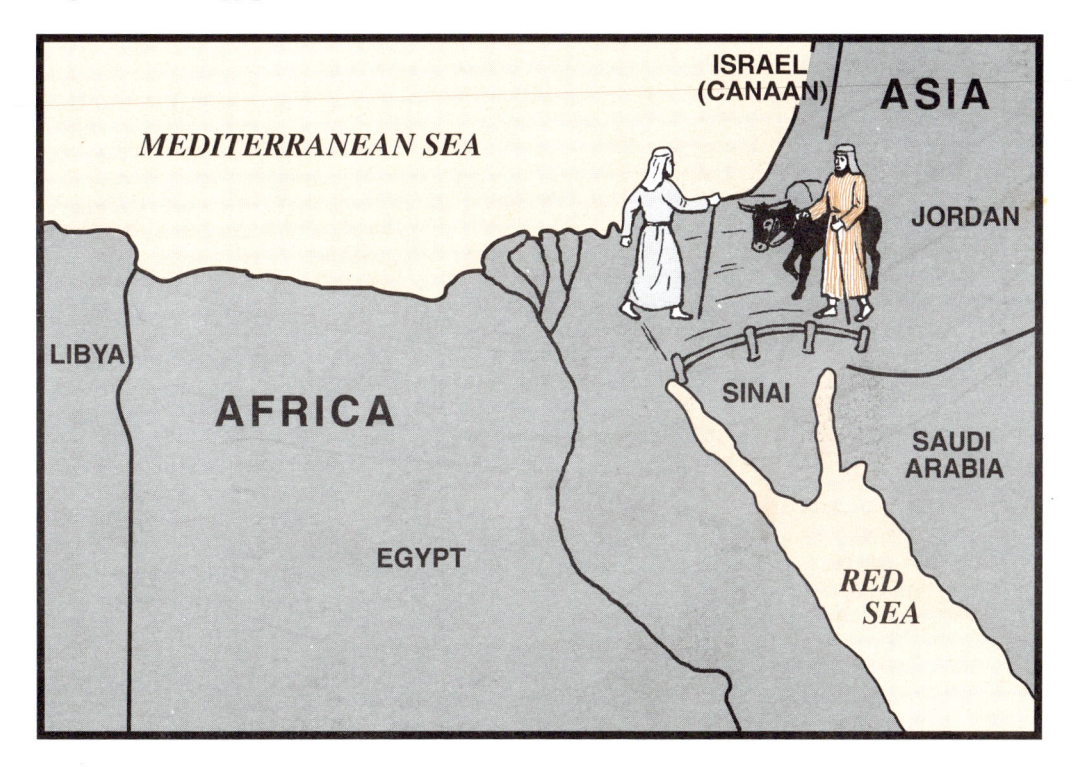

The land of Sinai is a **peninsula** (pə nin´ sə lə). A peninsula is a body of land with water almost all around it. What body of water lies to the north of the Sinai Peninsula?

South of the peninsula, find the northern end of the Red Sea. At this place, the Red Sea divides into two bodies of water that look like the ears of a rabbit. The Sinai Peninsula is between these two narrow bodies of water.

Perhaps you wonder how the Red Sea got its name. No one knows for sure, but we have some ideas.

Hot winds often blow clouds of desert sand across this sea. The dust settles in large reddish-looking streaks across the water. Some people believe the name "Red Sea" describes this sight.

Others believe the name comes from the red seaweed and the tiny reddish sea animals that live in the Red Sea. Still other people think the name comes from the reddish hills along the edges of the sea. Perhaps all of these things helped people long ago to name the Red Sea.

God helped the Hebrews to cross the Red Sea at the beginning of their trip. "And Moses stretched out his hand over the

Exodus 14: 21, 22a

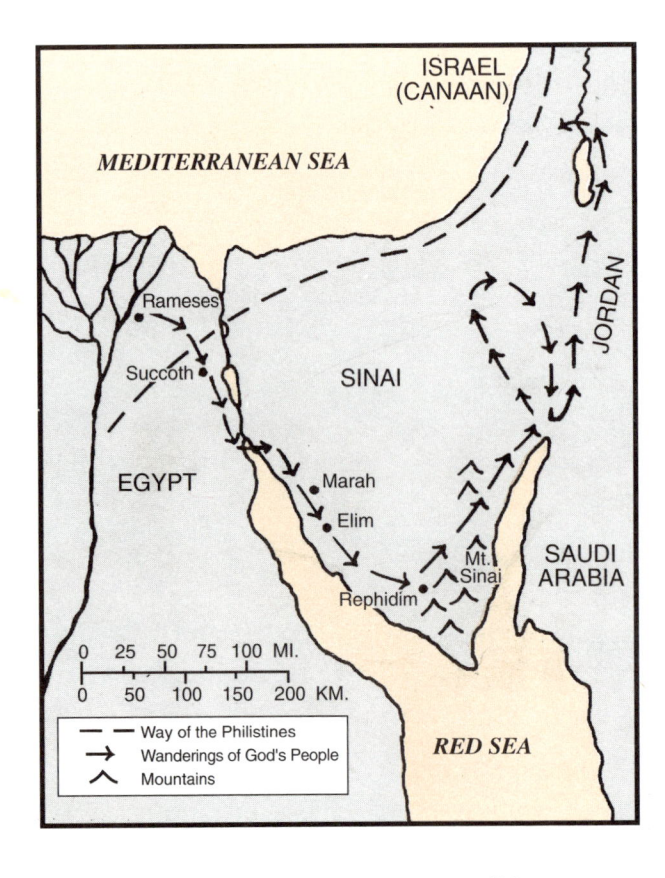

On this map the line of dashes shows the shortest way from Egypt to Canaan. Why didn't God lead the Hebrews that way? With your finger, trace the way God did lead them. Learn the names of the places where the Hebrews stopped along the way.

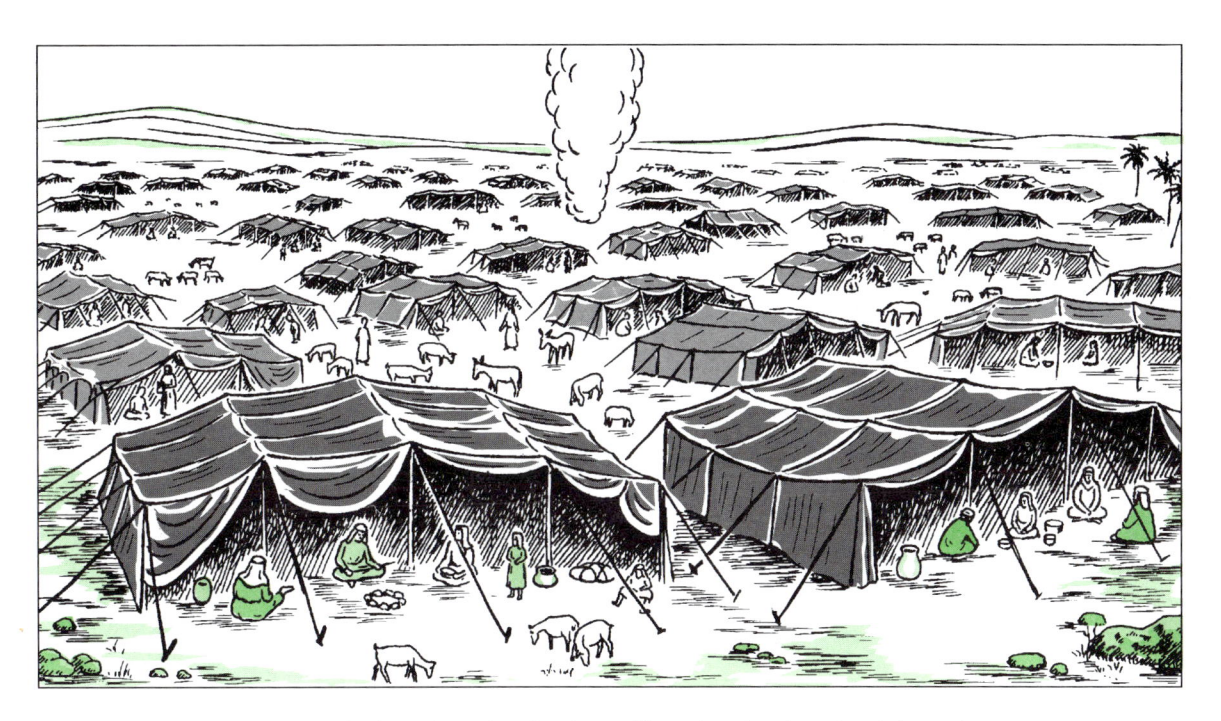

"And the Lord went before them by day in a pillar of a cloud, to lead them the way; and by night in a pillar of fire, to give them light; to go by day and night: He took not away the pillar of the cloud by day, nor the pillar of fire by night, from before the people" (Exodus 13:21, 22).

sea; and the LORD caused the sea to go back by a strong east wind all that night, and made the sea dry land, and the waters were divided."

The shortest way to Canaan was along the northern coast of the Sinai Peninsula. But enemies called Philistines (fi′ lə stēnz) lived there. The Hebrews were not prepared to fight. God did not lead them that way.

"God led them not through the way of the land of the Philistines, although that was near; for God said, Lest peradventure the people repent when they see war, and they return to Egypt."

Exodus 13:17b

God led the Hebrews toward the south instead. See the symbols for mountains at the tip of the peninsula on page 76. Find Mount Sinai. God led the Hebrews toward this mountain.

In the desert, the Hebrews had to learn new ways of living. Moses had traveled through the desert of Sinai before. He had learned about desert life. Now he could use that part of God's training. God helped him teach the Hebrews new customs. They learned to live like **nomads.**

Nomads camp in the desert where they find water to drink and grass for their cattle. They often camp at an oasis. Nomads move to another grazing spot when there is no more food for their cattle.

The Hebrews were different from other nomad people. God told them when to move and when to stop and set up camp. God also gave the Hebrews many of their customs. He wanted them to be His nation and live His way.

Nomad people still camp in the Sinai Peninsula today. They still live much like the Hebrews must have lived in the desert. Their customs help us understand Hebrew desert customs of long ago.

In this chapter, you will meet make-believe nomad friends. They will help you learn how the Hebrews really lived in Bible times when they traveled through the desert.

SHOW YOUR KNOWLEDGE

1. What route did traders and the Hebrews travel to get from Africa to Asia?
2. What body of water lies to the north of the Sinai Peninsula?
3. What body of water did the Hebrews cross at the beginning of their trip back to Canaan?
4. God led the Hebrews toward the south:
    a. because He wanted them to take the shortest way to Canaan.
    b. so they could find the best places to camp.
    c. to keep them from being discouraged by enemies.
5. In the desert, the Hebrews learned to live like _____.
6. How were the Hebrew nomads different from other nomad people?

SHARE YOUR KNOWLEDGE

1. The Sinai Peninsula is shaped most like a (square, triangle, circle).
2. Why is the Sinai Peninsula sometimes called a bridge?
3. List three things that might have given the Red Sea its name.
4. From Exodus 19:2, you learn that the Bible word _____ means the same as the word "desert."

"And what one nation in the earth is like thy people, even like Israel, whom God went to redeem for a people to himself, and to make him a name . . . ?" (2 Samuel 7:23a).

God's Nation in the Desert

"Please, Raman [rā´ man], may I have a drink? Just one small swallow of water," pleaded Meribah (mər´ ə bə). How she wished the journey would soon end. For weeks the weary Hebrews had tramped over hot desert sands.

"Only enough to wet your tongue and no more," Raman replied. He swung the skin water bottle down from his shoulder. "This water must last until we reach the next oasis," he said.

But before Meribah could lift the bottle to her lips, she heard a shout from up the line.

"Oasis! Oasis! An oasis called Rephidim [ref´ ə dim] is just ahead!"

The thirsty crowd hurried forward. By the time Meribah's family got to the oasis, an angry group stood around Moses shouting, "Why did you bring us out of Egypt to kill us? There is no water here!"

Moses cried to God. God told him to strike a nearby rock with his rod. Sparkling water gushed from the rock and splashed onto the dry sand. Angry murmurs turned to joyous shouts.

Nomads still live in lands where the Hebrews lived. They live in sackcloth tents much like the Hebrews had in Bible times.

The murmuring of the people bothered Raman. "Why do they always complain?" he asked himself. "God had done wonderful things for them in Egypt. Surely He wouldn't let them die in the desert. Isn't Moses a good leader?"

There was no time for questions. Raman's family needed his help to unpack. The pillar of cloud had stopped. The Hebrews would camp.

SETTING UP THE TENT

Raman and his father lifted a black cloth pack from the back of a donkey. This black bundle was a tent cloth called **sackcloth**. Sackcloth is woven from the hair of goats.

Raman helped to spread the large heavy tent cloth out on the ground. He and his father lifted it up over the tall tent poles. While his father pounded **stakes** into the ground around the tent, Raman helped Meribah stretch ropes from the edges of the tent cloth to the stakes.

Raman's mother hung a sackcloth curtain in the tent to divide it into two rooms. One room was for the men and guests. In the other room the women would prepare food for the family to eat.

Things for inside the tent had to be easy to carry, because nomad families were always on the move. Meribah and her mother unrolled rugs to cover the tent floor. Raman unpacked straw mats for chairs. He unrolled an animal skin to be placed on the ground for a table.

The family carefully unpacked their **pottery**. Pottery is jars and bowls made from clay that has been baked in a fire.

Their lamps were also pottery. They were shaped like saucers. Each lamp had a handle at one end and a hole or pinched lip at the other end. A piece of cotton or linen called a **wick** was placed in the hole or lip. The saucer was filled with oil. At night when the wick was lighted, the lamp gave off a soft yellow light.

Raman unloaded the **mortar** and **pestle** (pe´ səl) his mother used to grind grain into flour. A mortar is a stone bowl, and a pestle is a heavy stick used to pound grain placed in the bowl.

Father placed a large pottery jar outside the tent. This jar was an oven. When Raman's mother was ready to bake bread,

The pottery lamps of the Hebrews looked much like this one.

The Hebrews pounded grain into flour with a pestle in a bowl called a mortar. The Bible says the Hebrews used mortars to make flour from the manna God sent from heaven.

Nomads scraped out a hole in the sand to make a hearth for a fire. The women set dishes on stones for cooking.

she would build a fire inside the jar. After the jar was hot, she would take the fire out and pat flat loaves of bread against the hot inside walls of the jar.

Meribah hung the family water bottles on a tent pole. The bottles were made from goatskins. In the desert, water was too precious to be spilled. Skin bottles did not break easily.

A goatskin bucket was hung from a tent pole also. This bucket was used to draw water from a well if there was one at an oasis.

Meribah could see other families setting up camp. The people were placing their tents in groups.

Meribah asked, "Why are the tents in each group always placed in a large circle?"

Father replied, "Nomads must protect their animals. At night, the animals can be kept inside the circle of tents. There they will be safe from robbers and wild animals."

82

It was time for the evening meal. Raman and his father set to work making a **hearth** (härth) for cooking.

Together they scraped out a hole in the sand near the tent. They gathered stones and placed them around the top of the hole. Mother soon had a glowing fire in the hole and a pottery dish of food on the stones. The job of setting up camp was finished.

SHOW YOUR KNOWLEDGE

1. How many rooms did a nomad tent have?
2. How was each room in a nomad tent used?
3. Why were mats and skins better for a nomad family than chairs and tables?
4. Where did a nomad lady place her bread to bake it?
    a. against the hot inside walls of the jar oven
    b. in a pan on the hot coals
    c. on a rack in the oven
5. Why did the nomads use skins to make their water bottles and buckets?
6. Why did nomad communities camp in circles?

SHARE YOUR KNOWLEDGE

1. Study Exodus 15:22-25. Also study verse 27. These verses give two places where the Hebrews had camped before coming to Rephidim. Fill in the blanks below.
    a. At the first oasis called _____ , the Hebrews were sad to find _____ water.
    b. At the second oasis called _____ they found _____ wells of water, and _____ palm trees.
2. In the *World Book Encyclopedia*, look up *palm trees*. List foods the Hebrews might have gotten from palm trees in the desert.
3. Place a white sheet of paper over the map on page 76 and trace it with your pencil. With a colored pencil, draw a line to show the way the Hebrews traveled to Rephidim. The Hebrews started their journey near Rameses in Egypt. Use the scale of miles to find out

how far they had traveled to Rephidim.
4. Study Genesis 21:14. What kind of bottle do you think Abraham gave Hagar for travel in the desert?
    a. a pottery jug
    b. a goatskin bag
    c. a stone jar

DESERT FOODS

Nomads sometimes stay at an oasis long enough to grow a few crops. But they usually get their food in other ways. Their animals give them milk and meat. They trade animals and animal products for wheat or barley. From these grains they make bread, their most important food.

The Hebrews had carried some food along from Egypt. When it ran out, the people had no place to trade for more. God had planned it this way. In the desert, God could teach the Hebrews to trust Him for their needs.

Raman remembered the first morning God had sent food. After the dew had dried up, the ground looked like it was covered with frost.

"Manna?" Raman's family had said when they saw the ground covered with something white. Other families were saying "manna," too. The word meant, "What is it?"

Exodus 16:15b, 16a

Moses had answered, "This is the bread which the LORD hath given you to eat. This is the thing which the LORD hath commanded, Gather of it every man according to his eating, an omer for every man." An **omer** was about two quarts.

Exodus 16:31b

The manna looked like small white seeds. "The taste of it was like wafers [thin cakes] made with honey."

Numbers 11:8a

"And the people went about, and gathered it, and ground it in mills, or beat it in a mortar, and baked it in pans, and made cakes of it."

Mother and Meribah prepared the evening meal while Raman and Father went to milk the goats. Meribah ground manna into flour with the mortar and pestle. Mother built a fire in the jar oven.

When the oven was hot, Mother took the fire out and placed loaves of manna bread against the hot sides of the jar. She made three kinds of loaves.

One kind of loaf was small like a bun. Another kind was large and round. The third kind did not look like a loaf at all. It was thin like paper. The family would use pieces of this thin bread instead of spoons for eating.

Raman and Father brought the goat milk. Mother placed some of it into a bowl with a little yeast. In about a day, the milk would sour and form white lumps called **curds**. These sour curds are a food called **leben** (lā´ bən). The word *butter* in the Bible sometimes stands for this food made from milk.

Nomads today eat lots of leben. It is their favorite food. They often serve leben to their guests.

Before the evening meal, Mother and Meribah made butter. Mother filled a goatskin bottle with milk and hung it between three poles. She and Meribah squeezed the bottle and shook it back and forth until the milk turned to creamy yellow butter.

Bread and milk are the main nomad foods. Nomad families in the desert eat very little meat because their cattle are like money to them. They can trade animals, wool, and milk for the

This picture shows the way nomads used a goatskin bottle to churn butter.

things they need.

God commanded the Hebrews to be very strict about the animals they used for food. He said, "Whatsoever [beast] parteth the hoof, and is cloven-footed [has a split in its hoof], and cheweth the cud, among the beasts, that shall ye eat."

Leviticus 11:3

Animals that chewed the cud and had split hoofs were called **clean.** All other animals were **unclean.** God commanded the Hebrews not to eat any unclean animals.

Cows were clean, because they chewed a cud and had split hoofs. Pigs had split hoofs, but did not chew a cud. Pigs were unclean. The Hebrews were not to eat pig meat.

To the Hebrew nomads, fruits were a special treat. At an oasis, they sometimes found grapes, figs, dates, or **pomegranates** (pä´ mə gra nəts). Pomegranates are red and shaped like apples. Inside they are filled with seeds and a sweet juice. Honey was another treat nomads did not find very often in the desert.

SHOW YOUR KNOWLEDGE

1. Why did God allow the Hebrews to run out of food in the desert?
2. What does the word "manna" mean?
3. How did the people use the thin kind of bread?
4. What are the main foods of the nomads?
5. Why do nomad people eat little meat?

SHARE YOUR KNOWLEDGE

1. Exodus 3:8 tells about the land to which God was leading the Hebrews. Study this verse and answer these questions.
    a. What two foods would the Hebrews find in Canaan?
    b. The word "flowing" means there would be (enough, more than enough, less than enough) of these foods in Canaan.
    c. Why would these two foods make nomad people believe Canaan was a *very good* land?
2. From Deuteronomy 8:7, 8, 9a, list other things God said the Hebrews would find in Canaan.

KEEPING ORDER IN THE HEBREW COMMUNITY

The evening meal was ready. Bread, butter, and leben were spread on an animal skin outside the tent.

Hands had to be washed. Raman poured water on Father's hands from a pottery pitcher. As Father rubbed his hands together, the dirty water fell into an empty bowl on the ground. The family took turns pouring water for each other until everyone had washed.

The Hebrews did not wash their hands in water that had become dirty. Since Hebrews ate with their fingers, their hands needed to be very clean. They believed fresh water poured on their hands helped to get them cleaner.

When nomads have visitors, the men eat first with them. The women and children eat by themselves later.

This evening, everyone in the Hebrew camp was too busy

The Hebrews needed to have very clean hands for eating because they ate with their fingers.

for visiting. Families ate together in the warm night air. Father thanked God for the food. Then as the family ate, he spoke to them about order in the Hebrew community.

"Our community is divided into groups called tribes," Father began. "The people in each tribe are related to each other."

"How did the tribes begin in the first place?" asked Raman.

"They began with the 12 sons of Jacob and their families," replied Father. "Their families grew and became the 12 large tribes of Israel. When we get to Canaan, God will give each tribe a part of the land."

Numbers 26:55

" . . . The land shall be divided by lot: according to the names of the tribes of their fathers they shall inherit."

Father began talking about tribal government. He said, "Each tribe has leaders called **elders**. They are the older men in the tribe.

88

"The elders in each tribe settle the problems of their own people. Sometimes elders from every tribe talk over community problems with Moses, who is the leader of all the tribes.

"Moses teaches us God's way for our community. God has also called Moses to be the community **judge**. When people have a disagreement, Moses decides who is right and who is wrong. He decides the punishments for those who wrong others."

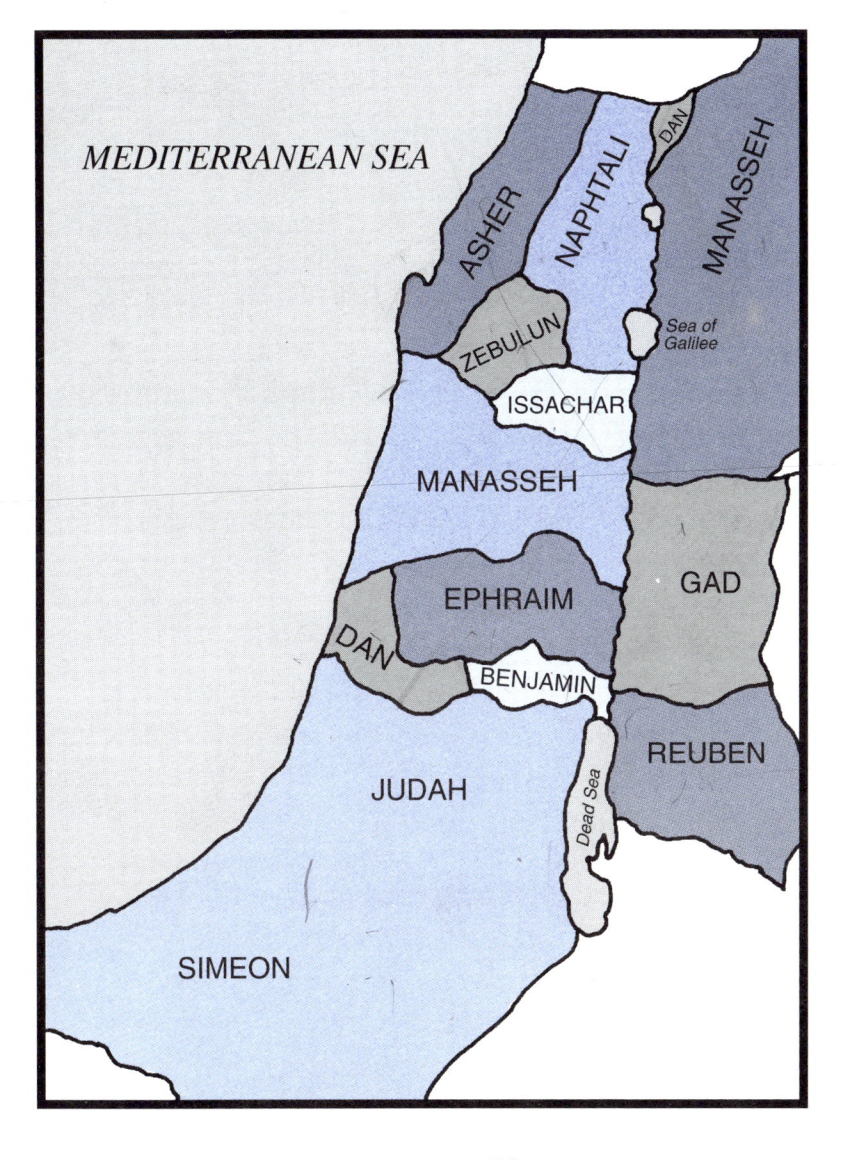

God gave each tribe its own piece of land when the Hebrews reached the land He promised them. This map shows where each tribe settled in the land of Canaan.

Moses went to the top of a mountain to watch the Hebrews fight the Amalekites. When Moses held up his hand, the Hebrews began to win the battle. They began to lose when he put his tired hand down. Moses sat on a rock. Aaron and Hur held up his hands until the Hebrews won the battle at the end of the day.

ENEMY TRIBES

Meribah said, "I heard that Moses is calling a meeting of the elders tonight. What community problem do they need to talk about?" she asked.

"Some of our men have spied another tribe coming across the desert toward our camp," Father replied. "They may attack and try to steal our cattle. Or they may try to drive us away from this oasis."

Father said, "If this tribe is friendly, their leaders will bring food to eat with our elders. By eating together, nomad tribes sometimes make a **covenant** [kə′ və nənt] to be friends and never harm each other. A covenant is an agreement between two people or two groups of people."

"Suppose the strange tribe is unfriendly?" asked Raman. "What will our tribes do if the men want to fight us?"

"God will tell us what to do," replied Father, getting to his feet.

The next morning, the strange tribe attacked. They were

enemies called **Amalekites** (a´ mə lə kīts). Because the Hebrews had been slaves, they were not used to fighting. God helped them win the battle. The battle taught the Hebrews to trust in God and not in their own strength.

SHOW YOUR KNOWLEDGE

1. What was the Hebrew custom for washing hands?
2. How did the 12 tribes of Israel begin?
3. When the Hebrews got to Canaan, each tribe would get a part of the _____ .
4. What did the elders in the tribe do?
5. Who was the judge for the community?
6. What was the work of the judge?
7. Suppose you visited a nomad tribe today. You could be *sure* of the nomads' friendship if:
    a. they lived at an oasis.
    b. they invited you to eat with them.
    c. they came out of their tents to meet you.
8. What lesson did the Hebrews learn when God helped them win the battle with the Amalekites?

SHARE YOUR KNOWLEDGE

1. Read the last sentence in 2 Kings 3:11. How does this sentence tell you that Elisha was Elijah's helper?
2. List the names of the 12 sons of Israel (Jacob). Find them in these verses from Genesis 49. Each son's family grew to be a large tribe.
    verse 3 _Benjameh_
    verse 5 _ruben_
    verse 8 _Josab_
    verse 13 _____
    verse 14 _____
    verse 16 _____
    verse 19 _____
    verse 20 _____
    verse 21 _____

verse 22 _____
verse 27 _____

3. Study Genesis 48:1. The tribe of Joseph later became two tribes from the families of his two sons. Their names were _____ and _____ .

4. Why did nomads sometimes worry when they saw a strange tribe coming toward their camp?

MOSES CHOOSES HELPERS

The land of Midian was not far from Rephidim. One day, Moses had a visitor from his old home in the desert. This visitor was Jethro (jeth´ rō), the father of Moses' wife.

Jethro watched Moses judge the people. All day, they brought their problems to him. Moses had no time to rest.

Exodus 18:17b, 18b

Jethro said to Moses, "The thing that thou doest is not good... this thing is too heavy [hard] for thee." Jethro gave Moses a plan for choosing helpers. Moses obeyed the plan.

Moses divided the Hebrews into small groups of ten people. He chose a judge for each small group and told them to settle all of the small problems.

Moses placed a judge over larger groups of 50 people to take care of hard problems. Judges over groups of 100 people looked into harder problems. Very hard problems went to

This is the Supreme Court Building. Judges have a court in this building to settle the hardest problems about laws in the United States. Judges in the towns and cities settle the smaller problems.

Photo: John D. Martin

This drawing shows how Moses divided large groups of 1,000 people into smaller groups. Judges over the smaller groups settled all the small problems. The judges from the largest groups brought only the hardest problems to Moses.

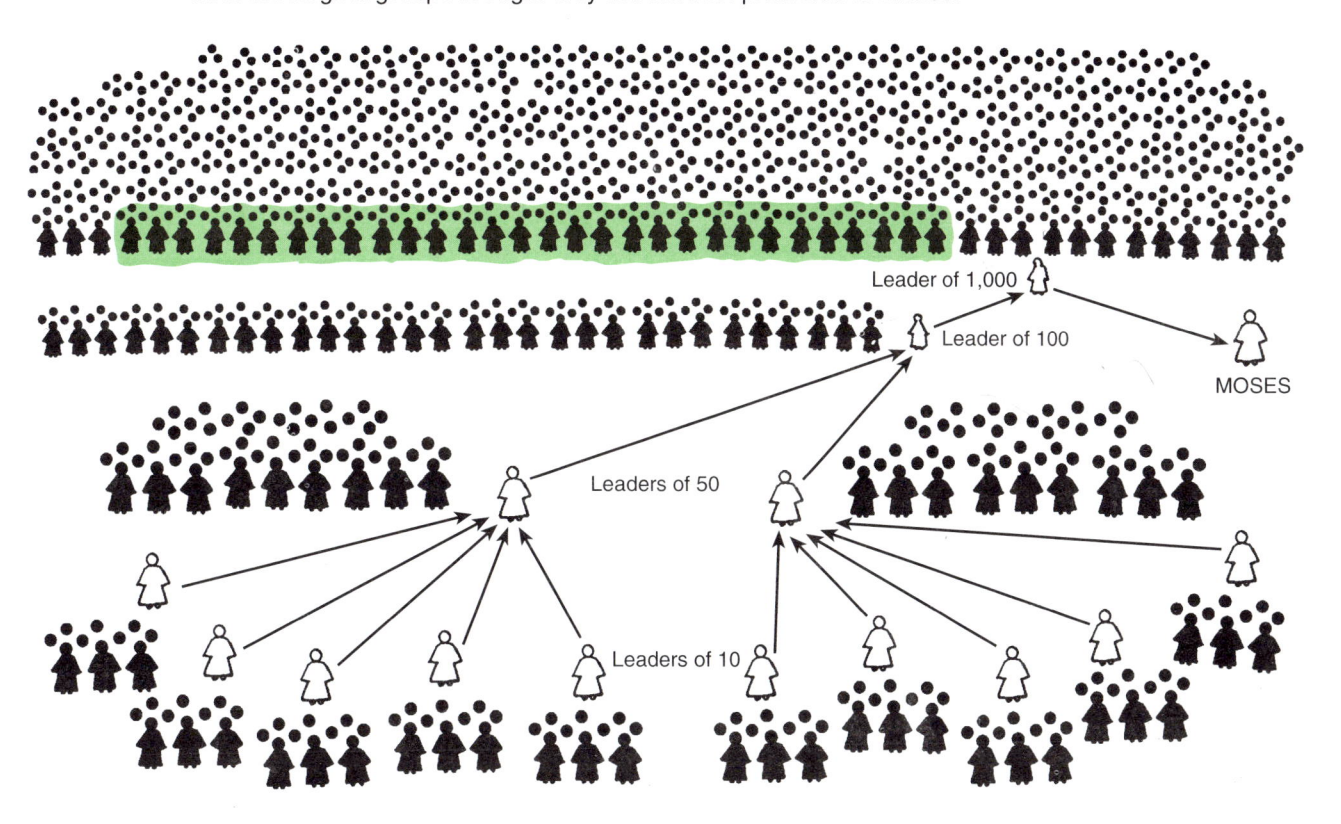

judges over groups of one thousand people. The people brought only the hardest problems to Moses.

This plan worked so well that judges ruled Israel for many years. The people did not need a king. God wanted judges and elders to be the leaders of His nation.

Today, our nation and many other nations use a plan somewhat like the plan Moses gave to the Hebrews.

Our nation has **courts** where people who disobey laws are judged. Small courts in towns judge small problems. Larger courts in cities judge harder problems. The hardest problems are judged in the **Supreme Court** at the capital of our nation. God's plan for judges still works today.

GOD GIVES HIS NATION LAWS

God gave the sign for the Hebrew camp to move. Raman and Meribah helped Father and Mother take down the tent and pack their belongings. The camp moved from Rephidim to Mount Sinai. On the map on page 76, find Mount Sinai at the tip of the Sinai Peninsula. The Hebrew nation camped at Mount Sinai for almost a year.

God's nation had leaders. But nations must have laws, too. Leaders usually make the laws for a nation. But God made the laws for the nation of Israel. He wanted other nations to learn about Him by looking at His nation and His laws.

God wrote His laws on two tablets of stone. He gave them to Moses on top of Mount Sinai. Today these laws are called the Ten Commandments. You can find them in Exodus 20 and in Deuteronomy 5 in your Bible.

Father explained the Ten Commandments to his family.

He said, "These ten laws show us which ways of living are right and which ways are wrong. Such laws are called **moral**

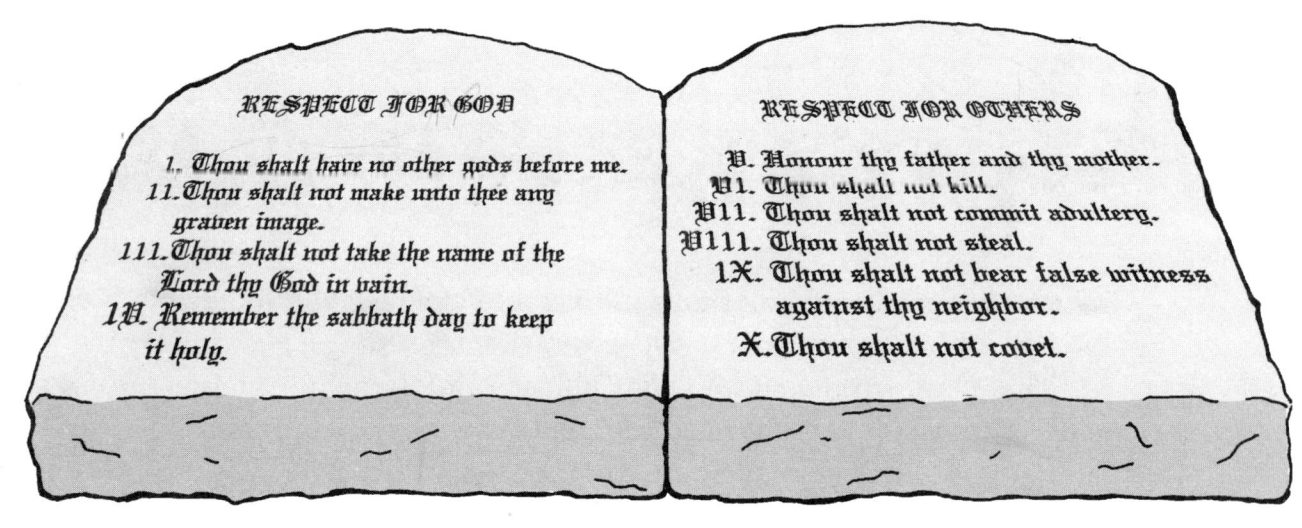

RESPECT FOR GOD

1. Thou shalt have no other gods before me.
11. Thou shalt not make unto thee any graven image.
111. Thou shalt not take the name of the Lord thy God in vain.
1V. Remember the sabbath day to keep it holy.

RESPECT FOR OTHERS

V. Honour thy father and thy mother.
VI. Thou shalt not kill.
VII. Thou shalt not commit adultery.
VIII. Thou shalt not steal.
IX. Thou shalt not bear false witness against thy neighbor.
X. Thou shalt not covet.

God wrote the Ten Commandments on tables of stone. Moses broke the stones when the Hebrews broke God's Law and worshiped the golden calf. Moses had to write the commandments himself as God gave them to him the second time.

laws. God's ten moral laws are divided into two parts.

"The first four laws show us how people must respect God.

Exodus 20:3 The first law says, 'Thou shalt have no other gods before me.' People must believe in the only true God first. Only then will they obey the rest of His laws.

"The last six laws show us how people must treat each other. All of these laws are against selfish actions. God knows that selfishness causes many community problems.

Exodus 20:17a "The tenth law says, 'Thou shalt not **covet**.' A person covets when he wants something he should not have. People covet before breaking the other five laws about treating others right."

Father finished by saying, "Obeying the first law and tenth law will help to keep a person from breaking any of the other eight laws."

God's laws are the best community laws ever written. This is because God made the people who need the laws. He understands people better than leaders who usually make laws for communities.

Some leaders today see that God's laws are best for their people. When these leaders make laws, they use many of God's laws. Many moral laws of our nation were taken from God's moral laws in the Bible.

When people obey these laws, God blesses our nation. We have trouble in our nation when people forget or disobey God's moral laws.

"By the blessing of the upright the city [or nation] is exalted [lifted up]: but it is overthrown by the mouth of the wicked." **Proverbs 11:11**

SHOW YOUR KNOWLEDGE

1. To make Moses' work easier, Jethro:
    a. decided they should have a king.
    b. gave Moses a plan for choosing helpers.
    c. made some new laws for the Hebrews.
2. Israel was ruled by (judges, priests, prophets) for many years.
3. (*True* or *False*?) Our nation uses a plan somewhat like Moses' to judge problems.
4. God made the laws for the Hebrew nation because:
    a. God wanted His nation to show other nations His will about right and wrong.
    b. Moses asked Him to do it.
    c. the Hebrew leaders did not know how to make laws.
5. God could make the best moral laws because:
    a. leaders do not care about right and wrong.
    b. He doesn't want anyone else to make laws.
    c. He knew more about people than anyone else did.

SHARE YOUR KNOWLEDGE

1. In Matthew 22:35-40, Jesus gave two great laws that will help us obey all of the Ten Commandments. Copy each law. Under each one, list the numbers of the commandments in Exodus 20 that it will help you obey.
2. Why do we have so much trouble in our nation today?

PUTTING LAWS TO WORK

"Laws do not help a nation if the people disobey them," Father told the family one evening when they were eating together. "So God told Moses how lawbreakers should be punished."

Raman said, "Egypt had punishments for lawbreakers too. But their punishments were not fair.

"I remember, Father, how you borrowed an ox once to do some work," he said. "It got sick and died. You were punished just as hard as the man who killed one of our goats on purpose."

Father replied, "God's punishments are more fair than the punishments of any other nation. If a person kills someone's ox by accident, he must give the owner another ox. But he must give the owner five oxen if he killed the ox on purpose."

"How will we know if a person breaks a law on purpose or

by accident?" asked Raman. "Who will decide the punishments?"

"The judges will study each case," replied Father. "The judges will decide how the law was broken. They will decide the punishments."

In the Bible, we can find God's punishments for broken laws. They are written in Exodus, Leviticus, and Deuteronomy. Leaders today sometimes use ideas about fair punishment from these books.

THE TENT OF GOD

God wanted a place to meet with the Hebrews. He wanted to live right in the middle of their camp.

On Mount Sinai, God said to Moses, "Let them make me a sanctuary [holy place]; that I may dwell among them . . . and there I will meet with thee."

Exodus 25:8, 22a

God gave Moses plans for making a special tent called a **tabernacle** (ta´ bər na kəl). The Hebrews made every part of God's tent just like He told Moses it should be.

The people gave materials they had brought from Egypt. Using red, blue, and purple thread, workmen wove tent cloths and curtains. They made furniture from wood. Many pieces were covered with gold. The beauty of God's tent reminded the nation of God's glory.

The tribe of Levi always camped around the tabernacle. God chose **priests** from this tribe to care for His tent.

The priests talked to God for the people. They killed sheep, goats, and bulls to burn upon an altar outside the tent.

These **sacrifices** (sa´ krə fis əz) showed that the people were sorry for their sins and believed God would forgive them. The blood of each sacrifice reminded the people that sin always brings death.

The tent of God always stood in the center of the camp. The 12 tribes camped around it. The tabernacle reminded them that God was with them.

Over the tabernacle, God placed a sign to show that He was there. "The cloud of the Lord was upon the tabernacle by day, and fire was on it by night."

Exodus 40:38a

THE TABERNACLE

1. Courtyard — any Hebrew man could go into this place.
2. Altar of burnt offering — the Hebrews offered all their sacrifices on this altar.
3. Laver — the priests washed here before doing their duties in the tabernacle.
4. Holy place — only the priests could go into this place to look after the candlestick, the table of shewbread, and the altar of incense.
5. Holy of holies — only the high priest could go into this place once a year to sprinkle the blood of a sacrifice. The ark of the covenant with the mercy seat was the only furniture in this place.

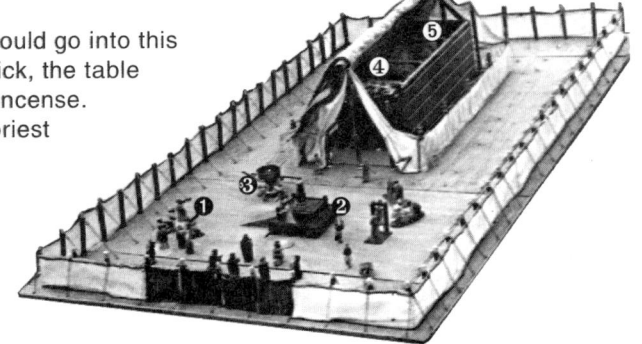

Photo: Library of Congress/Matson Photo Service

When the cloud began to move, the Hebrews rolled up their tents and followed it.

Numbers 9:17a "And when the cloud was taken up from the tabernacle, then after that the children of Israel journeyed."

Numbers 9:17b When the cloud stopped, the Hebrews set up camp. "And in the place where the cloud abode [stayed], there the children of Israel pitched their tents."

2 Samuel 7:6b Wherever the Hebrews went, they carried God's tent with them. God "walked in a tent and in a tabernacle" with His nation in the desert.

For over 40 years, the Hebrews lived as nomads in the desert. Finally, God led them into the land of Canaan. There the people no longer needed tents. They began to live in houses of stone or brick. In time, they built a stone temple to take the place of God's tabernacle tent.

In the United States, the words "In God We Trust" are on every coin. Do you think these words are true for most people? What will happen to this nation if the words are not true?

Photo: Kevin and Bethany Shank

98

At first, the Hebrews found enemies living in Canaan. God made a covenant or agreement with His nation.

God told them that if they obeyed His laws, He would bless them and help them win the land from their enemies.

The children of Israel often broke their covenant to obey. But when they turned to God, He always kept His part of the covenant and blessed His nation.

SHOW YOUR KNOWLEDGE

1. Laws do not work unless lawbreakers are _____ for disobedience.
2. The punishments God gave His nation were better than the punishments of any other nation because they were ____ .
3. Why did God want the Hebrews to make Him a tabernacle?
4. The priests who cared for the tabernacle were from the tribe of _____.
5. The priests helped the people kill animals for _____ to show that they were sorry for their sins.
6. What sign did God place over the tabernacle to show that He was there?
7. What did God promise to do for His nation if the people obeyed His laws?

SHARE YOUR KNOWLEDGE

1. Why did God ask the Hebrew nomads to make Him a tent, instead of a stone house, in the desert?
2. How did the Hebrews know when to move, where to go, and when to camp?

Name the countries Israel has for neighbors. Through the years, the people in these countries were often enemies of the Israelites. Many times God let these enemies take land from Israel to punish the Israelites for their sins. Look at the dashed spaces on the map. Until 1967 enemies of Israel ruled these lands. But in 1967, the nation of Israel took over these lands again and kept them for a number of years. Today, the nation of Israel covers much of the same land the country had in the time of Jesus.

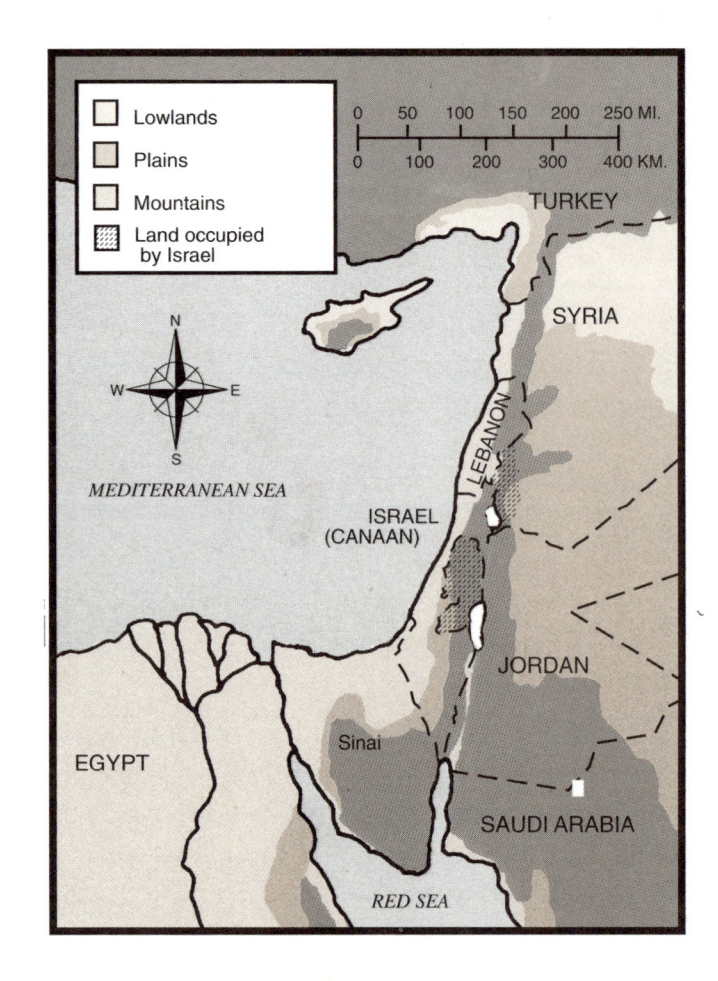

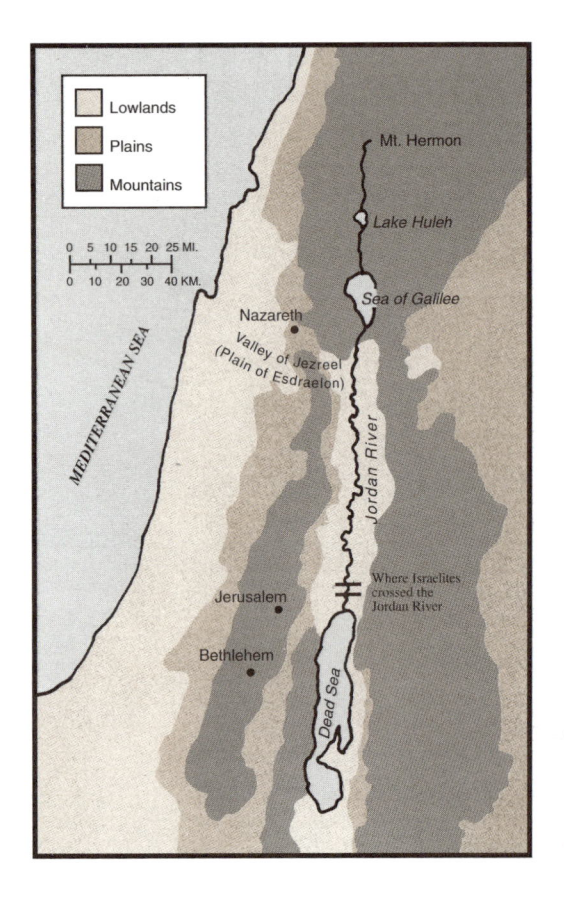

Israel is one of the smallest countries in the world. But God chose this very small country to be the homeland for His Son, Jesus Christ. Most of the happenings in the Bible took place in this land. People today know more about this small country than they do about many larger countries of the world.

"From Chinnereth [Sea of Galilee] even unto the sea of the plain, even the salt sea [Dead Sea]" (Deuteronomy 3:17b).

Palestine, Land of Two Seas

Find the country of Israel on the map on page 100. Find it on your globe. Israel is a small country. On a globe, you can cover almost all of Israel with the tip of your finger.

This small country was once called Palestine (pa´ lə stīn). In Bible times, people called Philistines lived in part of this land. The name *Palestine* means "land of the Philistines."

Long ago, God promised this land to Abraham and his children. God said to Abraham, "I will give unto thee, and to thy seed [children] after thee..., all the land of Canaan." Canaan

Genesis 17:8a

Jesus often looked out across the Sea of Galilee. On a clear day, He could see the snowy peaks of Mount Hermon far away to the north. The icy waters from this mountain flow south into the beautiful blue Sea of Galilee. Jesus' disciples, Peter, Andrew, James, and John, often fished in the deep, cool waters of this sea.

Photo: Library of Congress/Matson Photo Service

is also known as Palestine.

The Hebrew nomads belonged to Abraham's family. God kept His promise to them about the land. He led the Hebrews out of the desert of Sinai and into the land of Palestine.

On the map on page 100, find the Jordan River. Find the place where the Hebrew nomads crossed the Jordan River to enter Palestine.

The Jordan River is the largest river in Israel. With your finger, trace the Jordan north to its **source** at Mount Hermon.

From Mount Hermon, a clear, sparkling stream flows south a short way to a small body of water called Lake Hula (hü´ lə).

The land around Lake Hula is almost flat. The Jordan River leaves the lake slowly and peacefully. But the river soon reaches a steep drop in the land. Its waters dash swirling and foaming down through a deep valley.

A few miles to the south, the Jordan again reaches a flat plain. The river makes a few twists and turns and then dumps its waters into the clear blue Sea of Galilee.

Look at the shape of the Sea of Galilee on the map on page 100. Do you think it has the shape of a harp? The Hebrews thought so. Old Testament people named it the Sea of Chinnereth.

The Jordan River makes many twists and turns before it empties into the Dead Sea. On the picture you can see the jungle along the sides of the river. The bottom of the picture is near the place where Jesus was baptized.

Chinnereth (kin´ ə reth) is the Hebrew word for "harp-shaped."

The Sea of Galilee has **fresh water**. Fresh water is not salty. The sweet fresh water of this sea is full of fish. Many men make a living there by catching fish to sell.

In Bible times, the fish were dried. Then the fishermen carried them to cities in Palestine to trade them for other things.

The Sea of Galilee is not always peaceful. Sometimes icy blasts of wind sweep down on it suddenly from the snowy top of Mount Hermon. Without warning, the calm waters become a storm of lashing waves.

The Jordan River drops downhill fast as it flows south from the Sea of Galilee. The name *Jordan* means "something that comes down." The name helps to tell the river's story.

Down over steep hills, the Jordan rushes south toward the Dead Sea. Along its path are many waterfalls.

The Jordan wanders back and forth like a giant snake squirming its way along. The many twists and turns make the Jordan about 200 miles long. That is more than two times as long as it would be if it ran straight.

You can see why the Jordan has never been a good river for boats and travel. People in Palestine traveled mostly by land.

SHOW YOUR KNOWLEDGE

1. How did the land of Palestine get its name?
2. When God promised Palestine to Abraham He called it _____ .
3. The source of the Jordan River is at _____ .
4. The (size, shape, place) of the Sea of Galilee helped give it one of its names.
5. There are many fish in the (salty, fresh) water of the Sea of Galilee.

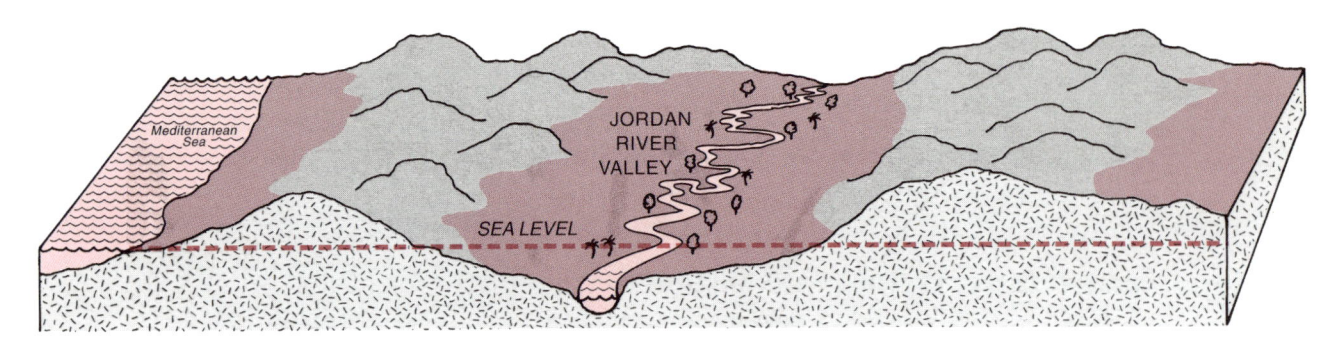

The Jordan River is below the level of the Mediterranean Sea. So we say it is below sea level. Lot, in the Bible, chose the well-watered plains in the Jordan River valley for his cattle. Read the story in Genesis 13:10, 11.

6. How does the name "Jordan" help to tell the Jordan River's story?
7. The Jordan River ends at the _____ .

SHARE YOUR KNOWLEDGE

1. Study Luke 5:1. In Jesus' time, the Sea of Galilee was sometimes called _____ . This name came from the name of a nearby city.
2. You studied about the Nile River in another chapter. In what ways are the Nile River and the Jordan River different?

LANDS NEAR THE JORDAN RIVER AND THE DEAD SEA

The Jordan River flows through a wide **valley.** A valley is a low area of land between hills. Down both sides of the Jordan River valley, mountains stretch out like high walls.

Streams flow into the Jordan from both sides of the river. These streams water the Jordan River valley and make it a wonderful garden for crops.

Exodus 3:8b

The waters of the Jordan helped to make Palestine a "land flowing with milk and honey" in Bible times.

A deep crack runs through the middle of the Jordan River valley. It is one of the deepest cracks in the earth.

The Jordan flows through this deep crack. Its waters are lower than the waters of the nearby Mediterranean Sea. So we say that the Jordan River is below **sea level**.

Trees, bushes, and grass grow thick along the Jordan. Years ago, men named the deep crack where the river flows, the "Jungle of the Jordan." Lions and other wild animals lived there.

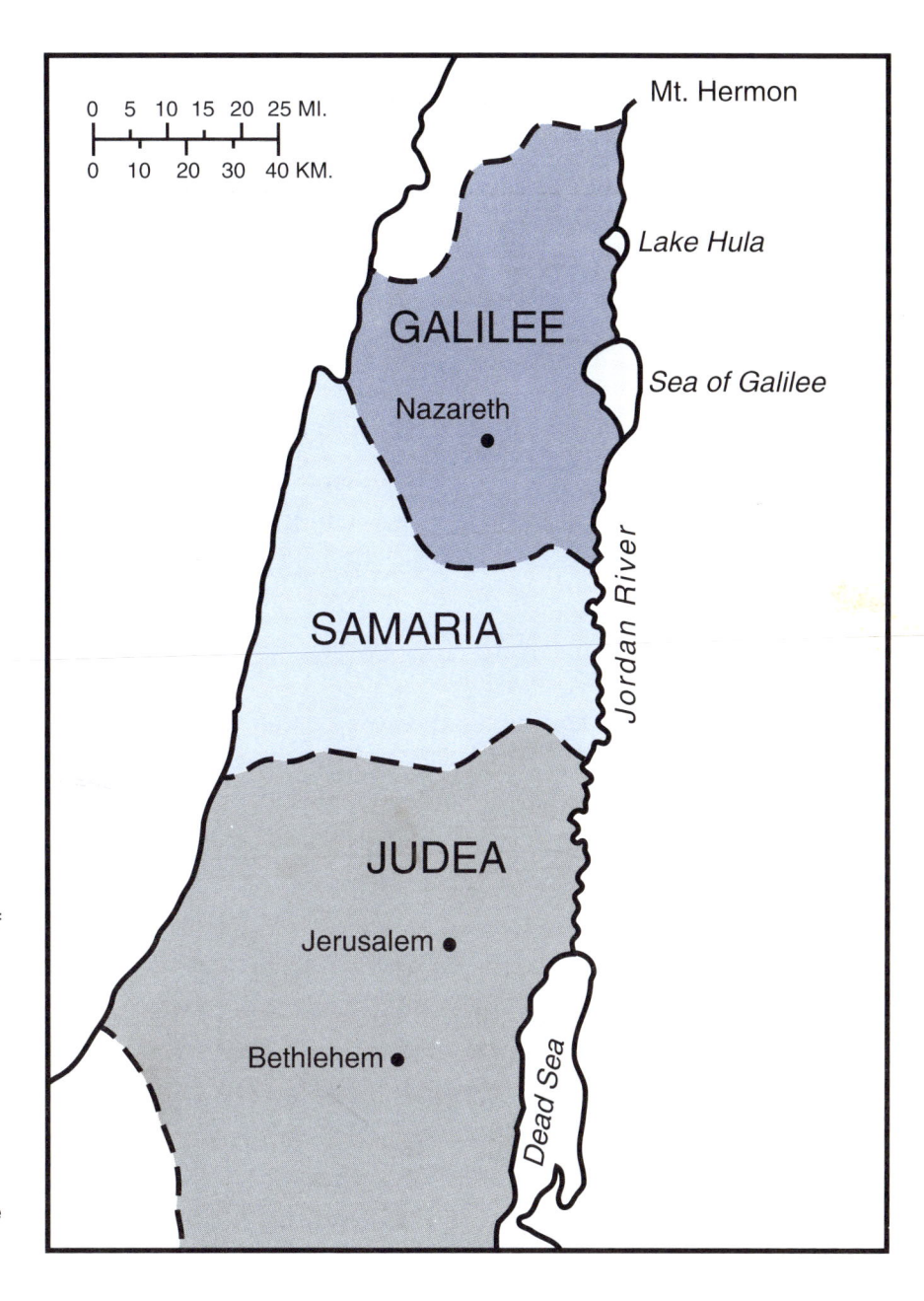

In the time of Jesus, the land of Palestine had these three parts. Name the part where Jesus was born. Name the part where He grew up. How many miles is it between the Sea of Galilee and the Dead Sea?

Each spring, the river overflowed and flooded the jungle. The flood drove the wild animals out. They came up into the valley and frightened the people who lived there.

Jeremiah 49:19a

The Bible speaks of this happening when it says, "Behold he [God] shall come up like a lion from the swelling [flood] of Jordan."

The Jordan River ends at the Dead Sea. Day after day, the Jordan pours millions of gallons of water into this sea. But no water can ever flow out of it, because the Dead Sea has no outlet.

In the hot sun, water from the sea **evaporates** (i va′ pə rāts) and goes into the air. The salts in the sea are left behind. You can see how the Dead Sea became the saltiest sea in the world. No fish can live in its salty waters.

The land beside the Dead Sea is a hilly, dry wilderness. In Bible times, nomads wandered in this desert with their flocks.

God gave the land between the Dead Sea and the Mediterranean Sea to the tribe of Judah. This southern part of Palestine came to be known as the land of Judah. Later, the name was changed to Judea (jü dē′ ə) in the time of Jesus.

The land in the north of Palestine was called Galilee. Galilee reached north to Mount Hermon. It reached south to a slanting wall of mountains called Mount Carmel.

This land in the north is also hilly. But between the hills of Galilee lie beautiful valleys with rich farmland. In Bible times, the people of Galilee grew many olive trees. They made some of the best olive oil in the world.

The land between Galilee and Judea was called Samaria. Before the time of Jesus, the people who lived there had married heathen. Because of this, the people of Galilee and Judea disliked the Samaritans.

Travelers between Galilee and Judea would not walk through Samaria. Instead, they went out around Samaria by using the highway along the eastern side of the Jordan River.

In this chapter, you will visit a city in Palestine. You will meet new make-believe friends. You will see how people of Palestine lived in the time of Jesus.

SHOW YOUR KNOWLEDGE

1. Why is the valley of the Jordan River a good place to grow crops?
2. Below sea level means:
    a. below the Dead Sea.
    b. at the bottom of a sea.
    c. lower than the waters of most other seas and oceans.
3. Salts in the sea are left behind when the water in the Dead Sea _____ .
4. Why did the people of Galilee and Judea dislike the people of Samaria?

SHARE YOUR KNOWLEDGE

1. Look at the map on page 105. Lake Hula is at sea level. Using the facts you know about the Jordan River, answer these questions:
    a. Is the Dead Sea below sea level?
    b. Is the Sea of Galilee below sea level?
2. The Dead Sea was given this name because:
    a. its waters are too salty for most living things.
    b. the Jordan ends there.
    c. the sun makes the water too hot for fish.
3. Study Joshua 15:2. In Bible times the Dead Sea was called the _____ .
4. Study John 4:4, 5. What did Jesus do that other people in Palestine would not do? What do you think He was trying to show?

FOR YOU TO DO

Find out how salty the water in the Dead Sea is. Put 1/3 cup of salt into a small bowl. Add 1 cup of warm water. Stir until the salt is melted. Taste it. The many kinds of salt in the Dead Sea make its water taste even worse.

Put an egg into the salt water. Then put the egg into water without salt. Does this help you understand how swimmers can float in the Dead Sea?

"Jerusalem is builded as a city that is compact [crowded] together" (Psalm 122:3).

Jerusalem, a City Community in Palestine

"Uncle Gareb [gär´ əb], how far is it yet to Jerusalem?" asked an excited little boy leading a donkey loaded with dried fish.

"Just over the top of the next hill, Benoni [ben ō´ nē]," his uncle replied. "See, the sun is just beginning to rise. We'll be at the city gate soon after the sun is up."

At the top of the hill, Benoni and his Uncle Gareb stopped to rest. In front of them was the holy city of Jersualem.

The golden front of the temple gleamed in the morning sun. Groups of people and loaded donkeys moved toward the city gate.

See the slots in the wall above the gate in the picture. Guards stood behind these slots to defend the city.

People met at the gates for many reasons. Prophets often shouted God's message to the people at the gates. God told Jeremiah, "Go and stand in the gate of the children of the people, . . . And say unto them, Hear ye the word of the Lord" (Jeremiah 17:19b, 20a).

Photo: David Wagler

THE CITY GATES

A high stone wall stood all around the city of Jerusalem. The wall helped to keep the city safe from enemies.

People went in and out of the city through large iron gates. The gates were closed each night. Men locked them with heavy iron bars.

Above the gates of Jerusalem, men had built towers. Day and night, guards watched from these towers for enemies.

2 Chronicles 26:15a One king of Israel "made in Jerusalem engines . . . to be on the towers . . . to shoot arrows and great stones withal [besides]." Enemies could not overthrow the city unless they could break down its gates.

Every morning, men swung the gates open. All day long, busy crowds of people could be seen at the gates.

Beggars sat at the gates and begged money from people going in and out of the city. People stood at the gates talking to friends and strangers. **Criers** shouted news from the city gates. The gates were important meeting places.

Judges sat on stone seats inside the gates. God said, **Deuteronomy 16:18a** "Judges . . . shalt thou make thee in all thy gates, . . . throughout thy tribes: and they shall judge the people."

The judges helped to settle disagreements between people.

They decided punishments from God's Law for lawbreakers. People brought their problems to the judges at the gates.

From the top of the hill, Benoni saw a **caravan** or group of traders moving toward one of the gates. Their camels were loaded with spices and perfumes from faraway lands.

The city shopkeepers met the caravan at the gate. They bargained with the traders for their **wares** or goods. The shopkeepers would trade the wares again with city people in the market.

People crowded around the traders at the city gate. What news would they tell? Would they know anything about happenings in Egypt? Had they met robbers along the way? The people had many questions.

Traders always carried exciting news from city to city. And people always listened eagerly to their stories. This is the way news traveled in Bible times.

Jerusalem had no newspapers. Benoni knew that criers would shout the important news up and down the city streets.

SHOW YOUR KNOWLEDGE

1. Why was it good to have a wall around Jerusalem?
2. When were the city gates closed?
3. What did the guards in the towers do?
4. The gates helped to protect the city, and they were also important _____ .
5. What government leaders sat at the gates to help people with their problems?
6. The camels in a caravan carried _____ and the men carried _____ from city to city.

SHARE YOUR KNOWLEDGE

1. Study Deuteronomy 21:18-21. Parents were to bring a wicked son to the city gate:
    a. to see him leave the city on a journey.
    b. for him to be judged by the elders.
    c. to meet good friends from a faraway country.

2. Revelation 21:25 tells about the city in heaven where God's people will live. The gates of this city will never be ____ . Why not?
3. Make a list of the things you could have seen happening at the gates of Jerusalem.

THE MARKETPLACE

Uncle Gareb and Benoni pushed their way through the crowds at one of the gates. On the other side of the wall was a large open space called the **marketplace.** Here shopkeepers traded their wares—fruits, olives, jars, baskets, cloth, and many other things.

Uncle Gareb and Benoni had brought fish from Galilee. They quickly unloaded dried, salted fish from their donkeys. Then they set up a **booth** to keep the hot sun off the fish. They made the booth by putting palm leaf mats over the tops of four long poles.

At the marketplaces in Palestine, people bargained until both the buyer and the seller could agree on a price.

Suddenly Benoni heard a voice he knew. Someone was calling, "Benoni! Benoni! Welcome to Jerusalem!"

Looking up, Benoni saw his cousin Moshe (mō shā´) running toward him. Moshe lived in Jerusalem. He was older than Benoni.

Benoni was visiting the city for the first time. Uncle Gareb didn't need any more of his help for the morning. He let Benoni explore the city with his cousin Moshe.

The boys stopped at a nearby booth to watch a farmer selling grain. A woman wanted to buy an **ephah** (ē´ fə) of barley. An ephah is a little more than a half bushel.

The woman wanted to trade one pigeon for the barley. The farmer wanted three pigeons. They began to **bargain** back and forth. "An ephah of barley for three pigeons is cheap," shouted the farmer.

Children played games between the booths at the marketplaces in Palestine. Jesus could remember games that were played in the marketplace when He was a boy. Jesus once said the stubborn Jews were like children playing funeral in the marketplace. He said, "They are like unto children sitting in the marketplace, and calling one to another, and saying . . . we have mourned to you, and ye have not wept" (Luke 7:32).

"I can buy barley cheaper at another booth," the woman replied.

The farmer finally agreed to trade the barley for two pigeons. Carefully he filled his basket measure. He pressed the grain down with his hand and tapped the basket on the ground.

For good measure, the honest farmer piled grain on top of the measure until it began to run over the edges. The farmer knew what the Law said about honest measure:

Deuteronomy 25:15b
Leviticus 19:36b

"A perfect and just measure shalt thou have: that thy days may be lengthened in the land which the LORD thy God giveth thee." "A just ephah . . . shall ye have."

114

The woman handed the farmer her two pigeons. Then she held out a loose part of her skirt, and the farmer filled it with the ephah of barley.

Most people bought things in the marketplace this way without using money. Such buying by trading is called **barter.**

The marketplace was very noisy. Buyers and sellers shouted as they bargained. A crier stood on a housetop and shouted the latest news. Children played games between the market booths. Donkeys brayed and sheep bleated.

No one seemed to mind the noise. Everyone seemed to enjoy what he was doing in the marketplace.

SHOW YOUR KNOWLEDGE

1. If the Jews gave honest measure, the Law said that:
    a. their enemies would starve to death.
    b. God would let them live in Palestine a long time.
    c. God would give them more and more land.
2. When people trade things in the marketplace without using money we say they _____ .

SHARE YOUR KNOWLEDGE

1. The gates into Jerusalem had names. Some gates got their names from the marketplaces near them. Each marketplace got its name from the thing traded there most. From Nehemiah 3, study the verses below. Tell what was traded most at the marketplace near the gates in these verses.
    verse 1 _____   verse 3 _____
    verse 28 _____
2. Make a list of the things you could have seen at a marketplace in Jerusalem.
3. Study Luke 6:38. Copy it onto your paper. Try to memorize it.

AT THE POOL OF SILOAM

In the cool morning, men and women hurried to their work. Benoni and Moshe caught up with a long line of women. On their heads, the women carried baskets of clothes to be washed or jars to be filled with water.

"Let's follow them to the pool of Siloam [sī lō´ am]," said Moshe. "People get their water from this man-made pool inside the city wall.

"Before men made the pool, the people got water from a spring outside the city wall," said Moshe. "But during times of war, the city gates were closed. At such times, people inside the city could not get water. Many people would die.

"A king named Hezekiah [hez ə kī´ ə] found a way out of the problem. He had his workers make a tunnel under the wall. He also had them build a pool inside the city to store water."

2 Kings 20:20b "He made a pool, and a conduit [tunnel], and brought water into the city."

Moshe explained how the work was done. He said, "Workers began digging from the spring outside the wall. Other workers dug from the pool inside. The workers met at the middle of the tunnel. Finally, water could flow from the spring outside the wall to the pool of Siloam inside."

Benoni saw women around the pool washing clothes. The women dipped the clothes into the water. Then they rubbed the clothes on stones. Washing clothes looked like hard work.

Other women filled their water jars with fresh water pouring from the tunnel.

The women talked while they worked. Today, they talked in hushed, angry voices about the Romans. The Romans were people from a nation called the Roman Empire.

Rome ruled Palestine. Roman soldiers guarded every road and every city in Palestine. The Jews had to obey Roman laws. They had to pay Roman taxes. The tax money went to pay the soldiers the Jews disliked so much.

Benoni heard one woman say bitterly, "Our money belongs to God. Why should we give it to heathen people from Rome?"

Another woman spoke up, "The **publican** tax collectors are worse than the Romans. They are Jews, but they work for the Romans and give our money to our enemies."

The Jews despised the publicans! They disliked the Romans. The Jews wanted their nation to be free again. But God was using the Romans to punish the Jews, because they had not obeyed His laws.

Soldiers from Rome kept the Jews from setting up their own nation again. This soldier is a centurion. A centurion had charge of one hundred soldiers under him. The Jews disliked the Romans who ruled their country.

SHOW YOUR KNOWLEDGE

1. King Hezekiah had his workers make a _____ under the city wall. Also, he had them build a _____ inside the city to store water. This pool is called the _____.
2. This made it possible for the people to have water during times of _____ when the city gates were closed and they could not go to the _____ for water.
3. The Jews (did, did not) like to be ruled by the Romans.
4. The Jews despised the publicans because:
    a. they were not Jews.
    b. they guarded roads and cities.
    c. they were Jews who worked for the Romans.
5. Why did God let the Romans rule Palestine?

SHARE YOUR KNOWLEDGE

1. Study Mark 12:17. Caesar (sē´ zər) was the Roman ruler. Jesus said the Jews (should, should not) pay taxes to Caesar.
2. Jesus' disciple Matthew was also called Levi. Study Luke 5:27. Matthew was a (doctor, lawyer, publican, fisherman, tax collector). Pick out two right answers.

A JEWISH SCHOOL

"Let's visit a **synagogue** [si´ nə gäg] next," said Moshe, pulling at Benoni's arm.

Benoni went with Moshe. A synagogue was a building used for worship services on the Sabbath days. During the week, the synagogue was used for a school.

A Jewish boy started to school when he was five years old. By the time he was 13, he could read, write, and do arithmetic. His only schoolbook was the Law of Moses—Genesis, Exodus, Leviticus, Numbers, Deuteronomy. He learned to say long parts from these writings by memory.

A 13-year-old boy had to know the Law well. At that age, a Jewish boy went to a service called a **bar mitzvah**.

At the bar mitzvah service, the boy promised to obey all

Jewish boys sat on the floor to study in a synagogue school.

Photo: Library of Congress

Scribes spent many hours copying by hand the Law of Moses onto scrolls.

the laws of Moses. From that time on, he was punished if he broke a law.

Benoni and Moshe entered a synagogue with a group of schoolboys. The boys sat in a half-circle on the floor. After a few minutes, the **rabbi** entered. A rabbi was a Jewish teacher whom everybody respected.

The boys showed their respect by standing to their feet. Together they said the **Shema** (shə mä´). The Shema was a part of the Law which said:

"Hear, O Israel: the LORD our God is one LORD: and thou shalt love the LORD thy God with all thine heart, and with all thy soul, and with all thy might."

Deuteronomy 6:4, 5

Everybody sat down and school began. The youngest boys were learning to write the Hebrew alphabet. With sharp pieces of metal, they scratched letters on broken pieces of pottery.

The older boys were learning to read the Law. They read from **scrolls.** Scrolls were long pieces of animal skin or papyrus rolled on two sticks.

In Palestine, scrolls were very scarce. **Scribes** spent many hours copying them by hand. The scrolls were safely kept in wooden chests.

All of the older boys read aloud at the same time. The rabbi took turns listening to each one. Jewish pupils learned by asking questions. They began asking questions almost

God's Law said, "Thou shalt bind them [God's laws] for a sign upon thine hand, and they shall be as frontlets between thine eyes" (Deuteronomy 6:8). The Jews did this by putting parts of God's Law in boxes called **phylacteries** (fə lak′ tə rēz). Jesus talked against Jews who wore phylacteries to make a show. God wanted His Law to be in the hearts of His people most of all.

Photo: Matson Photo Service

before the rabbi had a chance to sit down.

The rabbi took turns answering the boys' questions. He explained hard parts of the Law to them.

School ended before lunch. Benoni and Moshe stood with the other boys. Together they said the Shema again. Then all of the boys quietly left the synagogue.

Benoni hurried back to the marketplace to help Uncle Gareb pack up. The next day would be the Sabbath. Uncle Gareb wanted to stay in Jerusalem overnight.

Moshe hurried to his home. His father Caleb (kā′ ləb) was a brother to Uncle Gareb. Caleb went back to the marketplace with Moshe.

Uncle Gareb stopped his work when he saw his brother, Caleb. He turned to Caleb and said, "Peace be on you, brother."

"And on you peace," Caleb replied. Then Caleb kissed Uncle Gareb and Benoni. These were the usual Jewish greetings.

"You and Benoni must stay with my family tonight," said Caleb.

Uncle Gareb agreed.

Caleb led the way to a small stone house. At the door, they each stopped to touch a small box fastened to the door frame. This box was called a mezuzah (mə zü′ zə). Inside the mezuzah was a copy of the Shema.

Deuteronomy 6:9

God had said, "Thou shalt write them upon the posts of

thy house, and on thy gates."

The Jews believed using the mezuzah was one way of obeying this command. Touching the mezuzah was a good reminder for people to think about God's Law.

SHOW YOUR KNOWLEDGE

1. List two ways that a synagogue was used.
2. What was a Jewish boy's only schoolbook?
3. A Jewish boy needed to know the Law well by the time he was 13 because:
    a. at that age he was expected to obey all of it.
    b. he quit going to school at that age.
    c. he began studying other things after that.
4. Why did the Jews take good care of their scrolls?
5. What would you find inside a mezuzah?

SHARE YOUR KNOWLEDGE

1. Study Acts 22:3. Paul says he was "brought up...at the feet of Gamaliel." We can see that Gamaliel must have been (a rabbi, Paul's father, a preacher).
2. Ezra 7:6 tells us that Ezra was a:
    a. Jewish teacher.
    b. great king of Palestine.
    c. man who copied things onto scrolls by hand.
3. Study Jeremiah 36:2. God told Jeremiah to write down His words:
    a. on a scroll.
    b. in a book like this one.
    c. on a round piece of pottery.
4. Study Ezra 6:1. The king told his men to look in:
    a. a bakery.
    b. a library of scrolls.
    c. the house where he lived.
5. In what ways was a Jewish school different from your school? In what ways are they alike?

VISITING A JEWISH HOME

Caleb led his guests into the **courtyard** of his house. The courtyard was an open space surrounded by walls. Doors in the walls led to the rooms of the house.

Uncle Gareb and Benoni left their donkeys in the courtyard. They followed Caleb up an outside stairway to the flat roof of his house.

The houses in Palestine were often small and crowded. In warm weather, Jewish families spent much time together on the roofs of their houses.

The flat roofs were made from clay. On top of a layer of clay, workers sprinkled stones and sand. Then they rolled the roof with a stone roller to make it smooth.

Benoni saw the roller standing at one side of the roof. After each rain, Caleb rolled the roof again.

Around the edge of the roof was a low wall. God's Law commanded each owner to build this **battlement** around the roof of his house.

Deuteronomy 22:8

"When thou buildest a new house, then thou shalt make a battlement for thy roof, that thou bring not blood upon thine house, if any man fall from thence [that place]."

God's Law helped His people to think about safety. A battlement kept people from falling off a roof and getting hurt.

There was a small room built at the corner of the roof. This was the guest room where Benoni and Uncle Gareb would sleep.

Moshe brought a pitcher of water and a basin. Benoni and Uncle Gareb took off their **sandals** and Caleb washed their dusty feet. Servants most often did this job. By doing the job himself, Caleb showed that he wanted to be a servant to his guests.

The sun was going down in the west. Suddenly, the sharp blast of a ram's horn sounded from the synagogue. This meant that the Sabbath was about to begin. The Law commanded that no work should be done on the Sabbath.

"Six days may work be done; but in the seventh is the sabbath of rest, holy to the Lord: whosoever doeth any work in the sabbath day, he shall surely be put to death."

Exodus 31:15

Caleb brought clean clothes to the guest room. Uncle Gareb and Benoni rubbed their bodies with sweet-smelling oil and dressed in the clean clothes. Everybody changed clothes at the beginning of the Sabbath.

On pleasant days, the Jews liked to work, eat, and sleep on the flat roofs of their houses. Why did the Jews put walls around the edges of their roofs?

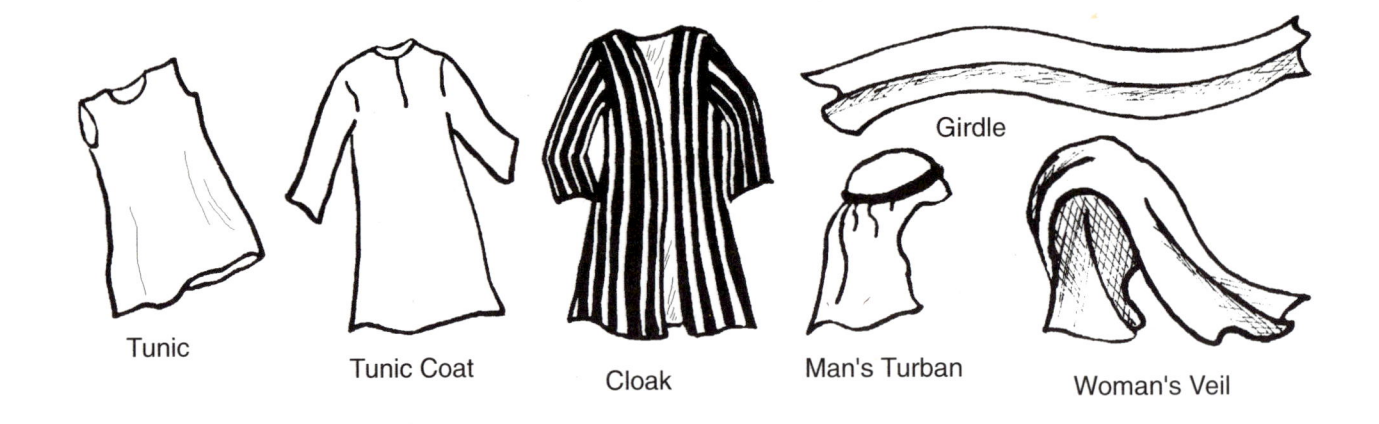

Tunic Tunic Coat Cloak Man's Turban Girdle Woman's Veil

CLOTHING IN PALESTINE

First, Benoni put on a linen **tunic.** A tunic was a shirt with no sleeves. It reached a little below his knees.

Benoni slipped a **tunic-coat** over the tunic. The tunic-coat had long sleeves and reached to his ankles.

Around his waist, Benoni tied a wide linen belt called a **girdle**. The girdle helped to hold the tunic-coat.

Sometimes a boy wanted to shorten his tunic-coat to make working or running easier. He could **gird** up his tunic-coat by tucking some of it up under his girdle.

Over the tunic-coat, Benoni put a heavy **cloak** with long sleeves. The cloak was sometimes called a mantle or robe. The cloak kept people warm in cool weather. Men used it for a cover at night.

Benoni placed a **turban** on his head. A turban was a small piece of cloth tied around the head.

Deuteronomy 22:5a

God's Law commanded men and women to dress differently. His Law said, "The woman shall not wear that which pertaineth [belongs] unto a man, neither shall a man put on a woman's garment."

The tunic-coat of the women was longer than the one worn by the men. The women wore long flowing **veils** (vālz) on their heads instead of turbans. Their clothing was more brightly colored than men's clothing.

SHOW YOUR KNOWLEDGE

1. Why did the people of Palestine spend much time on the roofs of their houses?

2. God's law about building battlements helped His people think about _____ .
3. Which is *not* a reason why Caleb washed his guests' feet?
    a. to clean their dusty feet
    b. the guests were too tired to do it
    c. to show his willingness to serve
4. How did Jewish women dress differently than Jewish men? Find three ways.

SHARE YOUR KNOWLEDGE

1. Study Nehemiah 13:19. What happened to the gates of Jerusalem on the Sabbath? Why?
2. Study Exodus 22:26, 27. If a man took another man's cloak, he had to give it back by _____ . Why do you think God wanted him to have it back by then?

KEEPING THE SABBATH DAY

The ram's horn sounded again. Now the Sabbath began. Caleb lighted the special Sabbath lamps.

Caleb's wife appeared at the top of the stairs with the Sabbath loaves of bread. Caleb's three small sons joined the group.

Caleb prayed, "Blessed be thou, O Lord God, who bringest bread out of the earth."

After the Sabbath meal, everybody said the Shema together. Then the men and boys older than 13 went to a short service at the synagogue.

The next morning, everybody went to the synagogue. A low wall divided the synagogue into two parts. The men sat on one side and the women sat on the other side.

The service began with everyone saying the Shema together. Then the ruler of the synagogue asked one of the men to pray. The man praying stood before the chest where the scrolls were kept.

Then the ruler brought a scroll from the chest. He could call on any man or boy to read from the Law. This morning he called on Benoni, because he was a visitor.

Benoni walked to the front of the synagogue. He climbed the two steps to the platform and read in a loud, clear voice:

Deuteronomy 11:26, 27a, 28a

"Behold, I set before you this day a blessing and a curse; a blessing, if ye obey the commandments of the LORD your God, . . . and a curse, if ye will not obey the commandments of the LORD your God."

Benoni finished reading and sat down. Next, someone would read from the prophets.

The ruler of the synagogue called on Uncle Gareb. Uncle Gareb read from the Prophet Isaiah.

After reading, Uncle Gareb sat down and explained what he had read. The synagogue service ended with another prayer.

At home again, Caleb's wife brought food. She had prepared it the day before. It was a cold meal. No fires were to be lighted on the Sabbath.

Exodus 35:3

The Law said plainly, "Ye shall kindle [light] no fire

throughout your habitations [houses] upon the sabbath day."

After lunch, Uncle Gareb and Caleb sat on the housetop and talked. The boys and women sat and listened.

The father was the leader in each Jewish home. Wives and children were commanded to listen respectfully when he spoke.

Today Caleb and Uncle Gareb talked about slavery. Some rich Jews had slaves.

Sometimes a Jew would sell himself to another Jew to pay his **debts** (dets). Such Jewish slaves were to be set free every seven years.

"And if thy brother, an Hebrew man, or an Hebrew woman, be sold unto thee, and serve thee six years; then in the seventh year thou shalt let him go free from thee."

Deuteronomy 15:12

"Slaves can be happy," said Caleb. "because the Law commands masters to treat them kindly.

"Surely our people treat their slaves better than people in any other country do."

But Uncle Gareb said, "I believe that our slaves want to be free, just as we want to be free from the Romans."

Jesus likely saw women grind grain into flour on a mill like this one.

Uncle Gareb and Caleb talked for a short while. Then the family walked to the synagogue again with their guests. There they studied the Law all afternoon.

At twilight, the ram's horn sounded again. The Sabbath was ended. Caleb's wife got out her **handmill** to grind flour for the next day's baking. Caleb and his boys hurried to help Uncle Gareb and Benoni get ready to leave for Galilee in the morning.

SHOW YOUR KNOWLEDGE

1. How did the men and the women sit in the synagogue?
2. What did Uncle Gareb do after he had read from Isaiah?
3. Why did the Jews eat cold meals on the Sabbath day?
4. Why did some Jews become slaves?
5. What signal helped the Jews know when the Sabbath began and ended?

SHARE YOUR KNOWLEDGE

1. In what ways was the synagogue service like your church service? In what ways was it different?

2. Slaves were usually treated better by the Jews in Palestine than they were in Egypt because _____ .
3. Study Deuteronomy 15:13, 14. How did God want a slave to be treated when he was set free?

THE TEMPLE

In the morning, Benoni and Uncle Gareb started back to Galilee. On their way through the city, they passed the **temple.** The temple had been built by Herod, a Roman ruler of Palestine.

Herod wanted to win the Jews' respect. He tried to do this by building the Jews a temple much larger and more beautiful than the temple built by King Solomon many years before.

Above the front porch of the temple was a large golden eagle. The eagle was a Roman symbol. It made the Jews unhappy. To them, the eagle was an unclean bird. The Jews later destroyed the golden eagle.

In the temple, priests offered sacrifices for the people. Each year, the people brought **tithes** to pay the priests. A tithe is one out of every ten pennies, animals, or bushels of grain a person has.

God had said, "Bring ye all the tithes into the storehouse, that there may be meat in mine house." **Malachi 3:10a**

Tithes could not be paid with Roman money. The priests asked the people to pay their tithes with Jewish coins.

The people brought their Roman coins to **moneychangers** who sat in the temple courtyard. The moneychangers traded Jewish coins for Roman coins. Some moneychangers cheated the people to make a lot of money for themselves.

Many people came to Jerusalem from faraway places. These people could not very well bring animals so far for sacrifices. In the temple courtyard, men sold animals to these travelers.

Three times each year, the Jews made trips to the temple

at Jerusalem for important feasts.

The most important feast was the **Passover Feast** in the spring. At this feast, the Jews killed and ate a lamb. God said they should "eat it with **unleavened bread** and bitter **herbs**."

Numbers 9:11b

Unleavened bread is made without yeast. Bread made without yeast does not rise. The loaves stay flat and hard. This feast was sometimes called the **Feast of Unleavened Bread**.

The flat loaves reminded the Jews that the Hebrews left Egypt in a hurry. They did not have time to let their bread rise.

The bitter herbs or plants reminded the Jews of bitter sadness in Egypt.

The Jews kept the **Feast of Pentecost** (pen´ ti kòst) 50 days after the Passover. The name "Pentecost" means "fifty" or "fiftieth." This feast was also known as the **Feast of Weeks.**

At the Feast of Pentecost, the people celebrated the end of wheat harvest. A man from each village brought baskets of the best grain, bread, and fruit. He gave these to the priest for an offering.

During the feast, the priest waved two loaves of bread over the altar. This **wave offering** showed thanks to God for a good harvest.

The Jews kept the **Feast of Booths** in October after they picked the last fruit. At this feast, families lived in booths or tents made from sticks and branches. This feast was also called the **Feast of Tabernacles** or the **Feast of Ingathering.** Some families built booths on the house-tops of Jerusalem. Others placed their

130

booths in fields around the city. The booths reminded the Jews of nomad days in the desert.

For seven days, the Jews lived in the booths and feasted together. It was a happy time of thanksgiving to God.

SHOW YOUR KNOWLEDGE

1. Who was Herod?
2. Why did Herod build such a large, beautiful temple for the Jews?
3. Name one thing about Herod's Temple that displeased the Jews.
4. Moneychangers were needed because:
    a. Roman coins were not used in the temple.
    b. travelers from faraway did not bring money with them.
    c. Jewish money could not be used.
5. Why were animals sold in the temple courtyard?
6. Why did God want the Jews to eat unleavened bread and bitter herbs at the Passover Feast?
7. At the Feast of Pentecost, the people celebrated _____ .
8. What did the Feast of Booths remind the people of?

SHARE YOUR KNOWLEDGE

1. Study John 2:13-16 and Luke 19:45, 46. Whom did Jesus chase out of the temple courtyard? Why did Jesus drive these people out? Who were the thieves?

ON THE WAY HOME

Benoni and Uncle Gareb left Jerusalem at one of the eastern gates. They took the highway to Galilee along the eastern side of the Jordan River valley.

Not far from Jerusalem, Benoni saw small boys grazing sheep. Most families in the city kept several sheep for wool and milk. A young boy in the family took them to country pastures each day. His mother packed his lunch of bread and cheese in a small skin bag called a **scrip.**

Benoni could see farmers working in their fields. The farmers had their fields **terraced** on the hillsides.

Terraces look like steps going up a hill. The farmers had made walls of stone at the front of each terrace step.

The flat terraces kept water from rushing down the hillsides and causing erosion. On each flat terrace, rains had plenty of time to soak into the ground.

Some hillsides were covered with olive trees. "Olive trees live for many years," Uncle Gareb told Benoni.

He said, "Olives are used to make olive oil. Each October men use sticks to knock the ripe black olives from the trees.

The workers gather the olives and place them into the large stone **vat** of an oil press.

"A pole fastened to a heavy stone wheel is hitched to a donkey. The stone wheel turns round and round on top of the olives. Oil is squeezed from them. The olive oil pours from a hole in the bottom of the vat," Uncle Gareb explained.

Benoni also saw **vineyards** of grapes on the hillsides.

"The people in our country eat many fresh grapes," said Uncle Gareb. "Workers dry some grapes to make **raisins**," he went on. "They press some grapes to make grape juice and wine."

Along the highway, Benoni and Uncle Gareb met a Roman soldier with a pack on his back.

"Stop, in the name of the law," commanded the soldier. "Carry my pack," he said to Uncle Gareb.

Uncle Gareb obeyed. A Roman law said that a Roman soldier could make a Jew carry his pack for one mile.

At the end of a mile, Uncle Gareb put the pack down. The soldier could not make him carry it any farther.

Benoni had a lot to think about on the way home.

"Why does God let the Romans rule Palestine?" he wondered. "Is it because so many Jews would not obey God's Law?"

The rabbi at home said that God would send a Messiah to save the Jews from their sins.

"Will this king help drive out the Romans?" Benoni asked himself. "Will the Jews have a nation of their own again?" Benoni and the Jews hoped so!

SHOW YOUR KNOWLEDGE

1. Why did the farmers make terraces on the hillsides?
2. How did the people of Palestine use olives?
3. List three ways the people of Palestine used grapes.
4. According to Roman law, how far did a Jew have to carry a Roman soldier's pack?
5. What did the rabbi say the Messiah would do?
6. What else did the Jews hope the Messiah would do when He came?

SHARE YOUR KNOWLEDGE

1. Study Matthew 5:41. The word *twain* in this verse means "two." In this verse, Jesus was telling the Jews to:
    a. disobey the Roman soldiers.
    b. do more than the Roman soldiers asked them to do.
    c. get as far away from the Roman soldiers as they could.
2. Study the law in Exodus 23:10, 11. Every seven years, the Jews were to let the land _____ .

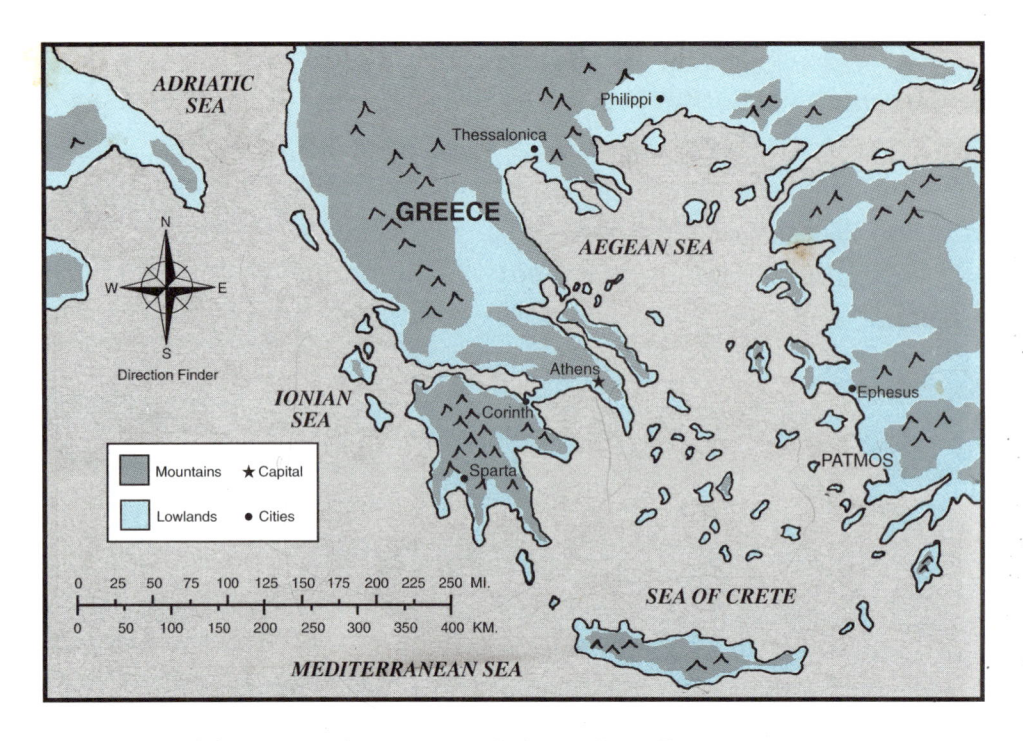

The country of Greece is a large peninsula in southern Europe.
Find Greece on the globe map at the left below.
Find Greece on the map above.
At the bottom of this page you see a picture of Greece taken many miles away from the earth. Pictures like this help men make maps.
Find the city of Corinth on the map. Find Athens, the capital of Greece. Water touches Grece on three sides. How did this help Greece become a nation of traders?

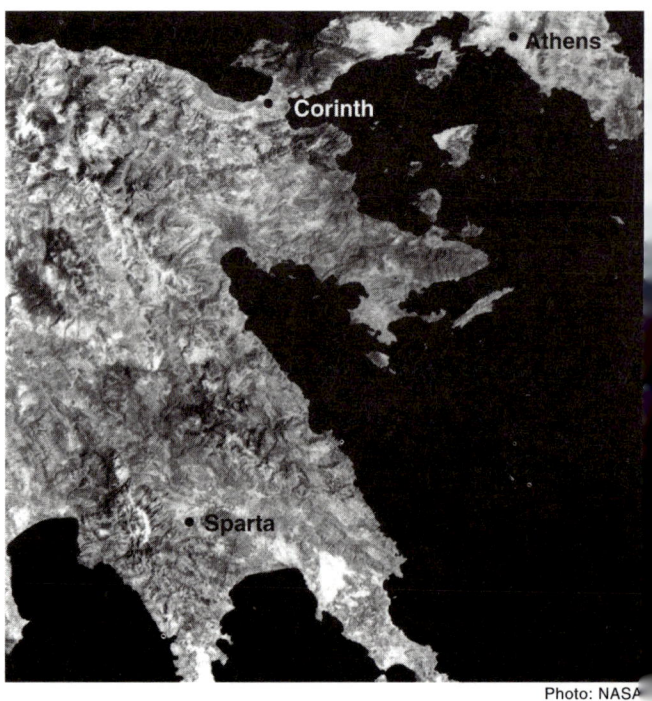

"And when he [Paul] had gone over those parts . . . he came into Greece" (Acts 20:2).

Greece, A Land Between Seas

Greece is a country in the southern part of Europe. On the map on page 134, you can see bodies of water on three sides of the country. Greece is a **península**.

Find the Aegean (i jē´ ən) Sea on the east side of Greece. Warm breezes blow from this sea across the land in the winter. In the summer, cool breezes come in from the sea. These **sea breezes** help to give Greece a mild climate.

On the west side of Greece is the Ionian (ī ō´ nē ən) Sea. What sea lies on the south side of the country?

Look at the coast of Greece where the land meets the water. As you can see, the coast is very crooked. All along the coast, fingers of land reach out into the sea. Between these fingers of land are small bodies of water called **bays**.

The water in a bay is peaceful and calm much of the time. Quiet bays are good places for ships to stop. The ships come to load and unload at places called **ports**.

The coast of Greece has many bays and ports. Years ago, the Greek people built many ships.

The ships carried goods from Greece to countries around the Mediterranean Sea. There the goods were traded for things the Greeks needed. Trading helped Greece to become rich and strong.

Most of the land of Greece is hilly and there are many mountains. Only a few valleys have good land for farming. The Greeks needed to get food from other lands. Trading was important for the Greek people.

The country of Greece has two parts. Find the place where the country looks almost squeezed in two. At this place a

People passed the city of Corinth when they traveled north or south across the land. People passed Corinth going east and west across the water. The city of Corinth was at a very good spot for the people in the city to make a living by trading.

narrow strip of land joins the two large parts of Greece. Such a narrow strip of land is called an **isthmus** (is′ məs).

Two large bays cut into the land on both sides of the isthmus. Large bays are called **gulfs.** Find the names of the two gulfs on the map above.

In Bible times, the isthmus had a port on each side. Find the city of Corinth between the two ports. Corinth was at one of the best places to become a great trading city.

Traders came to Corinth from many other lands. Egyptians, Jews, Romans, and people from other countries could be seen on the streets of the city almost any time.

The traders stayed in the city for a few days or weeks to do business. Then they went back to their home countries.

Paul saw these buildings while he was preaching on a hill called Mars' Hill at Athens.

Photo: Abner Stoltzfus

Sailors stayed in the city for a few nights until their ships were loaded and ready to sail again.

Corinth was a good place to spread the Gospel. People who came there from other lands would carry the story of Jesus back to their homelands. From Corinth, the Gospel story could be spread far and wide.

The Apostle Paul went to Greece on his second missionary journey. In Acts 17 of your Bible, you can find a sermon Paul preached at Athens. Find the city of Athens on the map.

From Athens, Paul went to the city of Corinth. There he worked hard to start a church.

Later, Paul wrote two letters to the new church at Corinth. People in the church were having problems. In his letters, Paul told the people what to do about these problems. Find the two letters to the **Corinthians** (kə rin´ thē ənz) in your Bible.

In the next chapter, you will learn about the community at Corinth in Bible times, You will see how badly the people of Corinth needed to know about Jesus.

SHOW YOUR KNOWLEDGE

1. Greece is on the continent of _____ .
2. The country of Greece has a mild climate because:
    a. it has a very crooked coast.
    b. it belongs to the continent of Europe.
    c. it is near seas.
3. A country with a crooked coast will likely:
    a. be dangerous for ships.
    b. have many good ports for trading with ships.
    c. not have good farms.
4. Why did Greece need to trade with other lands?
5. Write the word that means:
    a. a narrow strip of land joining two larger bodies of land. It has water on both sides.
    b. a good place along a sea for ships to stop
    c. a large bay
    d. a body of land with water almost all around it
    e. a part of a sea or lake reaching into the land

6. Why was Corinth a good place for spreading the Gospel?

SHARE YOUR KNOWLEDGE

1. Study Acts 16:1. Timothy's mother was a _____ , but his father was a _____ .

"And many of the Corinthians hearing believed [on Jesus], and were baptized" (Acts 18:8b).

The Two Communities at Corinth

A large ship moved through the Gulf of Corinth. There was no wind. The sails hung limp. The afternoon was hot.

Along the sides of the ship, three rows of oars moved in perfect time. Inside the ship, slaves sat chained to rows of benches. Sweat ran down their backs as they pulled at the oars together.

Together! Pull! Lift! Together! Pull! Lift! It was an endless job.

The master of the ship was in a hurry. Crack! His whip came down on the back of a slave who could not keep up. The master had no pity for tired or lazy slaves.

The ship was nearing land. A rough-looking slave tossed a rope from the shore. The rope was tied to the ship. A line of slaves on the shore tugged together on the rope. Slowly the ship floated into the port two miles east of Corinth.

The ship had sailed from Rome to Greece. The trip had taken two weeks. The tired passengers hurried to the city of Corinth for a good meal and rest. But a tall boy and a small girl stayed behind. They were Jews from Rome. Find Rome on the map on page 164.

The girl looked up to her brother and asked, "Cletos [klē təs], why did we have to come to Corinth?"

"Sophia [sō fē´ ə], I have told you often," Cletos replied. "The ruler of Rome does not like the Jewish people," he said. "He ordered all of the Jews to leave Rome.

"Mother and Father sent us here to Corinth where we will be safe. They will come later after selling Father's pottery shop. Until then, we will find a home with other Jews here at Corinth."

CROSSING THE ISTHMUS

Near the port, Cletos and Sophia saw busy slaves hard at work. They were moving a small ship from the water onto the land.

Sailors saved a lot of time by dragging their ships across the tramway near Corinth. The tramway also saved ships from the long, dangerous trip around Greece. See map on page 141.

140

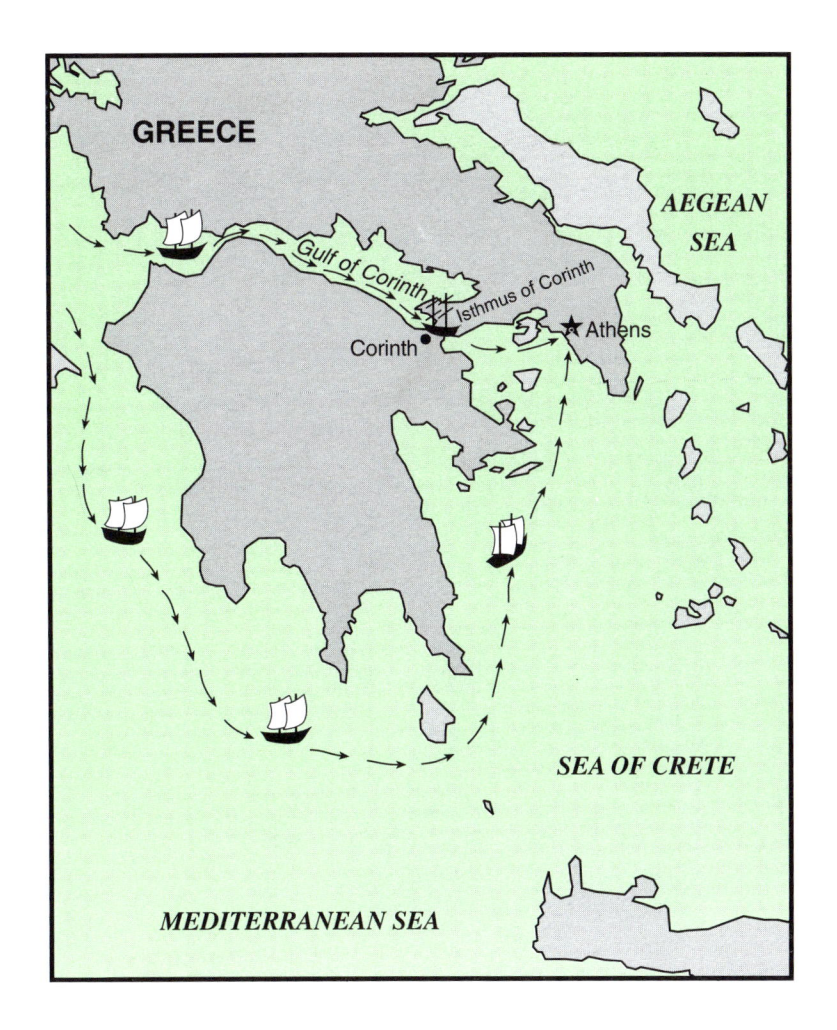

Slaves laid wooden rollers in front of the ship at the edge of the water. Then a large group of slaves tugged and strained at ropes tied to the ship. Inch by inch, the ship came up onto the rollers.

Cletos pointed to a stone track that looked like a narrow road across the isthmus.

He said, "The slaves will pull the ship to the other side of the isthmus on that stone **tramway**."

The children watched the ship begin the slow trip over the tramway. The wooden rollers creaked and clattered over the stones. Slaves kept carrying rollers from behind the ship to the front again.

"Why do the men take ships across the land?" asked Sophia.

Cletos said, "The men on this ship want to sail east. They could have gone around the southern part of Greece. But that

Since workers dug this canal across the isthmus of Corinth, ships no longer need to be dragged across the land on a tramway. Now ships can take the shortcut by water.

Photo: David Wagler

long trip takes many days. And besides, storms and rocks along the coast make the trip very dangerous.

"The isthmus is only four miles wide here. The tramway across it saves sailors much time and danger."

Cletos went on. "The tramway also helps the city of Corinth," he said. "Money or **toll** must be paid for each ship that crosses here. The money is paid to men in the city."

"Look what is happening to our ship from Rome!" cried Sophia.

Slaves were unloading barrels of olive oil onto donkeys.

Cletos explained, "Our ship was too large to be pulled across the isthmus. The donkeys will carry the **cargo** across. At the other side, slaves will load the barrels of oil onto another ship.

"The Romans tried once to dig a large **canal** through the isthmus to let ships sail to the other side," said Cletos. "But the job was too big. The workers gave it up."

Many years later, men finished the canal started by the Romans. Today ships get from one side of the isthmus to the other by water. They no longer need the tramway and the hard work to cross the land.

SHOW YOUR KNOWLEDGE

1. Why did the Jews have to leave Rome?
2. The Greeks moved ships and cargoes across the isthmus:
    a. to sell them at Corinth.
    b. to keep sailors from making a long, dangerous trip.
    c. because Corinth needed a way to make money.
3. Today ships use a _____ instead of a _____ to get to the other side of the isthmus.

SHARE YOUR KNOWLEDGE

1. Study Acts 18:1-3. Answer these questions.
    a. A man named _____ and his wife named _____ had come to _____ from _____.
    b. Italy is the country where you can find the city of _____. Use the map on page 164.
    c. This man and his wife made _____ for a living.
    d. _____ was the leader who sent all the Jews from Rome.
2. On the map on page 136, find the two ports that were on the east and west sides of the isthmus. Look up the two names in your glossary and learn to say them.

HOW CORINTH GREW

The two seaports near Corinth helped the city to grow. Ships could bring materials the people at Corinth needed.

Corinth did not have many natural resources. Ships brought wood, tin, copper, and other natural resources.

Workers in the city used these natural resources to make goods that people needed. Natural resources used this way are called **raw materials.**

Tin and copper are raw materials. They are soft metals. Workers at Corinth melted these two soft metals together to make a harder metal called **bronze.**

Making goods from raw materials is called **manufacturing** (man yə fak´ chər ing). Workers at Corinth manufactured hot pieces of bronze into knives, hoes, and other tools.

The manufacturing took lots of work. A worker spent a lot of time hammering a hot piece of bronze into the shape of an

THE WAY A MANUFACTURING BUSINESS GROWS

| Worker buys raw materials for shovel | Worker melts tin and copper to make bronze | Worker pounds hot bronze into the shape of a shovel | Raw materials make two shovels | Worker sells the shovels | Worker makes enough profit to buy raw materials for three shovels |

| Worker buys the extra raw materials. | Worker spends time manufacturing shovels from the raw materials. | Worker sells the three shovels. | Worker makes enough profit to buy raw material for four and one-half shovels. |

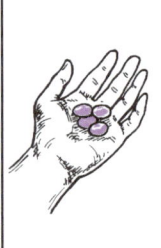

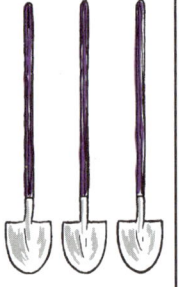

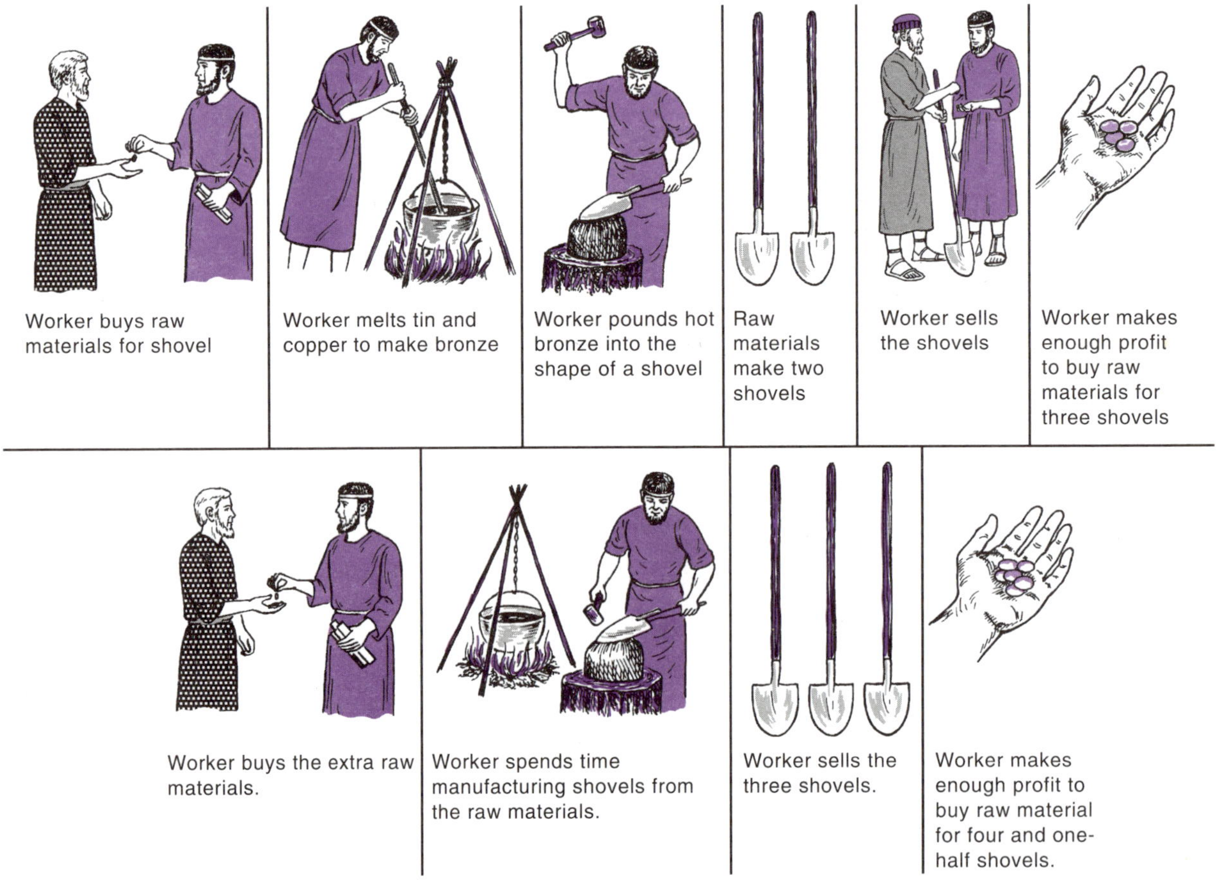

144

Greek merchant ships sailed all over the world to trade manufactured goods for raw materials.

ax or shovel. He got paid for the time he spent manufacturing each piece.

You can see that manufacturing costs money. The cost of manufacturing makes each piece worth more than the raw materials used to make it. The extra money a manufacturer makes on each piece is called **profit.**

A profit can be used to buy extra raw materials. With extra raw materials, workers can manufacture extra goods. Extra goods bring profits to buy more and more raw materials. You can see how a manufacturing business grows larger and larger.

Workers at Corinth also manufactured ships from wood. Traders loaded the ships with goods from Corinth. They sailed the ships to faraway lands to trade.

"They that go down to the sea in ships...do business in great waters."

Psalm 107:23

The goods traders took from Corinth are called **exports.** The men traded the exports for raw materials the workers at Corinth needed. The materials the traders brought back are called **imports**.

Now you know how the people of Corinth made a living.

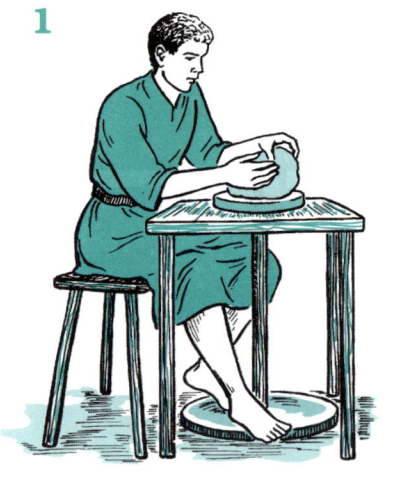

STEPS IN MAKING POTTERY

1. The potter centers the clay on the wheel.
2. The potter shapes the vase.
3. The potter smooths the vase, adds handles, and paints designs on it.
4. The potter bakes the vase in an oven until it is very hard.

They traded manufactured exports for the imports they needed.

The people found one good natural resource at Corinth. It was a sticky soil called **clay.** Clay is a raw material used to make pottery jars and dishes.

The clay at Corinth was white. Workers manufactured it into lovely white pottery. Artists painted pictures on the white jars and dishes. People all over the world wanted the beautiful pottery manufactured at Corinth.

As manufacturing grew, more and more people came to Corinth for jobs. These people needed houses. This made more work for builders.

Photo: Library of Congress

146

Manufacturing and trade built Corinth. Corinth became a trading city because it was near the sea.

SHOW YOUR KNOWLEDGE

1. Write the word that means:
    a. the money a person gains from the things he sells after the expenses are taken off
    b. goods brought into a country from another country
    c. making useful goods from raw materials
    d. goods sent out of a country to be sold in another country
    e. a natural resource or other material used for manufacturing
2. The main thing that helped Corinth become a trading city was its (location, natural resources, raw materials).
3. A manufacturing business grows because:
    a. manufacturing is hard work.
    b. manufacturing costs money.
    c. profits can be used to buy extra raw materials.
4. Manufacturing helps a city to grow because:
    a. people come there to get jobs.
    b. such cities have no poor people.
    c. the city will need more and more raw materials.

A TRIP TO THE CITY

Cletos looked away from the busy slaves at the port.

"Come, Sophia," he said. "Let's walk to the city. We must find a place to stay for the night."

The children headed toward Corinth over a wide road of flat stones.

"The Romans built this smooth road," Cletos said.

Sophia looked puzzled. "Didn't you say the people here are Greeks?" she asked.

"Yes," replied Cletos. "But the Romans now rule over Greece and most other nations. The Romans rule Greece much like they rule Palestine.

"The Greeks must pay taxes to Rome. The Romans use some of this tax money to build roads like this through all the lands they rule.

"The Romans build good roads," said Cletos.

"First they put down a layer of flat stones. Next they cover this with a layer of crushed stones cemented together with lime. Then over these two layers, the workers fit flat stones together to make a hard, smooth road."

Cletos went on. "The Romans found that water ruins a road," he said. "Puddles of water make soft spots. Soft spots in a road soon become holes and ruts."

Cletos pointed to the sides of the road. "See those ditches," he said. "When it rains, the water drains into them. Soon after a rain, the road is dry again. The Romans know how to build roads that will last a long time."

The Romans built roads between the most important

The Romans built good roads in the countries they ruled. Do good roads help a government rule its people? How? How do good roads help God's people?

Photo: Erwin C. "Bud" Nielsen, Tucson, AZ

This agora which was built many years ago is still standing. Once the people of Corinth met here to buy and sell, talk, or settle problems. Sailors once came to this agora from the ports. Some people think a synagogue where Paul preached stood just outside this agora. Now only one market stall still stands. Just behind the stall is a part of the temple to a false god called Apollo.

cities. These good roads helped people like the Apostle Paul to spread the Gospel into many parts of the world.

The road from the port led to the marketplace of Corinth. The marketplace in each Greek city was called the **agora** (a′ gə rə). Just outside the agora, Cletos and Sophia passed a Jewish synagogue. Nearby they saw market booths. "Sophia!" Cletos cried. "There are Aquila and Priscilla! See! Aquila is selling a piece of tent cloth."

Aquila and Priscilla were Jewish friends who also had come to Corinth from Rome. Cletos and Sophia watched until the bargain was finished. The buyer paid Aquila with a Roman coin called a **denarius** (də nar′ ē əs). It had an image of Caesar (sē′ zər) on one side. Caesar was the ruler or **emperor** (em′ pər ər) of Rome.

The denarius was the most important Roman coin in Bible times. In the Bible, a denarius is called a penny. But it was worth much more than our pennies today. In Bible times, one denarius was good pay for a whole day of work.

"And when he had agreed with the laborers [workers] for a penny a day, he sent them into his vineyard."
Matthew 20:2

149

Aquila looked up and saw the children. "Why, Cletos and Sophia!" he said. "Welcome to Corinth."

Photo: Dr. Gleason Archer

SHOW YOUR KNOWLEDGE

1. In the time of Paul, Greece and most other nations were ruled by _____ .
2. Roman roads stayed in good shape for many years, because the Romans built them to stay (wet, rough, dry).
3. How did the Romans help Christians like Paul to spread the Gospel into many parts of the world?
4. The image of _____ , the ruler of Rome, was on the denarius.
5. In Bible times, one denarius was good pay for a whole (day, week, month) of work.

SHARE YOUR KNOWLEDGE

1. The synagogue at Corinth in the time of Paul makes us think:
    a. most of the people there worshiped the true God.
    b. Corinth did not need the Gospel.
    c. many Jews lived there.
2. Study Acts 18:4. Both _____ and _____ came to the synagogue at Corinth on the Sabbath day.
3. In Luke 10:35, study about the money the Good Samaritan paid the innkeeper for taking care of the sick man. The Good Samaritan paid the innkeeper two_____ .
   The Good Samaritan likely worked two (hours, days, weeks) for this money.
4. Study John 12:3-5. Mary anointed Jesus' feet with perfume worth _____ . To earn this much money in Bible times, a man would have worked _____ days or almost a (week, month, year).

150

The Greeks honored their heroes by placing statues of them along their roads. They also lined their roads with statues of the unholy gods they worshiped. The Greeks did not worship the true God.

WORSHIP AT CORINTH

Aquila and Priscilla asked Cletos and Sophia to stay with them. They lived outside the city.

On the way home, Cletos pointed to white statues of men along both sides of the road.

He said, "I saw statues like these all along the road from the port. What do they mean?" he asked.

Aquila replied, "Some are statues of men the Greeks thought were great. Many are images of false gods they worship."

Priscilla said, "The Greeks believe their gods are like people who often do wrong things. They do not believe in a **holy** God who never sins. Their worship is not holy either.

"The Greeks choose special gods for each city. The people of Corinth worship a false goddess called Aphrodite (a´ frə dī´ tē). They believe Aphrodite is the goddess of love and beauty."

Aquila pointed toward a very high hill beside the city.

"That hill is called the **acropolis** (ə krä´ pə ləs) of

151

Corinth," he said. "The people of Corinth go there for safety in times of danger from enemies. But they also go to the acropolis to worship Aphrodite, their false goddess.

"On the acropolis, the Greeks have built a beautiful temple with a statue of Aphrodite," Aquila explained. "But their worship customs are ugly and sinful," he added.

"One thousand evil women live on the acropolis. To worship Aphrodite, men leave their wives and live with these women for a short time. In the Bible, this sin is called **adultery.** And God's Law says, 'Thou shalt not commit adultery.'"

Exodus 20:14

"The people of Corinth break God's moral laws," said Priscilla. "Those who break moral laws are called **immoral** people. Corinth has more immoral people than any other city in Greece."

"Yes," said Aquila. "When a person is immoral in any other part of Greece, the people often say, 'He lives like a Corinthian.'"

This picture shows some of the ruins of ancient Corinth. The hill in the background is the acropolis, which had a temple of the false goddess at the top. Worship customs in this temple were very immoral and wicked. The Corinthians were some of the most wicked people in Paul's day.

Photo: Erwin C. "Bud" Nielson, Tucson, AZ

The seats in the stadium at Corinth looked much like these seats.

GAMES ON THE ISTHMUS

The people of Corinth had another false god named Poseidon (pə sī´ dən). They believed that Poseidon ruled the seas.

You have learned how Corinth depended on the seas for trading. The people believed Poseidon would keep their ships from harm if they worshiped him.

The people on the isthmus of Corinth honored Poseidon in a special way. Near Corinth they built a large round **stadium** (stā´ de əm). A stadium is a place where games are played. The stadium near Corinth had thousands of seats where people sat to watch the games.

Every two years, the Greeks played games in the stadium to honor Poseidon. These games were called the **Isthmian** (is´ mē ən) **Games**. People came to the Isthmian Games from every part of Greece.

All of the players in the games were men and boys. Each

player spent years getting ready for the games. He practiced hard for many hours every day. He ate only foods that would make his body strong and healthy. Each player wanted to be a winner.

At the beginning of the games, a sacrifice was made to the false god, Poseidon. Each player promised to play fairly. Then the contests began.

Runners raced around the track inside the stadium. Each runner strained every muscle to finish the race first.

1 Corinthians 9:24b "They which run in a race run all, but one receiveth the prize."

There were other contests. Players tried to throw spears farther than anyone else. They also threw round **discuses** (dis´ cəs əz). There were chariot races and boxing.

In each game, the winner was crowned with a wreath made from branches of fir. Criers announced the names of the winners all over the land. Statues of winners were placed along Roman roads.

The Jews knew many things about these games were sinful and wrong. Godly Jews never went to the Isthmian Games.

In the Isthmian Games, the winners received crowns much like this one. The Bible calls it a **corruptible** crown, meaning that it will soon wither and die. What kind of crown will Christians receive in heaven? Read James 1:12.

CLP Staff Photo

SHOW YOUR KNOWLEDGE

1. The Greeks believed their gods were like (people, the true God).
2. List two reasons why people went to the acropolis of Corinth.
3. The Greeks believed Poseidon would protect the _____ they used on the seas for trading.
4. Godly Jews (went, did not go) to the Isthmian Games.

SHARE YOUR KNOWLEDGE

1. Study the last part of 1 Corinthians 9:25. In this verse, Paul speaks about the players in the Isthmian Games.
     a. He says the players tried to win a _____ crown.
     b. Look up this word in your glossary.
   Such a crown:
        1. is worth a lot of money.
        2. will not last long.
        3. is ugly.

A VISITOR TO CORINTH

One Sabbath morning, a Jewish friend brought news to the house of Aquila and Priscilla.

He said, "A teacher named Paul has come from the city of Athens. Maybe he will speak in the synagogue this morning."

Cletos and Sophia were excited. It would be good to hear a new teacher.

First, the people listened to readings from the Law and the Prophets. Then the ruler of the synagogue asked the new teacher to speak.

Paul stood up.

"Men of Israel," he began. "Listen to me. Jesus is the Messiah we Jews have been looking for.

"Jesus did not come to free Palestine from the Romans," Paul told the Jews. "But Jesus died on a Roman cross to free people from their sins. He will rule in the hearts of people who believe on Him."

The Jews became angry. They wanted a king who would put the Romans down. They would not believe Jesus was the Messiah God had promised. They would not ask Jesus to forgive their sins.

Paul was sad to see the Jews turn against Jesus. He told them it would be their own fault if they were lost in their sins.

Paul left the synagogue.

Acts 18:6b

He declared, "From henceforth [now on] I will go unto the **Gentiles** (jen´ tīlz)."

Gentiles are people who are not Jews. Paul wanted everyone to hear the Gospel. He preached to the Jews first. When they would not listen, he turned to the Gentiles.

PAUL PREACHES TO THE GENTILES

A man named Justus lived in the house right beside the synagogue. Justus asked Paul to come and preach in his house. Many Gentiles came to hear Paul.

The Gentiles at Corinth had come from many different lands. They spoke different languages. Maybe you wonder how all these people understood Paul when he spoke.

God had a plan for getting the whole world ready to hear the Gospel.

You know how Greek ships and people traveled far and wide. People in other lands began to learn the Greek language and Greek ways. Soon people in many lands could speak Greek besides their own language.

In the time of Paul, people from Egypt spoke the Egyptian language. But many people from Egypt had learned to speak Greek also. It was the same way in most other lands.

Paul spoke the Greek language. Now you can see how people from many lands could understand his words.

The Jews did not like Paul's preaching. They blamed him for saying things against the law. Jewish leaders tried to find a way to stop him.

One day it happened! The Jews grabbed Paul. They marched him to the middle of the agora. There the Roman

It is believed that the Jews marched Paul to this bema where the Roman judge sat to settle problems made by lawbreakers. The Jews blamed Paul for breaking the Law of Moses by preaching about Jesus. They wanted Gallio, the judge, to punish him. Gallio would not judge Paul because Paul had not broken a Roman law. Then Paul knew the Roman laws would give him safety to preach the Gospel.

ruler sat on a platform called a **bema.**

In Paul's day, the Roman ruler of Corinth was Gallio (gal´ ē ō).

The Jews said to Gallio, "This fellow persuadeth [turns] men to worship God contrary to [against] the law."

Acts 18:13, 15b

But Gallio replied, "I will be no judge of such matters."

Gallio chased the Jews away from the bema. Paul had not broken a Roman law. Gallio would not punish him.

Paul went right on preaching. Many Gentiles believed on Jesus and asked Him to forgive their sins. These people became **Christians.** This means they let Jesus be the **Lord** or ruler of their lives.

When the people became Christians, their customs changed. Christians stopped going to the acropolis to sin. They quit worshiping idols.

157

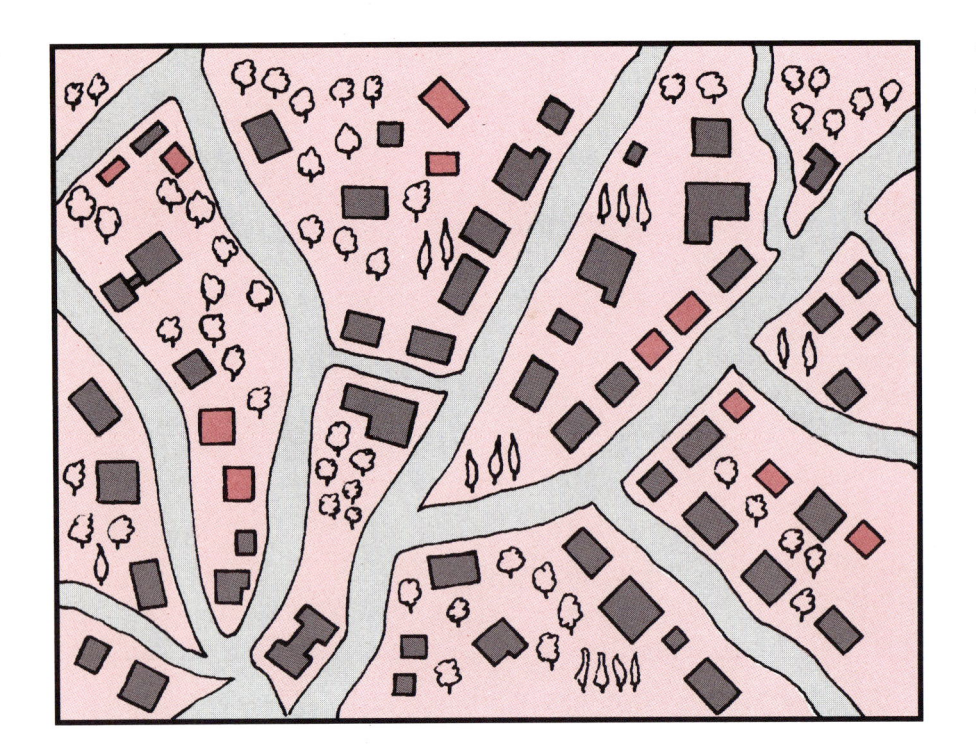

The gray houses show the homes of the people in the sinful community at Corinth. The red houses show the homes of people who belonged to the Christian community, the church. God wants the Christian community to live in the sinful community to tell the people about Jesus. But God does not allow Christians to copy the evil customs of the sinful community.

The Christians at Corinth began meeting together to worship Jesus. They had a Christian community right in the sinful community of Corinth. This Christian community was called the **church.**

SHOW YOUR KNOWLEDGE

1. Before Paul came to Corinth, he had been at _____ .
2. The Jews were hoping the Messiah would:
    a. live at Corinth.
    b. help the Gentiles.
    c. free them from the Romans.
3. When the _____ would not believe the Gospel, the _____ got to hear it.
4. In Paul's time, people in many lands could understand the (Jewish, Egyptian, Greek) language.
5. Gallio would not punish Paul, because:
    a. preaching about Jesus was not against Roman laws.
    b. Gallio was a good friend of Paul's.
    c. Gallio was a good Christian.

6. The Christians in the new Christian community lived by new _____ .

SHARE YOUR KNOWLEDGE

1. Study Acts 22:21 below. God sent Paul as a preacher to the _____ .
2. We are (Jews, Gentiles).
3. Study John 1:41 and answer these questions.
    a. The name *Messiah* was a word in the Hebrew language. The Greek word _____ means the same thing as the Hebrew word *Messiah*.
    b. When we say the name *Jesus Christ*, we mean *Jesus the promised* _____ .
4. Study John 4:25, 26. Jesus himself said that:
    a. the Jews should look for the Messiah to come later.
    b. the Messiah would tell all things.
    c. He was the Messiah the Jews were looking for.

THE CHRISTIAN COMMUNITY AT CORINTH

People at Corinth could see a great difference between the church and the sinful community.

Christians gave up immoral living. They became **pure** and free from sin.

Christians studied God's Word. They began telling others about Jesus and the Christian way.

Paul knew God wanted to see many differences between the two communities. The pure lives of the Christians would help sinners see how badly they needed Jesus.

Being different was a hard job. Paul knew he would need to teach the Christians many things about the new way.

Acts 18:11b   Paul stayed at Corinth "a year and six months, teaching the word of God." He stayed at the house of Aquila and Priscilla. Like them, Paul made tents to sell.

Cletos and Sophia liked to be around when Paul was at home. Often he talked while he worked.

One day, Paul talked about the Isthmian Games. To Paul, being a Christian was like getting ready for the games.

In the games, each runner tried to reach the finish mark first and win the prize.

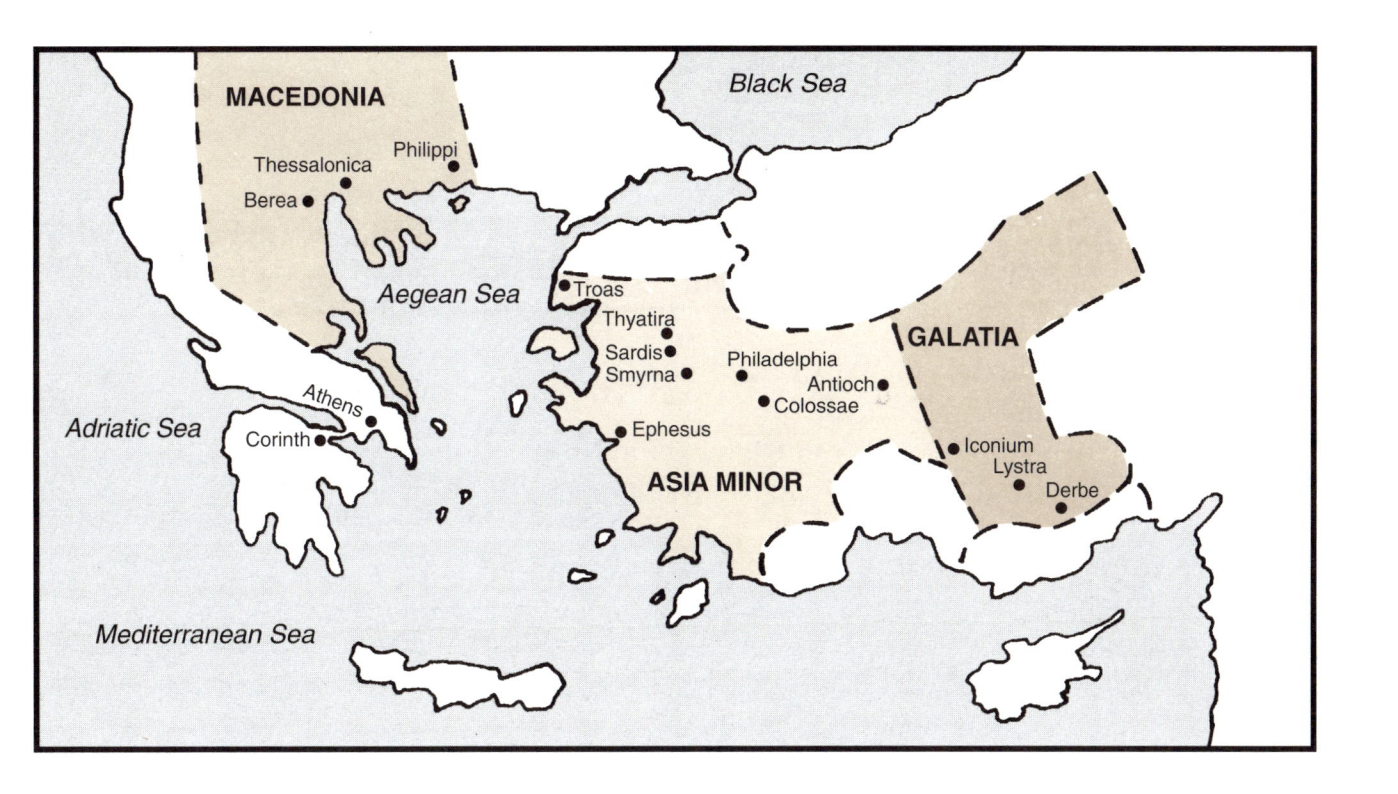

Paul said, "I press toward the mark for the prize of the high calling of God in Christ Jesus."

Philippians 3:14

Paul was using all his might to reach the finish mark of the Christian life. He wanted to win the reward God would give him.

The winners of the Isthmian Games were crowned with wreaths of fir. The players worked hard for this crown that would soon wilt and die.

Paul said, "They do it to obtain [win] a corruptible [wilting] crown; but we [Christians] an incorruptible [a crown that lasts forever]."

1 Corinthians 9:25b

One day Paul said it was time for him to leave Corinth. He wanted to preach in a city called Ephesus. Find it on the map on this page. Ephesus was in a land called Asia Minor. *Asia Minor* means "small Asia."

Paul asked Aquila and Priscilla to go with him. Cletos and Sophia had to stay behind and wait for their parents to come from Rome.

The children were sorry to see their good friends leave. The next day, they stood at the port west of Corinth and watched Paul's ship sail out of sight. Both children wiped a few tears. Then Cletos turned to his sister.

"Sophia," he said. "We really should be happy, not sad. Paul wants to start Christian communities in other lands. God will bless his work. Soon we will have Christian friends in many lands."

Sophia asked, "Will Christians from other places come to visit us here at Corinth?"

"Perhaps," answered Cletos. "Paul himself may come back with news about many new churches."

Two happy children walked back to the city. A family in the new Christian community had promised them a new home.

SHOW YOUR KNOWLEDGE

1. The Christians became _____ . They studied _____ . They told others about _____ .
2. How long did Paul stay at Corinth to teach the Christians?
3. What else did Paul do while he was at Corinth?
4. Paul thought the Christian life
    a. was the same as the Isthmian Games.
    b. was better than the Isthmian Games.
    c. was not as important as the Isthmian Games.
5. Why did Paul leave Corinth?
6. Paul preached in the lands of Asia Minor, Macedonia, and Galatia. See these lands on the map. Below are names of cities in these lands where Paul preached. Find each city on the map on page 161. Write the names of the cities on your paper. Put **A** beside the cities you find in Asia Minor, **M** beside the cities in Macedonia, and **G** beside the cities in Galatia.

Berea	Derbe	Thyatira
Ephesus	Philippi	Smyrna
Lystra	Troas	Thessalonica
Colossae	Iconium	Philadelphia
Antioch	Sardis	

SHARE YOUR KNOWLEDGE

1. Study 1 John 2:15 and answer these questions.
    a. In this verse, the sinful community is called the _____.
    b. People in the Christian community should not love the (people, customs) of the sinful community.

The map above shows the countries of Europe. The country of the Netherlands is one of the smallest countries in Europe. At the right, you can see a larger map of the Netherlands. Use the map key to find the land below sea level in the Netherlands.

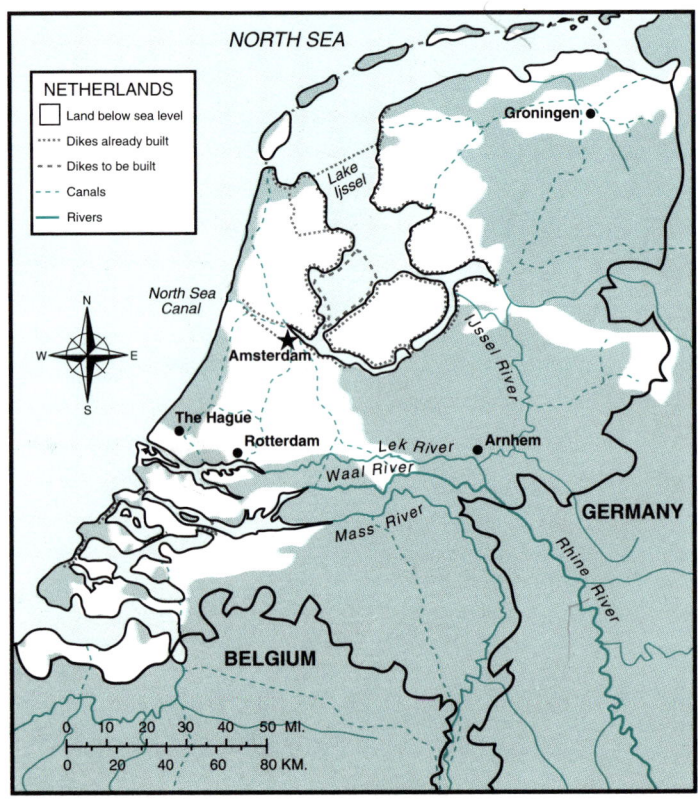

"Sing unto the Lord a new song, and his praise from the end of the earth, ye that go down to the sea, and all that is therein; the isles, and the inhabitants [people] thereof" (Isaiah 42:10).

Netherlands, Land From Under the Sea

In the northern part of Europe is a country called the Netherlands. This land is also called Holland. *Holland* means "hollow lands." Each piece of "hollow land" is like the bottom of a dish with sides around the edge. The people in this country are known as the Dutch. They speak a language called Dutch.

In some countries you have studied, the people have a problem finding enough water for their needs. The Dutch have always had the problem of having too much water.

THE LOWLANDS AND THE SEA

Several large rivers flow through the Netherlands and empty into the North Sea. You can find the sources of these rivers in other parts of Europe.

As these rivers flow along, they pick up silt. Each river drops the silt at its mouth. Over the years a delta forms like the Nile River delta in Egypt. Much of the Netherlands is delta land.

The name *Netherlands* means "low land." Delta land is flat and never much higher than the level of the sea.

On your map on page 164, you can find some land in the Netherlands that is even lower than the sea. We say that such land is below sea level. Most of the land below sea level is in the western part of the Netherlands.

Years ago, sea water could flow down into these lowlands. But God used the wind, sand, and sea to build up sides around the lowlands to keep out the water.

The wind and sea piled up sand dunes along the coasts of

the Netherlands. The sand dunes held back the sea water.

But the sand dunes could not always keep back the sea. Stormy waves sometimes broke through and flooded the lowlands.

KEEPING THE SEA IN ITS PLACE

The Dutch wanted to make their land safe from the sea. They piled up more sand and stones on both sides of the sand dunes to make strong walls. These walls are called **dikes.** The Dutch also built dikes along the sides of rivers to keep them from overflowing.

But the Dutch cannot always trust the dikes men build to keep back the water.

Job 38:8a
Job 38:11
Only God can "shut up the sea with doors" and say, "Hitherto [to here] shalt thou come, but no further: and here shall thy proud waves be stayed."

Storms sometimes send waves crashing through the dikes the Dutch have built. Houses are washed away, crops are ruined, and the land is spoiled.

Then the Dutch must set to work to repair the dikes, drain the land, and rebuild their homes.

The sea piles up sand dunes around the land below sea level. The sand dunes help to keep the sea from flowing over the lowlands. The drawing helps you see why the Dutch called the lowlands the "hollow lands."

The Dutch pile up rocks and soil to make walls of earth called dikes. The dike in the picture keeps the sea from spilling into the lowlands.

SHOW YOUR KNOWLEDGE

1. The Netherlands is on the continent of _____.
2. Another name for the Netherlands is _____.
3. The people and their language are called _____.
4. What natural resource makes a problem for the people of the Netherlands?
5. Where are the sources of the rivers that flow through the Netherlands?
6. Where are the mouths of these rivers?
7. Much of the Netherlands is _____ land.
8. The land of the Dutch is called the Netherlands because:
    a. much of this land is below sea level.
    b. the land is much higher than the level of the sea.
    c. it has sand dunes along the coast.
9. When the wind and sea made _____ along the coasts they helped to hold back the sea water.
10. What did the Dutch do to make their land safe from the sea?
11. Are the Dutch completely safe from floods now?

SHARE YOUR KNOWLEDGE

1. Study Jeremiah 5:22 and answer these questions.
    a. God has placed the _____ to be a bound (stopping mark) for the sea.
    b. The _____ cannot get past God's bound for them.
2. The Dutch make _____ to be a bound for the sea. How is this man-made bound different from the bound God placed for the sea?

CHANGING THE ZUIDER ZEE

On the map on page 164, find Lake Ijssel (i´ səl). Over a thousand years ago there was farmland where this lake is today. Then the sand dunes in the north broke. The sea rushed in and formed a body of water known as the Zuider Zee (zī´ dər zē).

The sea destroyed farms and villages. Then for many years the farmland beneath the sea was forgotten.

This large dike is 20 miles long. It closes Lake Ijssel off from the North Sea. The picture shows the North Sea on the right. You can see part of Lake Ijssel on the left.

Photo: John D. Martin

This picture shows a polder along Lake Ijssel. A polder is a piece of land claimed back from the sea. Find the dike the Dutch built first to keep out the sea. Find the canals that drain the land. How do the Dutch get the water from the canals up into the sea?

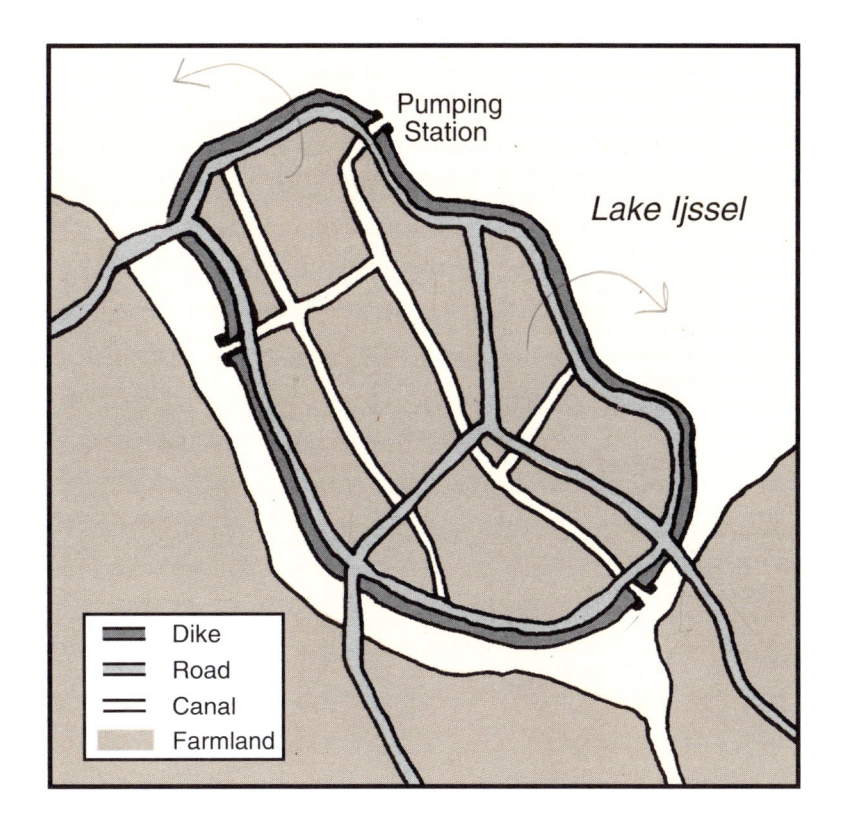

Finally, the Netherlands became filled with people. More farmland was needed for crops to feed everyone.

In the year 1920, the Dutch started work to get more land. Workers began a job that seemed impossible. They began working on a plan to get back the land that lay under the Zuider Zee.

First the Dutch built a long dike to close off the Zuider Zee from the North Sea. Find this dike on the map on page 164. This huge dike is 20 miles long and stands high above sea level.

The dike made a large lake out of the Zuider Zee. This is Lake Ijssel or Ijsselmeer.

The Dutch pumped the salt water from Lake Ijssel into the sea. Fresh water from the rivers took the place of the salt water. Today Lake Ijssel is a freshwater lake.

By pumping water out, the Dutch made the water level in the lake lower. Farmers began to drain water from the land along the edges of the lake. Little by little they got back pieces of land from under the sea. These pieces of land claimed from the sea are called **polders**.

DRAINING WATER FROM POLDERS

Draining a polder is slow, hard work. First, the Dutch build a dike around a piece of land that is still under the sea. Then they pump the water over the dike and into the sea.

Even after the water is pumped off, the land is soggy and wet. Water does not drain from land that is lower than the sea. Rains stay on the land and do not run off.

The Dutch solve this problem by digging canals through the polders. The water runs from the fields into the canals. Then the water in the canals must have a place to go.

The Dutch make other canals higher than the canals in

This is a Dutch farmhouse. A Dutch farmer built his barn and house together in one building. How would this be handy during cold winters? The canal drains the water from the farmer's fields.

Photo: John D. Martin

The farmland on this polder once lay under the sea. The Dutch built dikes around the polder and pumped out the sea water. Polder land is very flat. The soil on a polder grows good crops after the Dutch let the salt wash from the land.

Photo: John D. Martin

What looks strange about this picture? This sight is not strange to the people of the Netherlands. The Dutch built this high canal. They pump water up into this high canal from the lower canals. The high canal empties into the sea.

the fields. They use pumps to lift water from the low canals into the higher canals. The water can flow from these high canals into the sea.

The soil of a new polder has much salt in it. Farmers first scrape off some of the saltiest soil. Rains help to carry the rest of the salt into the canals. Then the farmers **fertilize** the land and plant crops. In five years farmers are growing crops in the rich, sandy silt of a new polder.

The Dutch built big dams between the islands along the southwest coast of their country. These dams help to prevent floods during storms.

The Dutch are still struggling with the sea as they have been for hundreds of years. They say, "Whoever cannot conquer the sea is not worthy of the land."

Find the city of Amsterdam (am´ stər dam) on the map on page 164. Amsterdam is the largest city in the Netherlands today.

In the next chapter, you will learn how Amsterdam grew from a small community into a large city. You will also learn about the Christian community which began at Amsterdam.

SHOW YOUR KNOWLEDGE

1. Long ago, the Zuider Zee covered _____ and _____ .
2. When the Dutch needed more farmland, they built a big _____ to close the Zuider Zee off from the _____ .
3. The new lake that was formed was called _____ .
4. The water in Lake Ijssel is (salt, fresh) water.
5. Number these sentences about making a polder in the order in which they would happen.
    a. ___ Men dig canals through polders.
    b. ___ Water is pumped over the dike and into the sea.
    c. ___ The water runs from the fields into the canals.
    d. ___ Men build a dike around a piece of land covered by the sea.
    e. ___ Water is pumped from low canals into higher canals and flows into the sea.
6. Crops cannot grow right away on a new polder because of _____ in the soil.
7. The Dutch built big _____ to help to prevent floods during storms.
8. What is the name of the largest city in the Netherlands?

SHARE YOUR KNOWLEDGE

1. Water does not drain off land below sea level because:
    a. land below sea level gets more rain than other lands.
    b. the water soaks into the soil.
    c. water cannot run uphill.
2. Water will drain into canals because the canals:
    a. are lower than the land.
    b. carry the water to the sea.
    c. are higher than the land.

This picture shows the city of Amsterdam the way it looks today. Amsterdam was built on lowlands. See the canals that drain the water from the land where Amsterdam stands.

> "All that will live godly in Christ Jesus shall suffer persecution" (2 Timothy 3:12).

The Story of Amsterdam

The place where Amsterdam now stands was once a lonely swamp beside the Zuider Zee. The land was below sea level.

The waters of the Zuider Zee nibbled away at the low sand dunes along the shore. Salt water tumbled over the sand dunes when the tide rose high.

The Amstel River flowed through the swamp. The Amstel often overflowed to flood the land. The land was soaked with water and covered with thick green brushwood.

The first people who lived there were fishermen. The fishermen lived in boats made from leather and ate fish from the Zuider Zee.

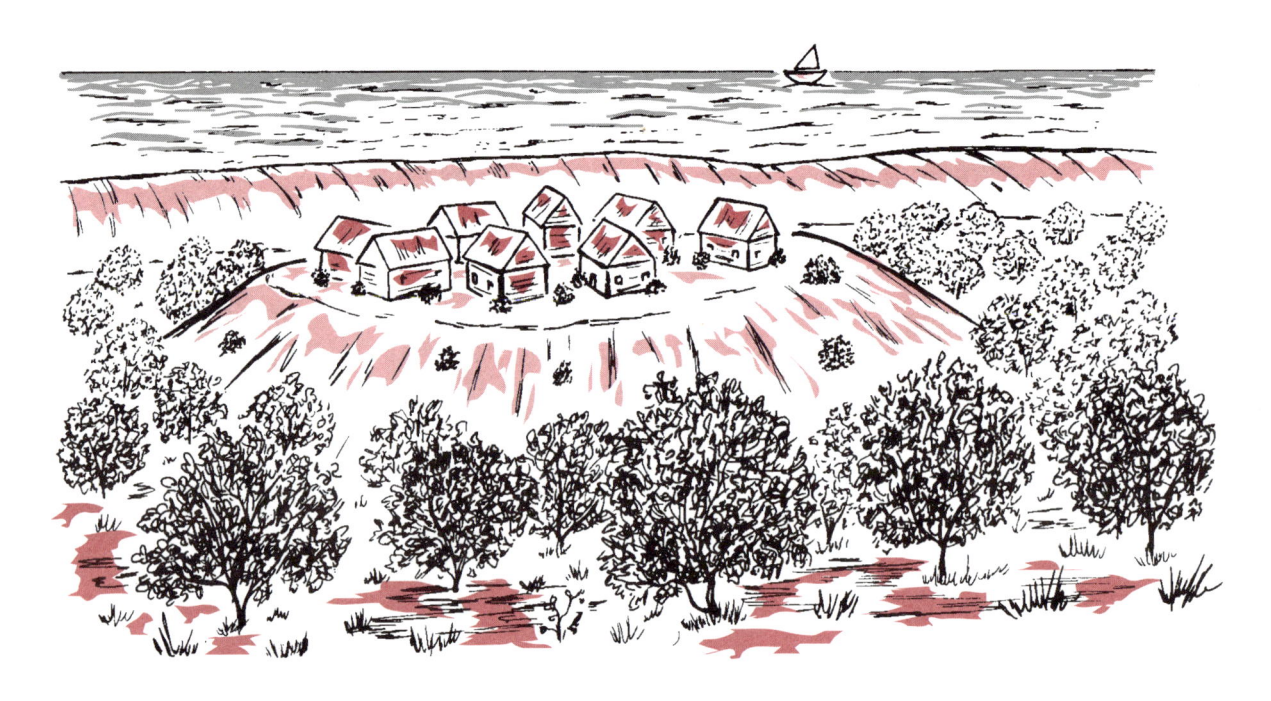

Long ago, settlers came to live on the land where Amsterdam stands today. These settlers kept their houses dry by building them on small hills called terpen.

Finally, some of the fishermen began to build houses. The people built their houses on mounds of earth. Sometimes they made mounds large enough for whole villages.

These early settlers fished and raised cattle. The floods made it impossible for them to grow crops.

No one can say for sure just how the city of Amsterdam began. But some people tell the story this way:

One day many years ago, a strong leader sailed up the Zuider Zee with his men and stopped at the villages on the swamp.

"This will be a good place for us to make our homes," he told his men. "We can build walls of earth along the sea and along the banks of the Amstel River to prevent floods. Then we can farm this land and grow crops."

He went on to say, "The water here is full of fish. We can make a living by trading fish with people in other lands."

The men set to work with wooden shovels. They piled up earth to make dikes. The men looked for rocks to make the dikes strong. But they could find no rocks on the swampy land. Using boats, they brought rocks from other lands.

FROM A SWAMP TO A VILLAGE

"We cannot build houses on this swampy land," said one of the workers.

The leader looked at the soggy soil. He said, "We will dig ditches to drain the water from the land."

The men set to work with their shovels. They dug a large circle of canals. Water filled the canals and the land began to dry off. But the soil was still too soft for houses.

One of the workers spoke up with an idea. "Let us drive wooden poles deep into the earth until they hit hard ground," he said. "These poles will make good hard bases for houses."

The leader and his men agreed. The workers pounded hundreds of poles called **piles** into the ground side by side. Then they built a village of houses on the land filled with piles.

Most of the houses were built from wood. But the workers built a stone castle for the leader. He became the first **lord** or ruler of the village.

The village beside the Amstel River became known as Amsterdam.

The lord of Amsterdam lived in a castle in the middle of the village. He made the village laws. He owned all of the land, and the people paid him **rent** for the land they used. In return, the lord promised to protect them.

The people also paid taxes to the lord. He used the tax money to build dikes, roads, canals, and other things the community needed.

Workers built a wall around Amsterdam to protect the people in times of danger. Outside the wall, the men made a ditch of water called a **moat.**

People had to cross the moat on a drawbridge to enter the town. When enemies attacked, the drawbridge was lifted so they could not enter.

Some men wanted to farm the land outside the village. They dug more canals in large half circles around the town.

The canals were below sea level. Water could not flow from the canals up into the sea. At first, men pumped the water into the sea by hand or with horses.

One day a man said, "The wind blows almost every day.

A moat of water surrounds this old castle. Long ago, the lords of Amsterdam lived in a castle with a moat and a drawbridge.

Someone should find a way to use the wind for pumping water."

Some men began working on a windmill that could run a pump. Before long they found a way to make it work. Soon windmills were pumping water from the canals. The windmills also gave power for grinding grain or sawing wood.

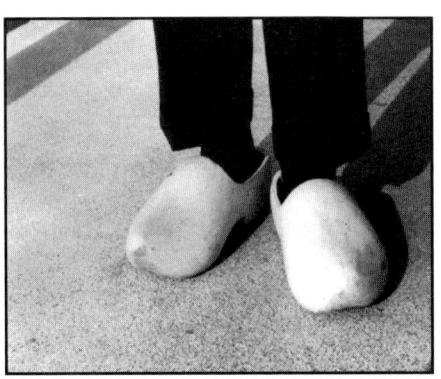

The soil in the lowlands was damp. The people knew that wooden shoes could keep their feet dry. Almost everybody in Amsterdam wore wooden shoes.

The Dutch word for wooden shoes is *klompen*.

Today the Dutch do not need windmills to run machines and pump water from the canals. Engines now do much of this work. But the Dutch want to keep some of the windmills to remind people of the way the Dutch lived in the Netherlands many years ago.

Photo: Carl Roger's Photography

SHOW YOUR KNOWLEDGE

1. Why did the first people beside the Zuider Zee build houses on mounds of earth?
2. Why didn't these first people do any farming?
3. What natural resource is missing at the place where Amsterdam is?
4. Some people say, "Amsterdam is built on an upside-down forest." They mean:
    a. the city builders spoiled a beautiful forest.
    b. the houses sit on poles made from trees.
    c. wood for building came from a southern country.
5. What did the lord of the castle do with the tax money the people paid to him?
6. In what three ways were windmills used?
7. Why did so many people in the Netherlands wear wooden shoes?

TRADE BUILDS AMSTERDAM

The village of Amsterdam was at a good place for ships to land along the Zuider Zee. The Dutch began building **merchant** ships for trading.

The sea near Amsterdam was full of small fish called **herring**. Dutch fishermen caught tons of herring. They salted the fish and packed them into wooden barrels.

Dutch merchants carried the barrels of herring to other lands by ship. There they traded and brought back ships loaded with spices, coffee, clothing, and foods the people of Amsterdam did not have.

As the fish trade grew, the village grew. That is why some people say, "Amsterdam was built on the backbone of a herring."

The fish trade made work for many people. The village

The Dutch added a new ring of canals to Amsterdam each time the growing city needed more land. Compare this drawing with the picture of Amsterdam on the top of page 173.

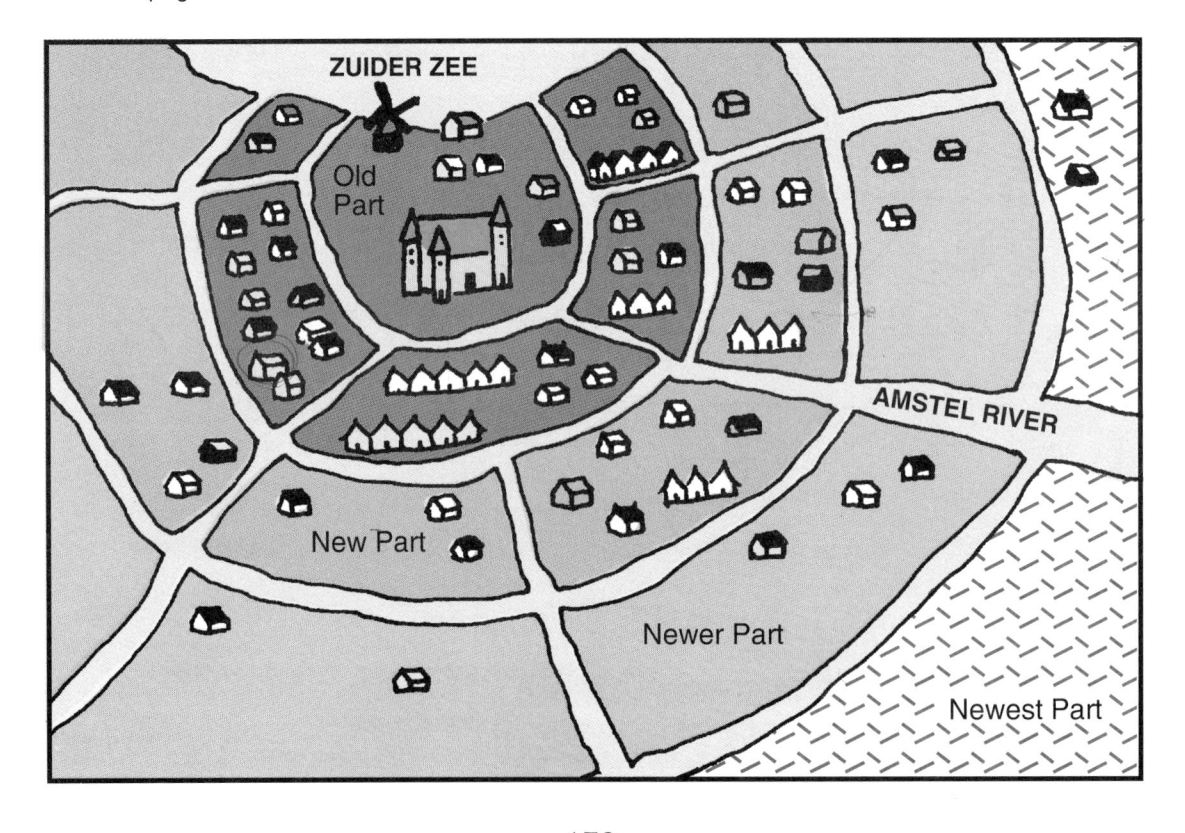

These boats are used by fishermen near Amsterdam.

needed **craftsmen** to make wooden barrels for the herring. More craftsmen were needed to build ships. Workers kept moving to Amsterdam until it became a small city.

The growing city needed more dry land for houses. The Dutch dug more canals around the outside edge of the city to drain more land. Each canal added a new ring of land to the city.

Ships began coming to Amsterdam from other lands. Dutch merchants in the city bought the goods on these ships. They loaded them onto small flat boats called **barges**.

Men floated the barges up the canals to large buildings called **warehouses**. There the merchants stored the goods until they could sell them for higher prices than they had paid.

The merchants made a profit by buying goods at a low price and waiting to sell them for a higher price. Amsterdam became one of the richest trading centers in the world.

Dutch merchants often paid for goods with barrels of herring instead of money. Herring became known as "Dutch gold."

In the next lesson, see if the rich people at Amsterdam used their power in the right way.

SHOW YOUR KNOWLEDGE

1. What natural resource helped Amsterdam grow?
2. How did the Dutch merchants use their warehouses?
3. Why was herring called "Dutch gold"?

SHARE YOUR KNOWLEDGE

1. Some people in Amsterdam became rich. Proverbs 22:7 teaches us that:
    a. rich people will never be poor.
    b. borrowers are always poor people.
    c. rich people and nations have power over others.
2. Now study Proverbs 22:9. A person with a "bountiful eye" receives God's blessing. This verse says such a person:
    a. rules over the poor.
    b. gives to the poor.
    c. gives away all of his bread.

GOVERNMENT PROBLEMS

As the years passed by, different lords ruled Amsterdam. Often the lords were unfair.

One lord would make taxes very high and keep most of the money for himself. The next lord would cruelly punish anyone who disagreed with him.

The lords often made unfair laws for the people. Sometimes the lords did not even obey their own laws.

Unless something was done, Amsterdam was headed for trouble, because God says, "By the blessing of the upright [faithful] the city is exalted [built up]: but it is overthrown by the mouth of the wicked."

Proverbs 11:11

The merchants decided to do something. They got together and wrote up an agreement called a **charter.**

The charter had rules to make the lord treat the people fairly. The merchants asked the lord to sign his name on the charter to show that he would obey it.

"We will not pay our taxes if you do not sign the charter," the merchants told the lord.

The lord needed tax money to run the government. He had to sign the charter. Then he had to obey it. When he did not obey, the merchants stopped giving him money. The charter made the people of Amsterdam safe from unfair laws and taxes.

The merchants made the lord of Amsterdam sign his name to a charter. The charter had rules for the lord to obey. These rules helped to keep the lord from being unfair to the people at Amsterdam.

Many years went by. Again some people in Amsterdam had to suffer.

These people were a small group of Christians. They were treated cruelly by leaders of a false church that did not obey all the teachings of the Bible.

The Christians believed it was wrong to fight back as the merchants had done. The Christians were called **nonresistant** people. This means they did not resist or try to make things hard for their enemies.

The Christians followed the words of Jesus, "Love your enemies, bless them that curse you, do good to them that hate you, and pray for them which despitefully [hatefully] use you."

Matthew 5:44

The merchants had not used the Bible way to make things better. The Christians were different. The Christians would not force the evil leaders to change. They showed only love to the people who made them suffer.

SHOW YOUR KNOWLEDGE

1. A charter has rules mostly for (merchants, poor people, leaders).
2. The merchants were able to force the lord to change his ways, because:
    a. kings do not like charters.
    b. the merchants would not pay their taxes unless he obeyed the charter.
    c. lords always sign charters.
3. How did the charter help the people?
4. Instead of using force, the Christians showed _____ to those who made them suffer.

SHARE YOUR KNOWLEDGE

1. Which of these would a nonresistant person do? Choose two.
    a. give good things to those who hate him
    b. refuse to pay taxes to an evil ruler
    c. say unkind things about someone who has said unkind things about him
    d. refuse to fight in a war

THE FALSE CHURCH AT AMSTERDAM

Most of the people at Amsterdam belonged to a church called the Roman Catholic Church. But the leaders in this church made the people do many wrong things. The Roman Catholic Church was a false church.

The Roman Catholic leaders wanted to baptize all the babies.

But some parents could not obey. These Christian parents knew baptizing babies was against Bible teaching.

Mark 16:16a

The Bible says, "He that believeth and is baptized shall be saved."

The Christian parents said, "The Bible tells us people

must believe on Jesus when they are baptized. Babies do not know about Jesus. They cannot believe on Him."

But the Roman Catholic leaders did not care what the Bible said. Baptizing babies helped to make sure everyone would belong to the Roman Catholic Church.

Most of the people of Amsterdam were Roman Catholics. But many of them did not give up their sinful ways.

The Roman Catholic leaders said that if people told their sins to a **priest** he would get forgiveness for them.

The Christians in Amsterdam knew priests could not forgive sins.

They said, "Only Jesus can forgive sins when people are sorry enough to stop sinning. The people in the Roman Catholic Church tell their sins to a priest. Then they go right on doing the same sins."

Praying to an image will never help anyone.

The Roman Catholic leaders put images of Jesus and His mother, Mary, in their churches. Roman Catholic churches also had images of people who had died.

The Roman Catholic leaders believed these people were in heaven and could help people when they prayed to them.

Such teaching was very wrong. The Bible says, "For there is... one mediator [helper] between God and men, the man Christ Jesus." No one but Jesus can talk to God for His people.

1 Timothy 2:5

But people did not often dare to disobey the Roman Catholic leaders. These leaders often worked with the government. The government gave the Roman Catholic leaders power to punish anyone who disobeyed their church laws.

Most of the people in Amsterdam obeyed. Hardly anyone had a Bible to show that the Roman Catholic leaders were wrong.

Bibles were hard to get. Amsterdam had no printing

presses. New Bibles had to be copied slowly by hand.

Besides, the Bible was written in a language called **Latin.** The Dutch people could not read Latin. The Roman Catholic leaders would not let anyone change the Bible to the Dutch language. The leaders did not want the people to find out about their wrong ideas.

> ## John 3:16 in Latin
>
> Sic enim Deus dilexit mundum, ut Filium suum unigenitum daret, ut omnis qui credit in eum non pereat, sed habeat vitam aeternam.

SHOW YOUR KNOWLEDGE

1. Why didn't the Christian parents want their babies to be baptized?
2. Why did Roman Catholic leaders want to baptize all babies?
3. The Christians knew that only _____ can forgive sins, not the _____ .
4. Only Jesus could be a _____ between God and men.
5. Why were most people in Amsterdam afraid to disobey the Roman Catholic leaders?
6. How did the Roman Catholic leaders keep people from reading the Bible? Why didn't they want people to read it?

A TRUE CHURCH RISES UP

At last in the country of Germany a man found a new way to print books. This man was Johannes Gutenberg (yō hän´ əs gü´ tən bərg). The first book he printed was the Bible.

Soon many Bibles were being printed for people to read. But these Bibles were printed in the Latin language. Most Dutch people could not read Gutenberg's Latin Bible.

Finally in 1522 a man named Martin Luther translated the Bible into the German language. The new printing presses began producing many German New Testaments. Some people in Amsterdam could read German. Men began studying the Bible and teaching people what it said.

The Bible teachers said to the people, "You were baptized when you were babies and that was wrong. You must turn from your sins and be baptized again."

Many people believed the Bible teaching. They confessed their sins and asked to be baptized again. A true church began to grow at Amsterdam.

The new Christians learned to read. They wanted to read the Bible for themselves so false leaders could not trick them again.

Here you see Johannes Gutenberg looking at the first page of the first printed Bible.

H. Armstrong Roberts

The Roman Catholic leaders hated the Christians. They gave the name **Anabaptist** (a nə bap´ təst) to any person who was baptized again.

The Roman Catholic leaders had government power to make laws against the Anabaptists. The government punished Anabaptists and tried many ways to make them give up their beliefs. Evil men beat some and burned others with hot irons.

Matthew 10:22

But the Anabaptists knew the Bible said, "... Ye shall be hated of all men for my name's sake: but he that endureth [stands] to the end shall be saved." The Anabaptists wanted to be saved. They chose to obey God rather than wrong laws.

The Roman Catholic leaders became angry. They chained some Christians to wooden stakes and burned them with fire until they died. They drowned others.

The Christians who died for their beliefs were called **martyrs** (mär´ tərz). The dying martyrs often prayed for their

The cruel leaders at Amsterdam put many Anabaptists to death. See the hard-hearted leader warming his hands at the fire. What are the Anabaptists doing as they die? You will read the story about this picture on page 187. One man in the fire is named Ellert Jans. After you read the story, see if you can tell which man is Ellert.

Martyrs Mirror

enemies. Many sang songs as they were being burned. The words and songs of the martyrs made others want to be Christians.

The Christians at Amsterdam had to hide from government leaders. They met at night to worship in secret. Some Christians hid in fields to worship. One merchant preached to people in his boat on the water away from the city.

God blessed the Anabaptists and their church grew. The Roman Catholic leaders could not stop it.

SHOW YOUR KNOWLEDGE

1. When the printing presses produced German New Testaments, men began _____ the Bible and people _____ what it said.
2. Why did new Christians want to be able to read?
3. The Anabaptists were ready to suffer and die rather than obey laws against the Bible, because they:
    a. could not disobey the Bible and be saved in the end.
    b. did not respect the evil leaders who made the laws.
    c. wanted other people to see them suffer.
4. When the Roman Catholic leaders treated the Anabaptists unkindly, it made their church (get smaller, grow).

ELLERT JANS DIES FOR HIS FAITH

(a true story)

"Ellert Jans! (el´ ərt yans). Have you been baptized again?" shouted an angry voice from the street.

Ellert looked up from the coat he was sewing. In the doorway of his shop stood a government leader of Amsterdam and two soldiers. The swords by their sides shone in the morning sun.

Ellert knew they had come to take him. Without fear he

said softly, "Yes, I confessed my sin and was baptized as the Bible teaches us."

"Then you must come with us to prison!" the angry leader shouted again.

The two soldiers tied Ellert's hands with a rope and shoved him roughly from the doorway of his shop.

Thump! Thump! Ellert's wooden leg sounded on the stone sidewalk as he slowly limped along between the soldiers.

People stopped along the street to watch. Some hissed the name "Anabaptist" through their teeth. Others stared at Ellert with pity. They knew he would never come back.

At the prison, the soldiers stopped, keys jingled, the lock screeched, and the iron gate clanged shut behind Ellert.

Roughly, the soldiers pushed Ellert to a dark, damp, dirty cell. There he was shut in with other Christian prisoners.

Day after day, the prisoners got only small pieces of bread to eat and water to drink. Every day, priests came and tried to talk them out of their Bible teachings. But all stayed true to God.

One day men came and dragged Ellert to the **torture**

room. Some Roman Catholic leaders were waiting there.

"Give up your beliefs or we will hurt you!" the leaders told Ellert.

"I will not," replied Ellert. "You can hurt my body, but God will save my soul."

The men squeezed Ellert's fingers with iron clamps until the blood ran. They stretched his body with ropes until pain shot through his arms and legs. But Ellert would not believe their lies. Finally they took him back to his cell. He was bleeding and sore, yet singing praises to God.

One dark night, Ellert was awakened by a noise. Two men were breaking the bars from the prison window.

"We have come to free you," they whispered in the dark.

The men outside had a brother in the cell. This brother cried out softly, "Oh, my dear brothers. How can we ever thank you? I only wish you would also give up your sins and be baptized."

"Stop preaching to us and hurry up!" one of the men muttered.

The two men let the prisoners down from the window with a rope one by one. But when Ellert Jans' turn came, he would not go.

He said, "I am ready to die for Jesus, and I shall never be happier than I am right now. Besides, I would soon be caught again because of my wooden leg."

Before long, a day was set for Ellert Jans to be burned at the stake. Hundreds of people followed him as soldiers led him out and placed him in a cage. Ellert soon spied his cousin Jan (yan) in the crowd.

"Greetings in the name of Jesus, brother Jan," Ellert cried

with joy. "Indeed, this is the happiest day of my life," he said.

Ellert pushed his New Testament through the bars for his cousin. An evil leader saw him.

"Where is the book?" the leader roared. But the little book was quickly lost in the crowd.

Ellert spoke bravely to his cousin.

"Jan, do not believe the lies of the Roman Catholic Church. Read the New Testament I gave you. Obey its teachings and be saved."

Soon the soldiers dragged Ellert from the cage and tied him to a wooden stake. As the fire leaped high around him, he sang a joyful hymn. The song came to an end and Ellert's spirit went to be with God.

Jan Jans walked slowly away. Ellert's cheerful words and song rang in his ears. He believed his cousin's words. Before many days, he also believed on Jesus.

♪ *Faith of our fathers...* ♪♪
We will be true to thee till death!

FREEDOM FOR CHRISTIANS

Most of the people at Amsterdam did not become Anabaptists. But many people pitied the brave Christians and did not think they should have to suffer for their beliefs.

Some men said, "The job of the government is to keep order in the community. The Christians do not make trouble. The government should make laws to keep good people safe and not laws to punish them."

"That's right," said some others. "The Roman Catholic Church should not have government power to make laws against Anabaptist beliefs."

The Anabaptists agreed. They said, "The government and the church have different jobs.

"Government leaders must punish bad people to keep order in the community. God wants His church to teach bad people about Jesus and His love. The two jobs do not go together."

The Anabaptists did not work in the government. They did not believe God wanted them to help punish bad people.

The Anabaptists said, "God wants Christians to help the government by obeying its laws, paying taxes, and praying for its leaders."

Once the government at Amsterdam needed a lot of money to build some dikes. The suffering Christians gave the leaders a large gift of money for this job.

At last, a king named William of Orange became the leader of the Netherlands. He did not think the government should make laws against people's beliefs about God.

William of Orange put a stop to punishments for Christians. The Netherlands became the first country to have freedom of religion for all people.

In the years after William of Orange, the church grew rapidly and so did the city of Amsterdam. Suffering Christians came to Amsterdam from other countries. At Amsterdam they could obey the Bible without fear of punishment.

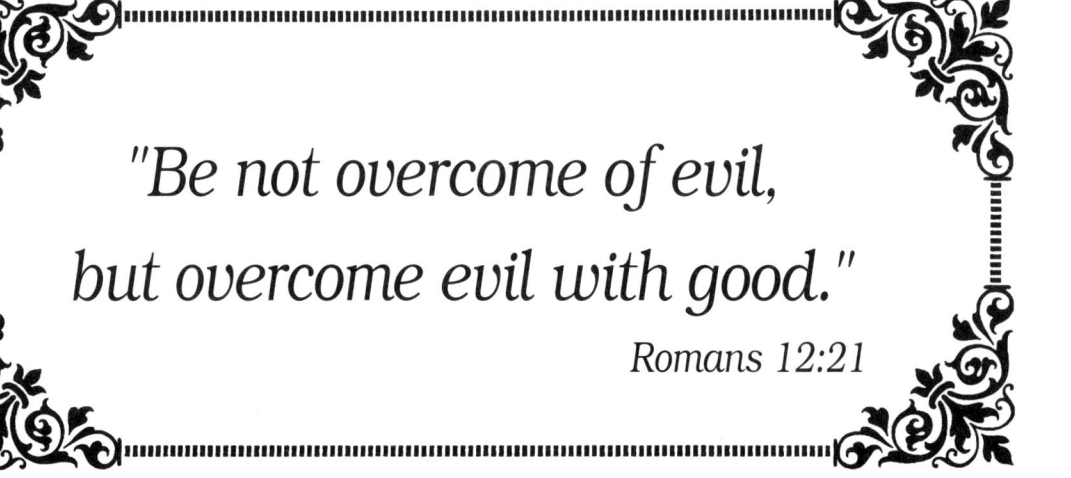

> *"Be not overcome of evil, but overcome evil with good."*
> *Romans 12:21*

SHOW YOUR KNOWLEDGE

1. Ellert knew men could hurt his _____ , but God would save his _____ .
2. What good thing happened to Ellert's cousin after Ellert gave up his life?
3. The Anabaptists believed the _____ and the _____ had different jobs.
4. The Anabaptists believed:
    a. God does not want Christians to be government leaders.
    b. God does not want Christians to help the government in any way.
    c. there should not be any government.
5. What did King William of Orange do for the Christians in the Netherlands?

SHARE YOUR KNOWLEDGE

1. Study 2 Timothy 3:12. Find *persecute* in your glossary and write the meaning of this word. The verse says persecution will come to those who _____ .

VISITING AMSTERDAM TODAY

The houses in Amsterdam are narrow and tall. This is because land for houses has always been scarce. Today some families live in houseboats along the canals in Amsterdam.

The streets of Amsterdam are along the banks of the canals. Over one thousand bridges cross the canals to join the streets together.

Most of the streets were built many years ago. At that time not many people lived in Amsterdam. But today the city is crowded with people. The narrow streets are crowded with traffic.

Many Dutch people ride bicycles. Bicycles are easier to handle than cars in the crowded streets. Children in Amsterdam learn to ride bicycles almost as soon as they can walk.

Amsterdam has fast electric streetcars called **trams**. A ride on a tram is one of the safest and quickest ways to get around in the city.

Barges still carry loads of goods on the canals of Amsterdam. Each Friday from spring to fall, barges loaded with cheese travel from Amsterdam to the town of Alkmaar (alk´ mär) where they are sold. From the market at Alkmaar, famous Dutch cheeses are shipped all over the world.

Cheese is one of the Netherlands' important exports. Milk to make the cheese is needed from many farms.

Dutch farmers graze herds of **dairy** cattle on grassy pold-

Moving day for a family in Amsterdam is different from moving day for a family in your community. The old houses in Amsterdam are very narrow and tall. The stairs in these houses are also narrow and steep. This picture shows how the Dutch get furniture into the upstairs rooms of these houses.

Photo: Netherlands Information Service

Many people ride bicycles on the old, narrow, crowded streets of Amsterdam today.

Photo: John D. Martin

Dutch farmers sell cheeses at the market in the town of Alkmaar. Some of these cheeses will go to other lands.

ers. Barges pick up the milk and haul it to the cities. There the milk is manufactured into cheese and butter.

In the spring, barges loaded with flowers travel through the canals of Amsterdam every day. Tulips, hyacinths, and daffodils are sold in the streets.

Dutch women buy some of the flowers to make their homes beautiful. But most of the fresh cut flowers are sold and shipped to other countries.

The Dutch grow flowers mainly for their bulbs. The flower bulbs are an important Dutch export. Dutch merchants ship millions of flower bulbs all over the world to be traded or sold.

Herring are still an important Dutch export. Barges loaded with these fish can still be seen on the canals. At stands along

This picture shows Dam Square in the oldest part of Amsterdam. The large building is the Royal Palace. It stands near the place where the castle of lords once stood. The Royal Palace is built on 13,659 piles pounded into the ground.

Photo: Royal Netherlands Embassy

the streets of Amsterdam, people often buy herring and eat them raw.

TRADE AND MANUFACTURING

When Amsterdam began, ships could travel from the city to the ocean on the Zuider Zee. Then the Dutch built the large dike to close off the Zuider Zee from the ocean. The dike blocked the way for ships.

The men at Amsterdam had to find another way for their ships to reach the ocean. They decided to build the North Sea Canal. Find this canal on the map on page 164.

The North Sea Canal is one of the widest and deepest canals in the world. The people of Amsterdam can ship goods to and from many countries through this canal.

The men of Amsterdam built another canal to the Rhine River. The Rhine River reaches to many countries in Europe. The canal to the Rhine River makes a way for ships to go from Amsterdam to these countries.

Barges on the Rhine River can now carry raw materials from many places in Europe to Amsterdam. The canal also gives Amsterdam merchants a way to ship Dutch goods to these places.

Many of the people in Amsterdam today work in factories. These Dutch workers help to manufacture steel, aircraft, food products, and many other goods.

Amsterdam merchants trade some of these manufactured goods with other countries for raw materials. Iron ore is one important raw material the land of the Dutch does not have. Iron ore must be imported for the factories at Amsterdam.

Today Amsterdam is a grown-up city. Manufacturing and trade helped it to grow from a small fish trading village to a large city. But the sea helped the most by giving the Dutch a way to trade. God made the sea. The people of Amsterdam should thank Him for all the blessings of their city.

"Oh that men would praise the LORD for his goodness, and for his wonderful works to the children of men!" **Psalm 107:8**

WHAT HAPPENED TO THE CHURCH?

At first the Christian church at Amsterdam grew rapidly. Some Christians became rich merchants and factory owners. Others became rich farmers.

The Bible warns about the danger of riches. Riches can cause people to think about the things of this world and make them forget God.

The Dutch Christians forgot God's warning. As the

This painting shows a Mennonite (me′ nə nīt) preacher and his wife. The Mennonites were a group of Anabaptists. A famous Dutch artist named Rembrandt painted this picture many years ago.

Christians became rich, many of them began to think much about their money and little about God.

Soon Christians were copying sinful customs from the community. The church and the sinful community became more and more alike.

After a while, the people who called themselves Christians were no different from the people who were not Christians.

Today most people in Amsterdam are lost and ungodly. Some people go to church, but many of them do not turn from their sins.

God can help the true church to rise up and grow again at Amsterdam. But He needs Christians who will preach His Word there again as the martyrs did many years ago.

SHOW YOUR KNOWLEDGE

1. Amsterdam has two problems:
    a. _____ is scarce.
    b. _____ are crowded.
2. The people of Amsterdam use _____ on the canals for the transportation of goods.
3. List four important Dutch exports.
4. When Dutch ships could no longer sail through the Zuider Zee to the ocean, men built the _____ .
5. Why did the Dutch build a canal from Amsterdam to the Rhine River?
6. List one natural resource that must be imported to Amsterdam.
7. Two things that helped Amsterdam to grow were _____ and _____ . But the _____ God made helped most of all.

SHARE YOUR KNOWLEDGE

1. What caused the Christians at Amsterdam to forget about God? Study Ephesians 4:28. What should the Christians at Amsterdam have done with their riches?

As cold waters to a thirsty soul, so is good news from a far country" (Proverbs 25:25).

America, the New World

Leaders in the Netherlands gave Christians the freedom of religion. But for many years, Christians in other parts of Europe had to suffer.

Some of these Christians wanted to leave their homes in Europe. They looked for a place where they could be free.

The suffering Christians trusted God to help them. God had said, "I will never leave thee, nor forsake thee." But the Christians did not know God had been planning a new land of freedom for His people.

Hebrews 13:5b

At that time, sailors from Europe were beginning to cross the Atlantic Ocean. These brave men came back telling stories about a new land they had found far across the Atlantic.

For years, people in Europe had been afraid to cross this large ocean. They kept their ships close to the coasts of well-known lands. People knew nothing about our land of America.

Merchants from Europe often traveled east to faraway

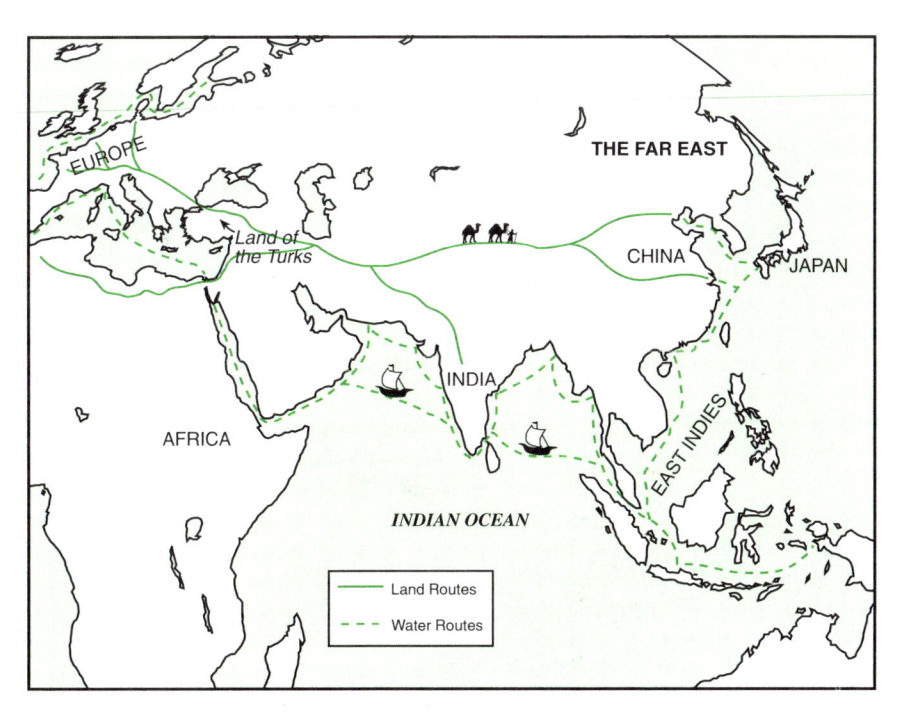

This map shows how the people of Europe traveled over the land to the East Indies. They had to cross the land of the Turks. Finally, the Turks closed the routes across their lands. The traders needed to find another way to get spices from the East Indies. Columbus looked toward the west. He said, "The earth is round. I can reach the East Indies by sailing my ships west around the earth."

Columbus and his men sailed three ships to America. The names of these ships were the *Nina*, the *Pinta,* and the *Santa Maria.*

Courtesy of Chicago Historical Society

islands in Asia. There they traded for peppers, cloves, and other **spices.** The islands in east Asia were called the Spice Islands, or the Indies.

The merchants passed through the lands of the Turks on their way to the Indies. Once the Turks closed the path through their lands. They would not let the merchants pass through. The people of Europe could not get the spices they needed so badly.

A man named Christopher Columbus believed the earth was round.

He said, "I can reach the Indies by sailing west."

Columbus tried to reach the East Indies by sailing west around the world. But today we know he sailed only part of the way around. The islands he found are called the "West Indies."

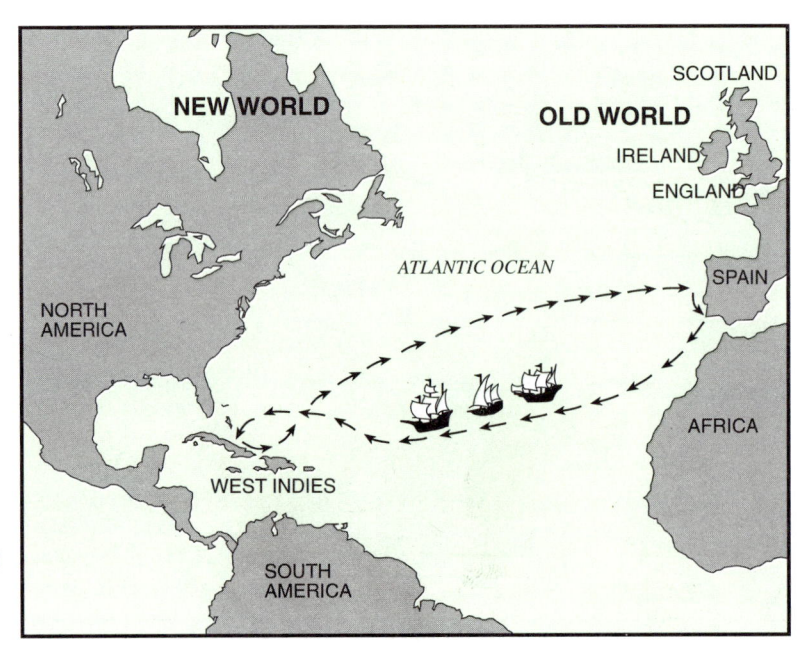

200

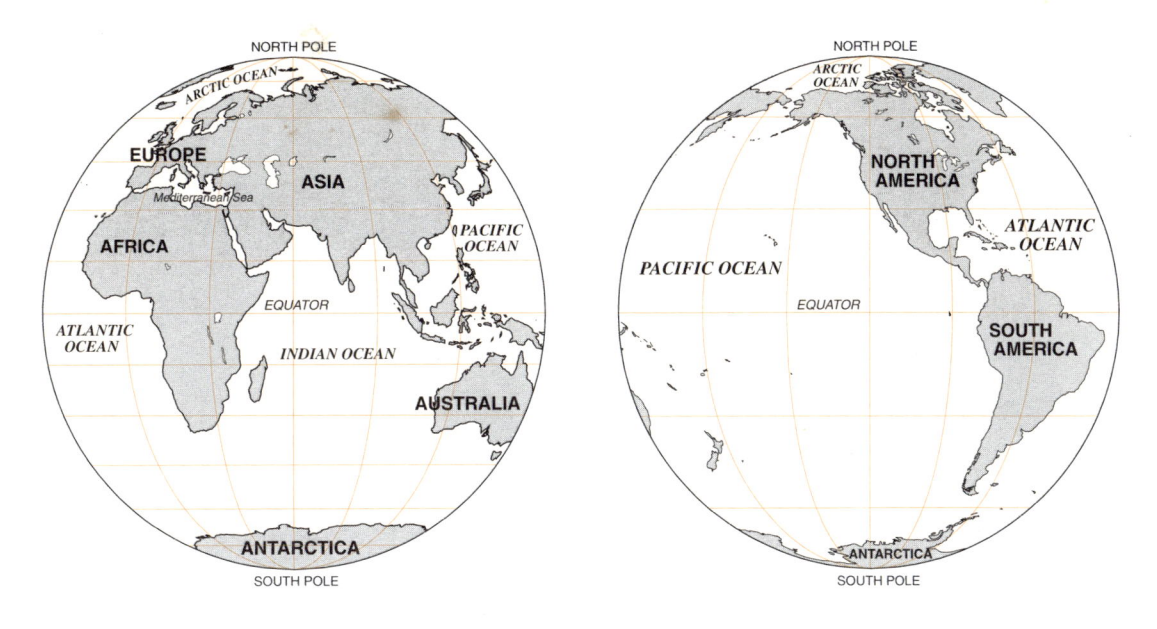

People have lived in lands of the Eastern Hemisphere since the beginning of the world. This is why these lands are called the Old World. Can you name some of these lands and the people who lived there in Bible times? Over 5,000 years went by before people in the Eastern Hemisphere knew about lands in the Western Hemisphere. Explorers from the Old World called these lands the New World.

The King and Queen of Spain believed Columbus. They gave him ships, men, and money.

Columbus and his men did what other sailors were afraid to do. They sailed out across the Atlantic Ocean to the west. Many people believed they would never return.

The ships sailed west for weeks. Day after day, Columbus and his men saw nothing but water. The men became afraid. They begged Columbus to turn back. But Columbus was sure they would soon reach the Indies.

He said to his men, "Sail on! Sail on!"

Two weeks after that, the weary crew saw land. When they stepped ashore, friendly copper-colored men greeted them. Columbus called these men **Indians.** He believed his ships had reached the Indies.

Today we know that Columbus landed on islands south of the United States. Now these islands are known as the West Indies. Columbus was trying to reach the East Indies. Find both groups of islands on your globe.

Columbus returned to Europe. He told the people about his trip. Other men began to sail across the Atlantic Ocean. One of these men was Amerigo Vespucci (ve spü´ che).

Amerigo Vespucci did not believe Columbus had reached

the Indies. He decided that Columbus had found new land. People in Europe began to call this land the New World. It became known as America, named after Amerigo.

Unhappy people were glad to hear about the New World. In Europe a few rich men owned much of the land. Most of the people were poor. Wars had destroyed many of their homes and belongings.

People began sailing from Europe to make new homes in America. Some came to get land and make money. But Christians had a better reason for coming.

Matthew 10:23a

Jesus had said, "When they **persecute** you in this city, flee ye into another."

Suffering Christians fled from many cities in Europe. They came to worship God in the free land He had prepared for them.

SHOW YOUR KNOWLEDGE

1. Why did some Christians want to leave their homes in Europe?
2. Study page 5 in your book. Why were sailors afraid to cross the Atlantic Ocean for many years?
3. Merchants from Europe traveled _____ to the Indies until the Turks _____ .
4. Columbus thought he could get to the East Indies by sailing west because he believed _____ .
5. What did the King and Queen of Spain do for Columbus?
6. Where did Christopher Columbus really land?
7. Why was the New World named America?
8. Give two reasons why people wanted to make new homes in America.

SHARE YOUR KNOWLEDGE

1. Study Acts 8:1, 4. Persecution sometimes _____ Christians into other places to spread the Gospel. How did persecution help God's plan for the Christians in Europe?

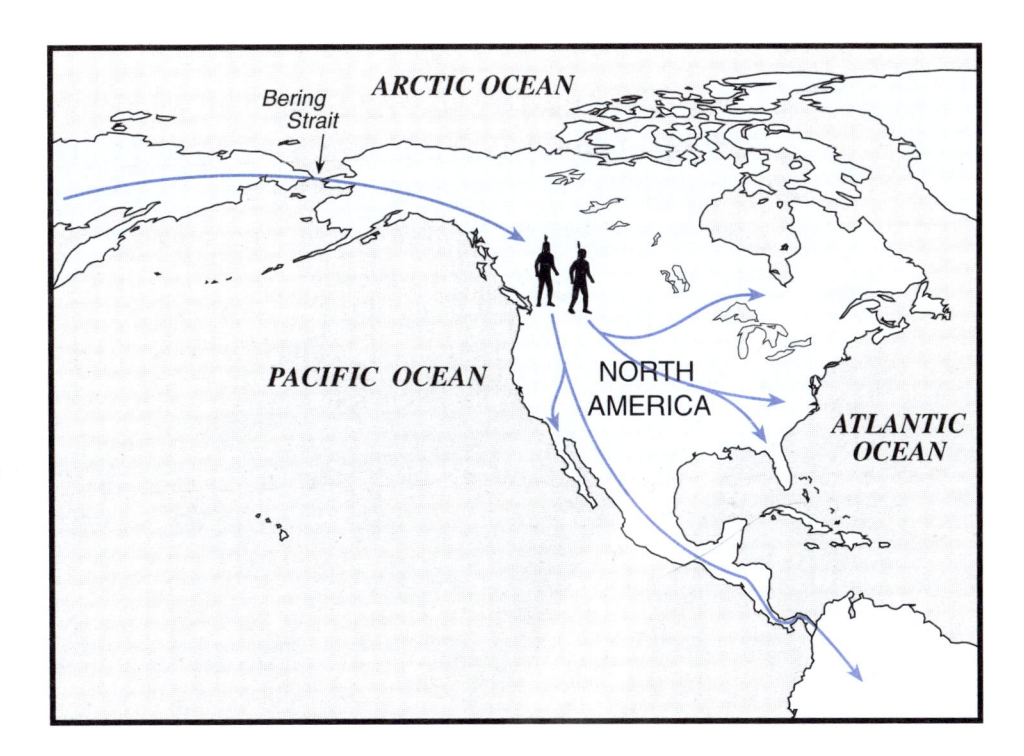

The lands of the Old World almost touch the lands of the New World at the Bering Strait. Perhaps the Indians moved across this narrow strait to America many years ago.

THE FIRST PEOPLE IN AMERICA

Tribes of copper-colored Indians lived in America long before the white people came. Many people think the Indians came to America from Asia.

The Indians may have come across the Bering Strait into Alaska. They may have walked across the ice. They may have sailed across the water.

Some tribes of Indians settled in Mexico and South America. Others settled in what is now the United States. The Indians became the first Americans or **natives** of our country.

Most Indian tribes were nomads. They lived by hunting, fishing, and gathering nuts and berries. These nomad tribes moved from place to place to find food.

After a time, some Indian tribes began to grow crops. They no longer needed to roam in search for food. They began to build villages.

A tribe of Indians lived in villages along the Delaware River. They became known as the Delaware Indians. Many of their customs were strange to the white people.

The Delaware Indians had not learned to use **metals.** They used hard **flint** stones for arrowheads and sharp cutting tools. They also made tools from bones and deer antlers.

The Delaware Indians built long houses big enough for several families. They drove thin poles into the ground for sides. They tied branches across the tops to make roofs. Sheets of bark covered their houses inside and outside. These large houses were called **longhouses.**

Each family had a spot in the longhouse for a cooking fire. The smoke from the fire escaped through openings in the roof. Bunks were built along the walls for sleeping. The Delaware Indians had little furniture.

Some Indian tribes built walls of logs called **palisades** (pal ə sādz´) around their villages for protection. But the Delaware Indians were a peaceful tribe. They did not build palisades around their villages.

The Delaware Indians cleared the land outside their villages for farming.

Most Indians were not peaceful like the Delaware Indians. Indians of fighting tribes built palisades around their villages.

With stone axes, they cut rings of bark from the trunks of large trees to kill them. They got rid of the dead trees by burning them.

The Indian women were called **squaws.** The squaws did the farming. With bone or stone hoes, they dug up the ground. In small hills of ground, they planted corn. Around the edges of the hills, they planted pumpkins or squash.

The Indian men were called **braves.** The braves did the hunting for meat to eat. Where the Delaware Indians lived, the forests were full of animals.

The Indians did not worship the true God. They believed there were spirits in water, earth, and fire. So the Indians worshiped nature.

No one had ever told the Indians about the true God and Jesus, His Son. God said, "I will set my glory among the heathen." God used the Christians to carry His story to the Indians of America.

Ezekiel 39:21a

God used Christians from the Old World to tell the Indians about Jesus Christ.

Historical Society of Pennsylvania

SHOW YOUR KNOWLEDGE

1. The American Indians may have come from _____.
2. The Indians may have traveled across the _____ _____ .
3. Indians quit being nomads when:
    a. they had no place to go.
    b. they became peaceful.
    c. they learned to grow crops.
4. What did the Delaware Indians use to make arrowheads and tools?
5. How was the Delaware Indian tribe different from some other Indian tribes?
6. Who did the farming for the tribe?
7. What did the braves do?
8. The Indians worshiped (braves, nature, the Holy Spirit).
9. Who told the Indians about the true God?

"When it goeth well with the righteous, the city rejoiceth" (Proverbs 11:10a).

Philadelphia, the City of Brotherly Love

In England a group of people were meeting for worship. These people called themselves Friends. Others called them **Quakers** (kwā´ kərz), because they feared God and sometimes trembled before Him.

A group of Quaker men stood talking before the meetinghouse door. The wide brims of their hats nodded quietly as they spoke together.

The men kept looking toward the door. An iron lock hung from the latch. Enemies had put it there to stop their meeting.

Men and women began gathering in the courtyard outside the building. Soon a large crowd of Quakers jammed the street beside the courtyard.

A young Quaker named William Penn climbed the meetinghouse steps and began to speak.

207

The King of England gave William Penn a written agreement called a charter. The charter made William Penn the owner of land in the New World.

Historical Society of Pennsylvania

At once, soldiers began to push through the tightly packed crowd. Firmly, they grabbed William Penn and marched him past his friends to prison.

Leaders in England did not like the Quakers. The Quakers were obedient people. But they would not fight in the king's army. Instead, they obeyed God and showed kindness to their enemies.

The Quakers did not copy the customs of the unsaved community. God's Word calls an unsaved community **the world.**

Romans 12:2a The Bible says, "Be not conformed to [like] this world."

The Quakers wanted to obey this Bible teaching. They did not copy the styles and **fashions** of people in the world.

The Quakers dressed in clothing made from plain dark cloth. The women wore dresses without ribbons or lace. The men wore hats with wide brims.

The people in England said the words *thee, thou,* and *thy* to ordinary persons. But they said the word *you* only to important people.

Proverbs 28:21a The Bible says, "To have respect of [make a difference between] persons is not good."

The Quakers tried to treat all people alike. They never used the word *you*. Quakers always said *thou, thy,* and *thee* to both important people and ordinary people.

You can see why many people of the world hated the Quakers. Like William Penn, Quakers were often put into prison.

PLANS FOR A NEW HOME

William Penn's rich father was not a Quaker. He was a good friend of the king. Once he had loaned the King of

England a lot of money.

When William Penn became a Quaker, his father became very angry. He made William leave home. But William Penn's father was dying when he heard William had been put into prison. He wanted to see his son. By paying money, he got William set free.

Six days after William went home, his father died. The King of England wanted to pay William the money he owed to his father. But William Penn had plans of his own.

"Give me land in America instead of money," he begged the king.

The King of England agreed. He gave William Penn a **charter** for a large piece of land in the New World.

The king named the land "Pennsylvania" (pen səl vā´ nyə). This name means "Penn's Woods." William Penn did not like this name, but the King would not change it.

William Penn made plans to set up a **colony** in Pennsylvania. A colony is a group of people who leave their own country to settle in a new land.

Penn believed the land belonged to the Indians who had lived there first. Others told him that this idea was foolish. The king had given him the land. But Penn wanted to be fair. He planned to pay the Indians for their land.

William Penn planned a city for the new colony. He wanted the city placed between two rivers. Rivers would help it become a city of trade.

The name for the new city would be "Philadelphia" (fi lə del´ fyə). The name *Philadelphia* means "brotherly love." Penn wanted Philadelphia to be a city where Christians would live together in peace and love.

The first Quaker settlers left for Penn's new colony in October, 1681.

Penn told them to choose a place for the city of Philadelphia. With the settlers, he sent a friendly letter to the Indians.

FOR YOU TO DO

The name "Philadelphia" comes from the Bible. Use a Bible concordance to find the place where the name is in the Bible. Write the Bible book, chapter, and verse where the name is found. On page 161, find the city of Philadelphia. Which part of Asia was it in?

SHOW YOUR KNOWLEDGE

1. Why did some people call the Friends in England "Quakers"?
2. Instead of fighting in the king's army, the Quakers showed _____.
3. The Quakers did not copy the styles of the world in the way they _____.
4. The Quakers did not make a difference between _____ people and _____ people when they talked.
5. William Penn's father (did, did not) like for him to be a Quaker.
6. What kind thing did William Penn's father do for him?
7. Instead of taking money, Penn asked the king for _____.
8. What does *Pennsylvania* mean?
9. After the King gave Pennsylvania to William Penn, Penn believed the land:
    a. still belonged to England.
    b. belonged to him.
    c. still belonged to the Indians.
10. Why did William Penn want the new city to be placed between two rivers?
11. Why did Penn name the city "Philadelphia"?

SHARE YOUR KNOWLEDGE

1. Study Philippians 2:3. The word *vainglory* in this verse means "pride." Why do you think William Penn did not like the name the King gave his land?
2. Study Proverbs 3:33. The word *habitation* in this verse means "place."
    a. The word _____ in this verse means "fair."
    b. William Penn was fair to the Indians. So he could expect God to _____ his land.

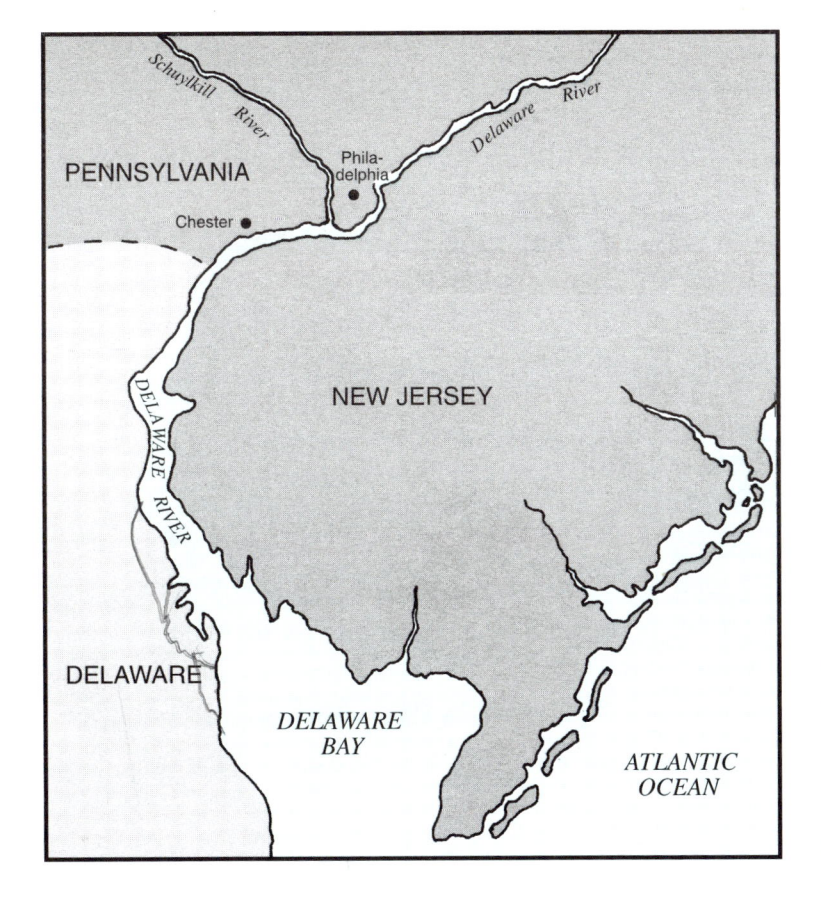

William Penn sent settlers to his land in the New World. These settlers laid out the city of Philadelphia between the Delaware River and the Schuylkill River. Why was this a good place for a city?

A PLACE FOR PHILADELPHIA

Two ships moved north along the eastern coast of America. Wind bulged the sails of the *John* and *Sarah*. Excited Quakers on the ships talked and pointed. They had spotted the wide mouth of a bay.

Boat boys scrambled to lower the sails. The ships moved slower and slower. With a swing to the left, they entered the bay called Delaware Bay.

Sailing up the Delaware Bay, the ships came to the mouth of the Delaware River. The Delaware River flows into Delaware Bay. William Penn's land lay west of the Delaware River.

The **pioneers** (pī ə nirz´) stopped at a town along the river now known as Chester. People called Swedes were living there. They had come from Europe years before.

The pioneers stayed at the town for the night. It was a cold night in December. During the night, the Delaware River froze over. So the pioneers had to stay all winter.

The next spring, the pioneers started up the Delaware River again. Soon they came to the mouth of a river flowing into the Delaware River. This was the Schuylkill (skü´ kəl) River.

The pioneers started the city of Philadelphia on the land between the Schuylkill and the Delaware Rivers.

BUILDING THE NEW CITY

A large forest covered the wilderness between the Schuylkill and Delaware Rivers. Huge trees shaded the forest floor. Tall grass grew in the rich soil of the open spaces.

The pioneers built cave shelters along the high bank of the Delaware River. They lived in these caves until the land was cleared for streets and better houses.

After cutting some of the trees, the pioneers **surveyed** the land and laid out streets. William Penn had carefully planned for these ahead of time. He wanted the city to have lots of space for trees and gardens. Philadelphia was to be a "greene countrie towne."

The settlers built wide streets running north and south. Crossing these, they built streets running east and west. Large square **city blocks** lay between the streets.

William Penn carefully planned the city of Philadelphia before he sent the first settlers to Pennsylvania. He drew this map to show how he wanted the streets and city blocks laid out. After you read page 213, find the public squares Penn planned for his city.

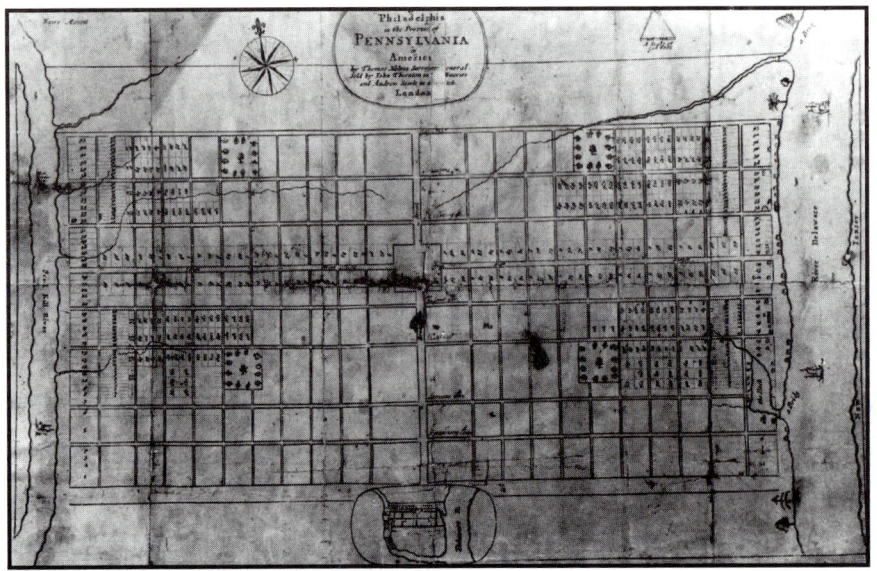

Historical Society of Pennsylvania

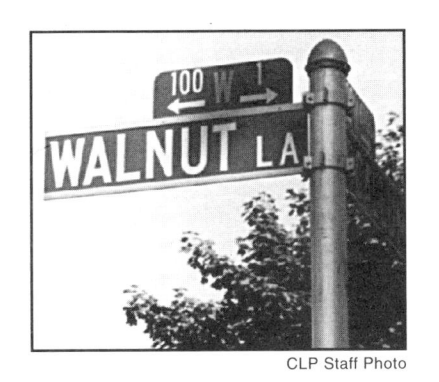

These signs tell the names of two streets in Philadelphia. How did the streets get their names?

Trees lined the streets. The pioneers gave some of the streets tree names such as Walnut Street, Chestnut Street, and Poplar Street.

The pioneers planted grass and flowers in five large city blocks. These pleasant gardens called **public squares** were for everyone to enjoy.

Houses were built in the centers of the city blocks. The people planted gardens around them.

Most of the settlers built log cabins from forest wood. Some of the richer people used red clay for bricks to build houses.

Careful planning helped Philadelphia become one of the most beautiful cities in America. Other cities had crowded houses, and crooked, narrow streets. But careful planning at the beginning gave Philadelphia plenty of space to grow.

Philadelphia still has the public squares William Penn planned for the city. On pleasant days, many people come to enjoy this square called Washington Square.

213

William Penn built a house for his family at a lovely spot north of Philadelphia. He called it "Pennsbury Manor." After William Penn died, the house fell into ruins and was torn down. Later, some men wanted to rebuild the house just as it was when William Penn lived there. They found drawings and plans Penn had made for his house and other buildings at Pennsbury Manor. Today visitors can see Pennsbury Manor the way it looked 300 years ago.

SHOW YOUR KNOWLEDGE

1. Why did the pioneers have to stay at the town of Chester all winter instead of for a night?
2. The Schuylkill River flows into the (Delaware Bay, Atlantic Ocean, Delaware River).
3. Where is the city of Philadelphia located?
4. Where did the pioneers live while they cleared the land?
5. Why did William Penn do so much planning for Philadelphia ahead of time?
6. What two things did the settlers use to build their houses?
7. Philadelphia was more beautiful than some cities in America because it was carefully _____ .

Corn was a new food to the pioneers from the Old World. The Indians taught the settlers to place a fish in each hill of corn. Why? The Indians also taught their white friends how to cook the new food.

GOD'S BLESSINGS IN THE NEW COLONY

The pioneers placed Philadelphia on the land of the Delaware Indians. Many Indian tribes in America were fierce fighters. But the Delaware Indians were one of the few peaceful tribes.

God knew that nonresistant settlers needed a peaceful home. The Bible says, "When a man's ways please the LORD, he maketh even his enemies to be at peace with him."

Proverbs 16:7

God led these pioneers who wanted to please Him to Pennsylvania. He led them to the land of the peaceful Delaware Indians.

The nonresistant settlers treated the Indians kindly and fairly. In turn, the Indians helped the settlers learn to live in the New World.

The Indians taught the pioneers how to make light canoes from skins or bark. The Indians showed them the best places to cross streams and mountains.

The pioneers did not know about corn. The Indians taught them how to plant, harvest, and cook this new food.

Corn became the most important American food. From the

215

Indians, the pioneers learned to make a mixture of corn and lima beans called **succotash.** The Indians also taught them how to pop popcorn and to make tapioca.

Psalm 37:3

These pioneers who wanted to please God were blessed with plenty. The Bible says, "Trust in the LORD, and do good; so shalt thou dwell in the land, and verily thou shalt be fed."

Even the poorest settlers had plenty of food. Wild deer were plentiful. The settlers ate lots of **venison** or deer meat. They gathered huge oysters from the rivers. They ate fat wild turkeys and pigeons from the forests.

William Penn always showed kindness to the Indians. He made fair trade with them for their land and promised to live in peace with them. Other settlers in America chased out the Indians and took their land unfairly. These settlers had many wars with angry Indians. But the Pennslyvania settlers and the Indians kept their promises and lived peacefully together for many years.

WILLIAM PENN VISITS HIS COLONY

The first settlers had been at Philadelphia almost a year before William Penn came to visit his colony. He came in a ship called *Welcome*.

The pioneers were glad to see their **governor** or ruler. The Indians were glad to see him, too.

William Penn soon called the Indian tribes together to make a peace agreement called a **treaty.** Penn wanted to "follow peace with all men" as the Bible teaches.

Hebrews 12:14a

The meeting was held under a spreading elm tree. Neither Penn's men nor the Indians carried weapons.

Penn's men brought a chest full of presents for the Indians. The chest contained knives, hatchets, and guns for the braves. It held kettles, hoes, scissors, and combs for the squaws.

The Indians sat in a half circle. In the center sat the Indian chief.

The Indians made speeches. They agreed to sell land to Penn. They made promises.

"We will live in peace with the white man as long as the sun and moon keep shining," they said.

The Indian chief gave William Penn a belt of **wampum** (wäm´ pəm). A wampum belt is made with tiny shell beads. This belt had a bead picture of a Quaker and Indian shaking hands. The belt was the Indians' sign of friendship.

William Penn also made promises. He gave gifts to the Indians from the chest. Penn kept his promises. The Indians kept theirs. The **Great Treaty** between the Indians and Quakers was never broken.

The Indians gave William Penn this wampum belt at the Great Treaty. How does the belt show the Indians' promise to be friends?

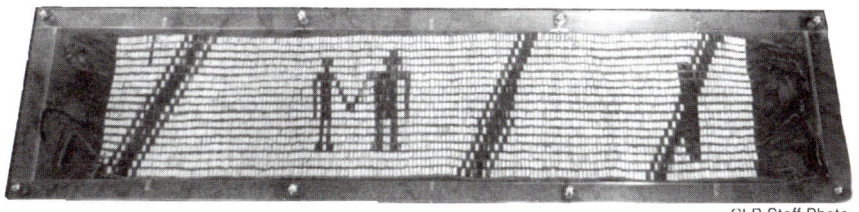

CLP Staff Photo

SHOW YOUR KNOWLEDGE

1. God led the nonresistant settlers to the land of the _____ Delaware Indians.
2. List three main things the friendly Indians taught the settlers.
3. List three kinds of meat the settlers ate.
4. The wampum belt with its picture was a sign of the Indians' _____ with the Quakers.
5. How long did the Great Treaty between the Indians and the Quakers last?

SHARE YOUR KNOWLEDGE

1. In your own words, tell how long the Indians promised to keep peace with the Quakers.
2. Study Proverbs 12:20. The word *counselor* means "leader."
    a. God promises _____ to a leader who makes peace.
    b. Who was the counselor of peace in Pennsylvania? How did this verse come true for him?

To make candles, pioneer women dipped strings into a fat called tallow and let them cool. One woman in this picture is making candles. What is the other woman making?

LIVING IN THE COLONY OF PENNSYLVANIA

The pioneers worked hard. At first they had no factories. Ships brought some manufactured goods from England. But these cost more than the settlers could pay. They learned to make what they needed.

The settlers cut logs for houses. There were no nails. The men made wooden pegs to hold the logs together. Instead of glass, the settlers learned to use oiled paper for windows.

Door latches were made from wood. The latch was always inside. A latchstring hung through a hole in the door to the outside. A person could open the door from the outside by pulling on the latchstring.

What did the latchstring show the Indians about the people living in this house? Why did the Indians save this house when they burned the village?

At night, the pioneers could pull the latchstring inside for safety. A latchstring hanging out was a sign of hospitality and welcome.

The pioneers had to make their clothes. The men and boys grew flax and raised sheep. They cut the flax and sheared the sheep.

With their spinning wheels, the women made thread from the linen and wool fibers. They wove cloth on **looms** by hand.

Many pioneer women made a cloth called **linsey-woolsey.** They made linsey-woolsey by mixing linen and wool thread together.

The women dyed threads to make colored cloth. They made the dye. Most of the settlers dressed in plain clothes of brown or gray.

Brown dye was made by boiling the bark of walnut, chestnut, or butternut trees. Cedar berries gave gray dye.

The settlers often had more venison than they could eat. They cured the extra meat so it would not spoil.

Women cut the meat into thin strips. They dried the strips on sticks over a fire. The pioneers called these strips of dried meat **jerky.**

Farmers bought land outside the city. They cut down trees and cleared the land. They tilled the rich soil with hoes and planted crops of Indian corn, wheat, and rye.

The pioneers needed a mill to grind flour. A Quaker named

Richard Townsend built this first gristmill near Philadelphia. Why did he build it along a stream?

Library of Congress

Pioneers in America often used logs to build roads over muddy places. Why were such roads called "corduroy roads"? Were they as good as Roman roads? Why or why not?

Richard Townsend built a **gristmill** along a stream. Water from the stream turned a waterwheel. The waterwheel turned the round stones of the mill.

Farmers brought grain to be ground into flour. They paid the miller with bags of grain.

The farmers took their goods to the market in Philadelphia. The roads to the city were bad. In rainy weather they were muddy. Some roads were only narrow Indian trails.

The settlers worked together to make better roads. Each farmer built a road ten feet wide through his land. At the muddy places, he laid logs side by side to make a dry path.

The pioneers had to work hard. But they did not mind. Hard work was better than persecution.

Many pioneers thought about suffering friends in Europe. Some sent letters telling friends to come to Penn's free colony.

Hundreds of Christians wanted to come. But many had no money to pay for the trip across the ocean.

God had blessed the pioneers with more than they needed. They wanted to be good stewards and use God's blessings the way He wanted them to.

God had said, "If there be among you a poor man of one of thy brethren . . . thou shalt not harden thine heart, nor shut

Deuteronomy 15:7-8a

thine hand from thy poor brother: But thou shalt open thine hand wide unto him, and shalt surely lend him sufficient [enough] for his need."

Pioneer farmers and craftsmen paid for the trips of poor Christians in Europe. The poor Christians agreed to work for the farmers and craftsmen to pay them back.

After four or five years of work, the Christian servants could go free. Their masters gave them tools and clothing to help them get started on their own. Many suffering Christians got a start in the New World this way.

SHOW YOUR KNOWLEDGE

1. Why did the pioneers make most of the things they needed?
2. What did the pioneers use instead of glass for windows?
3. If a settler said, "My latchstring is always out," he meant:
    a. you would be welcome in his house any time.
    b. he could not open his door from the inside.
    c. he didn't want visitors.
4. What two natural resources did the pioneers use to make their clothing?
5. Why did Richard Townsend build his gristmill along a stream?
6. The farmers gave the miller (flour, money, grain) for grinding their grain.
7. What did the settlers use to make their muddy roads better?
8. To get to America, many suffering people became (farmers, servants, Christians).

SHARE YOUR KNOWLEDGE

1. Like the children of Israel, the Pennsylvania pioneers sometimes took poor brothers for servants. Study Deuteronomy 15:12-14. Do you think the pioneers knew anything about this one of God's laws? Why do you think so?

SETTLERS AT GERMANTOWN

In 1683 a ship called the *Concord* set out for Philadelphia. On board were 13 families from Germany. Some of them were Christians called **Mennonites** (men´ ə nīts).

The Mennonites were Anabaptists from the Netherlands, Germany, and other countries in Europe. They got the name *Mennonite* from one of their leaders, a Dutch preacher named Menno Simons.

Like the Quakers, the Mennonites were nonresistant. The Mennonites also dressed in plain clothing. But they were different from the Quakers in some ways.

The Mennonites had Communion services. Jesus said, "This do in remembrance of me." The Quakers did not do this. **Luke 22:19b**

The Quakers also did not believe in water baptism. The Bible says, "He that believeth and is baptized shall be saved." **Mark 16:16a** The Mennonites obeyed this command.

The Mennonites were glad to leave suffering in Europe. They were ready to face the hard trip across the Atlantic Ocean.

Storms often tossed the small ships for days, making the passengers sick and fearful. Some people fell and broke bones.

Menno Simons was an Anabaptist church leader who lived in the Netherlands over 400 years ago. The people who followed his Bible teaching were called Mennonites. Many Mennonites in the Netherlands and Germany were persecuted because of their beliefs. Some of these persecuted Mennonites found new homes and freedom of religion in Pennsylvania.

Library of Congress

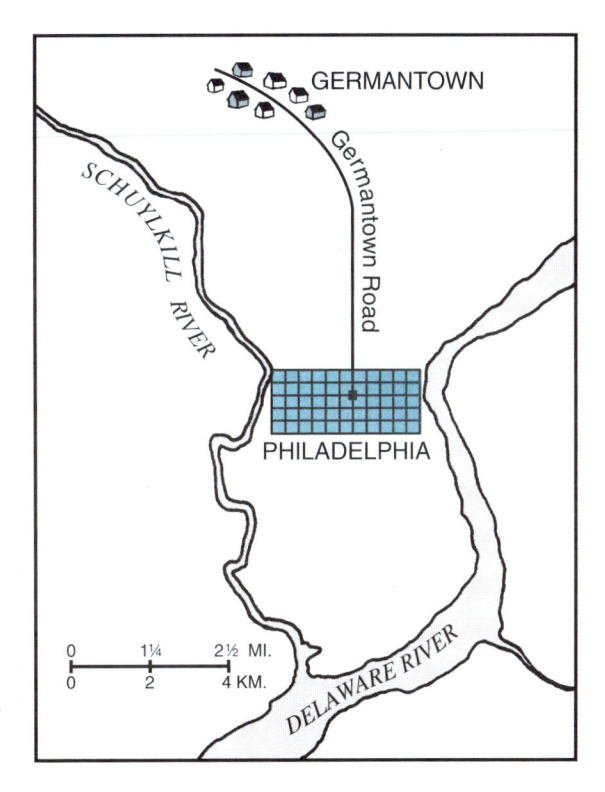

This is Markethouse Square in Germantown. Many of the first buildings are gone. But you can still see the cobblestones of the old Germantown Road.

The people of Philadelphia put up this monument to help them remember the first Germans who settled at Germantown.

On some of the trips, sickness spread and many people died.

The trip on the *Concord* took two long months. The food ran short. Worse than that, it spoiled. Water had to be saved. The passengers became very thirsty. They were glad to catch the first sight of free land.

A man named Francis Pastorius (pas tȯr´ ē əs) met the German passengers at Philadelphia. He and William Penn had chosen a place for them to live.

Pastorius led the Germans to land north of Philadelphia. Here they started a town called Germantown.

The German settlers built log cabins at first. But soon they found their land had rocks. They replaced the log cabins later with stone houses.

Most of the Germantown settlers were linen weavers. They planted flax. Soon they were producing cloth. The Germantown Road led to Philadelphia. The weavers sold their cloth at the Philadelphia market.

The colony needed paper. A Mennonite minister named William Rittenhouse (rit´ ən haůs) lived at Germantown. He built a paper mill along the Wissahickon (wis´ ə hik ən) Creek. He built a waterwheel to run the mill.

The paper was made from linen rags. First the rags were pounded in mortars by hammers. Other materials were added.

This building at Germantown is the oldest Mennonite meetinghouse in America.

This building at Germantown is the oldest Church of the Brethren meetinghouse in America.

Then the mixture was spread in a layer to dry. Making paper was a slow job.

For many years, William Rittenhouse made most of the paper in America. Once a flood destroyed his paper mill. The citizens of Philadelphia helped him rebuild it.

At Germantown, the Mennonites built their first church building in America. They built it from logs. Later a stone building was built in its place. This stone church building still stands today at Germantown.

Soon a group of Christians called **Brethren** came to Germantown. They believed much like the Mennonites. Sometimes the two groups worshiped together.

This picture shows one of the first German Bibles Christopher Sauer printed at Germantown.

Christopher Dock was a Christian teacher who taught his pupils to read the German Bible. He died while he was on his knees praying for his pupils at the end of a school day.

    A Brethren man named Christopher Sauer set up a printing press. He began printing a German newspaper.

    Christopher Sauer also printed German Bibles. He made the price low enough so many people could buy them. But some had no money.

    Christopher Sauer said, "For the poor and needy, there is no price."

    The German Christians started a school at Germantown. Francis Pastorius was the teacher.

    In other colonies, only boys went to school. But the German Christians believed everyone should learn to read the Bible. Both boys and girls went to the Germantown school.

    In a few years, a Mennonite named Christopher Dock came to America. He started a school along the Skippack River north of Germantown. He taught a school at Germantown a few summers.

    Christopher Dock was a Christian teacher. He taught his pupils to read the German New Testament. He also taught them to sing hymns. At the end of each day, he prayed for each pupil listed in his roll book.

    Christopher Dock was the first American to write a book about teaching. In it he tells how he tried to teach every pupil to fear God and obey Him out of love.

    Philadelphia grew larger and larger. Germantown also grew. The city and the town grew together. Today Germantown is inside the city of Philadelphia.

SHOW YOUR KNOWLEDGE

1. The first Mennonites came to America in the year _____ .
2. Where did the Mennonites get their name?
3. List two ways the Mennonites were different from the Quakers.
4. Why were Christians willing to suffer on ships to come to America?
5. Most of the Germantown settlers were (farmers, paper makers, linen weavers).
6. Who built the first paper mill in America?
7. The oldest Mennonite church building in America can be seen today at _____ .
8. Name the Brethren man who printed German Bibles.
9. Why were girls allowed to go to the school at Germantown?
10. Name the Christian teacher who started a school along the Skippack River.
11. What happened to the little town of Germantown?

SHARE YOUR KNOWLEDGE

1. List all the things that show that Christopher Dock was a Christian teacher.
2. Study 1 John 2:3 to find the following answer. Christians want to do (all, some) of the _____ of Jesus Christ.

LAWS FOR THE COLONY

The new colony needed laws. Penn planned for the settlers to help make the laws.

The people **elected** 200 men for a group called the **Assembly.** The men in the Assembly could not be servants or slaves. All of them had to believe on Jesus Christ.

The people also elected a smaller group called the **Council.** The Council was made up of 72 men.

The governor met with the Council. Together they

suggested laws the community needed. Then the men in the Assembly voted on the suggestions. A suggestion became a law if most of the men voted for it.

At first most of the people in Pennsylvania were Quakers. They tried to have a godly community by making good laws.

The Quakers helped to make laws against swearing, lying, and ungodly games. They made laws against working and playing on Sunday.

At first, most of the settlers were godly people. They broke very few laws. Only small **fines** were needed for punishments.

As Pennsylvania grew, more and more ungodly settlers came. Some Christians began to forget God. Sin began to cause great problems. Hard punishments were needed.

The Quakers believed God wanted them to love others, even lawbreakers. They were nonresistant. They did not want to help with punishments that hurt lawbreakers.

The Quakers had to make a choice. They would need to give up their nonresistant beliefs or give up their part in the government.

More and more Quakers left the government. They decided to let others keep order in the community.

The Quakers learned that good laws cannot make everyone live a godly life. They also learned that nonresistance and government do not go together. For the government carries out "wrath upon him that doeth evil." Yet God commands His people to "live peaceably with all men."

Romans 13:4b
Romans 12:18b

Workers at Philadelphia made barrels from wooden staves. Philadelphia merchants used these barrels to ship goods to other lands.

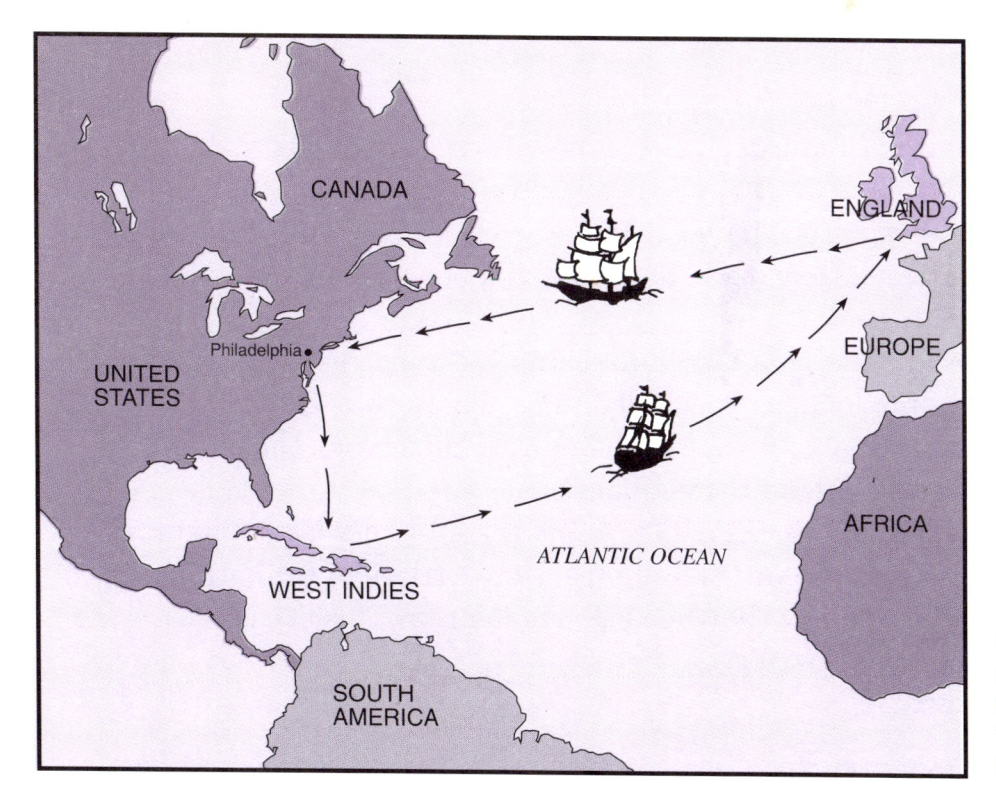

This map shows you the great "triangle of trade."

TRADE HELPED PHILADELPHIA GROW

The pioneers needed manufactured goods from England. They needed to trade.

Pennsylvania was covered with forests. England had few trees. The settlers could trade forest products for England's manufactured goods.

People in England also wanted animal furs. The settlers could get furs from the Indians by trading.

Sawmills were set up along the rivers. Some lumber was sawed by hand.

Men built ships from the lumber. Other men made narrow boards called **staves.** Staves were used to make wooden barrels.

The settlers got tar and turpentine from pine trees. They used the tar to make their ships watertight.

Merchants sailed ships to England loaded with forest products and furs. There they traded these products for glass, cloth, **hardware,** and other manufactured goods. Sometimes they even traded the ship itself for needed goods.

The merchants at Philadelphia also had grain, flour, pork, and beef to trade. But England did not need these products. The merchants had to find another place to trade.

You remember that Columbus landed on the West Indies.

A colony grew up there. The climate of the West Indies was warm.

The settlers on the West Indies grew **sugarcane**. From the sugarcane, they made molasses and sugar. England wanted these products.

The Philadelphia merchants shipped their grain, meat, and farm products to the West Indies. There they traded for sugar, molasses, and wine. Loaded with this cargo, the ships sailed on to England to trade again.

The path of the merchant ships looked like a large triangle. This **triangle of trade** helped the settlers to trade things they had for things they needed. Trade grew. The city of Philadelphia grew, too.

SHOW YOUR KNOWLEDGE

1. The government of Pennsylvania had two parts.
    a. The _____ decided what laws were needed.
    b. The _____ voted on the suggested laws.
2. The Quakers tried to have a godly community by making good _____.
3. When ungodly people needed harder punishments, the nonresistant Quakers decided:
    a. to help the government punish those who disobeyed.
    b. to let others keep order in the community.
    c. to start a new government.
4. How did the settlers make their ships watertight?
5. The pioneers exported forest products and furs to (England, the West Indies).
6. The pioneers imported manufactured goods from (the West Indies, England).
7. The pioneers exported grain, flour, pork, and beef to (England, the West Indies).
8. What products did the Philadelphia merchants ship from the warm West Indies to England?

PROBLEMS IN A GROWING CITY

Hundreds of Christians came to Philadelphia for freedom of religion. Hundreds of merchants came for trade. Soon Philadelphia was no longer a small "countrie towne."

More houses were needed. Many gardens disappeared. Houses took their places. Philadelphia was not as "greene" as before.

Fires began to be a problem. Houses stood close together. Fire from one house often spread quickly to others. Something had to be done.

The Council made a suggestion. The Assembly voted to make it a law.

The law said each house should have two leather buckets and a large piece of cloth called a **swab.** If a house was found without a swab and two buckets, the owner would have to pay a fine.

At the cry of fire, people threw buckets and swabs from their windows. Men formed long lines and passed buckets of water to the fire. They used wet swabs to beat out flames.

Animals caused other problems. Cows, pigs, and goats ran free in the streets and gardens. The government passed more laws.

Fences were built. Pigs had rings placed in their noses to keep them from digging ugly holes in the ground.

Many poor people came to Philadelphia. The Quakers wanted to have a city without one beggar. They gave jobs to the poor. They also built public **almshouses** for those who couldn't work.

Big problems began to bother the city. Indians often came to the city to trade furs, corn, berries, and baskets.

Ungodly men sold **whiskey** or strong drink to the Indians. The Indians became drunk. They could not stop drinking. Selfish men took all of their goods.

The government passed laws against selling whiskey to the Indians. The laws helped. But ungodly men soon found many other ways to mistreat the Indians, because there was "no fear of God before their eyes."

Romans 3:18b

The Quakers never broke their treaty with the Indians. But some of the other settlers treated the Indians more and more unfairly. Some Indians became angry. They attacked farms and villages on the **frontier** (frən tir´) or edges of the settlements.

Government leaders in Philadelphia wanted to raise an army to fight the Indians. But Quakers in the Assembly would not vote for such suggestions. The Quakers wanted to win the Indians by showing love.

More and more government leaders disagreed with the Quakers. Finally, they got enough votes to defeat them. Armies were sent to the frontier.

The Quakers were very sad. The people in Philadelphia were losing their brotherly love. They would no longer "follow after the things which make for peace, and things wherewith one may edify [build up] another."

Romans 14:19b

The Quakers gave up their part in the Assembly. Government could not solve the greatest problem. It could not change evil hearts.

Governments needed to use force. Christians needed to show love. The Quakers believed force and love did not go together.

SHOW YOUR KNOWLEDGE

On the left is a problem the people of Philadelphia had. On the right, find the way they solved the problem. Put the correct letter for each number.

1. Fires
2. Animals running free
3. Poor people
4. Indians drinking
5. Indian attacks

a. gave them jobs and built almshouses
b. men worked together with swabs and buckets
c. armies were sent to the frontier
d. passed laws against selling whiskey to Indians
e. fences were built

6. The Quakers gave up their part in the government because they believed that force and _____ did not go together.

SHARE YOUR KNOWLEDGE

1. Study Hebrews 12:14. Some people mistreated the Indians and wanted to fight with them. This verse says those who do not follow _____ with _____ men will never see _____ .

This is what part of Philadelphia looks like today.

PHILADELPHIA TODAY

The port of Philadelphia is 100 miles from the ocean. Yet it is one of the busiest ports in our country. Steel products and other goods are exported.

Philadelphia is a growing city. New houses keep going up. The city does not have as many trees as it used to have. But the people can still see lovely gardens and trees in the **city parks.** City parks are places where people can get away from the crowded feeling of living between tall buildings.

Today, the people of Philadelphia are tearing down worn-out parts of their city called **slums.** New apartment houses now stand where shacks and junkyards once stood.

Philadelphia was once the capital of our nation. Workmen have repaired some of the houses people lived in then. These old red brick houses remind people today of old times.

The people of Philadelphia want to keep their city clean. Garbage trucks haul trash to the city **incinerator** (in si´ nə rā tər) to be burned.

Many Quakers still live in the city. A few Mennonites still live in the part of the city called Germantown. But many people have forgotten the Christian beliefs of the first settlers.

At first, the people of Philadelphia had more brotherly love than the people of any other city in America. Then sin became

The people of Philadelphia repaired many old houses to make them look the way they did years ago when they were new.

In this "Bible House" in Philadelphia, workers help with the job of getting Bibles to people who need them. How are these people helping the city of Philadelphia the best way?

The people of Philadelphia can buy fresh vegetables and other foods in this Italian market.

a greater and greater problem. Today, Philadelphia has as many problems with sin as other cities do.

Christians forgot the job Jesus gave them when He said, "Let your light so shine before men, that they may see your good works, and glorify your Father which is in heaven."

Matthew 5:16

The story of Philadelphia shows us that good government can help a city. But it cannot solve the problem of sin. It cannot make people Christians. Only Jesus Christ can do that by changing sinful hearts.

Today, Christians can help Philadelphia most by witnessing for Jesus. By doing that, Christians can help bring true brotherly love back to the city.

SHOW YOUR KNOWLEDGE

1. Philadelphia is a busy _____ from which _____ products are exported.
2. Why do the people of Philadelphia like to have parks in their growing city?
3. The people of Philadelphia are tearing down _____ and building new _____ .
4. Philadelphia was once the _____ of our nation.
5. Some old houses in Philadelphia have been repaired:
    a. because too many people need places to live.
    b. because new houses cost too much money.
    c. to remind people of things that happened long ago.
6. Which of these would be the most important for a city to have?
    a. beautiful parks and buildings
    b. Christian people
    c. a good government

SHARE YOUR KNOWLEDGE

1. Study Luke 8:39 and answer these questions:
    a. What did Jesus tell the man to do?
    b. What did he do?
    c. What could Christians in Philadelphia learn from this man?

"I will make waste mountains and hills, and dry up all their herbs; and I will make the rivers islands, and I will dry up the pools" (Isaiah 42:15).

Israel, an Old and New Country

Did you ever go exploring in a large, old, run-down house? Perhaps the last family moved away long before you were born.

The house stood lonely and empty. You could see the sky through a hole where part of the roof had caved in. Mice scampered across rotted floors. Weeds choked out the grass of a lovely lawn.

People once worked hard to keep the place in good shape. But now everything slowly goes to ruin. No one seems to care. Such careless waste makes us feel sad.

Some years ago, visitors to the old land of Palestine felt this way. These visitors saw a wasted land.

Most of the trees had been cut from the hillsides. Rains had washed the topsoil away in many places. At some places rivers had become clogged. Water had flowed out over the land, turning good farmland into swamps. At other places water had not been

In Bible times, God's people made terraces like these on hillsides to let rains soak into the soil and not wash it away.

saved and used for crops. Good farmland had become desert.

The visitors felt very sad. They knew the land of Israel had once been a good land. God's people had lived there many years ago. The Bible says Israel was then a land of "milk and honey" or a land of plenty.

Exodus 3:8

Long years before, as Moses led God's people to the land, God had said, "The LORD thy God bringeth thee into a good land, a land of brooks of water, of fountains and depths that spring out of valleys and hills;

Deuteronomy 8:7-9a

"A land of wheat, and barley, and vines, and fig trees, and pomegranates; a land of oil olive, and honey;

"A land wherein thou shalt eat bread without scarceness, thou shalt not lack any thing in it."

God's people had built flat terraces on the hillsides to keep rains from washing away the soil. The terraces soaked up the rain for growing crops. The roots of trees also helped to hold the soil. Some farmers grew crops in the desert by irrigating the land.

Deuteronomy 11:12

God also cared for the land. "A land which the LORD thy God careth for; the eyes of the LORD thy God are always upon it, from the beginning of the year even unto the end of the year."

God knew the land would wear out if men misused it. He wanted to help keep the land fruitful, so He gave laws to protect it.

Leviticus 25:3-5

God said, "Six years thou shalt sow thy field, and six years thou shalt prune thy vineyard, and gather in the fruit thereof;

"But . . . the seventh year shall be a sabbath of rest unto

the land, a sabbath for the LORD: thou shalt neither sow thy field, nor prune thy vineyard.

"That which groweth of its own accord of thy harvest thou shalt not reap, . . . for it is a year of rest unto the land."

At first God's people obeyed His laws. They let the land rest every seven years.

Then slowly the whole nation of Israel drifted into sin. One sin was misusing God's land. The people disobeyed God and stopped letting the land rest.

God sent punishment. He scattered His people, the Jews, into other nations. He let enemies rule their land. It happened just as God had promised.

"Your land shall be desolate [wasted], and your cities waste. Then shall the land enjoy her sabbaths, as long as it lieth desolate, and ye be in your enemies' land; even then shall the land rest, and enjoy her sabbaths."

Leviticus 26:33b-34

For 70 years, the Jews lived in other lands. God did not pour out His blessings upon the land. Good farmland did not produce crops. The land rested.

At the end of 70 years, God brought His people back to their land. The Jews built up the land again. This time the Jews lived in Israel until the time of Jesus. In another chapter you learned about their ways of living.

In this book you also learned how the Jews looked for a

Titus, a Roman ruler, destroyed the city of Jerusalem in 70 A.D. His father had this arch built to celebrate the victory. It is named the Arch of Titus. Carvings on the arch show Jews being carried away from Jerusalem.

Photo: J. Otis Yoder

Messiah to free them from the Romans. But many would not believe on Jesus the Messiah, whom God sent to save them from their sin. So again God needed to punish the people who did not believe.

God let the Romans destroy the city of Jerusalem in 70 A.D. This means it happened 70 years after Jesus was born.

The cruel Romans killed many thousands of Jews. Roman soldiers pushed most of the Jews who were left out of their land. The Romans scattered the Jewish people into many other countries. There they lived for 1,900 years.

During all these years, the land was wasted. People cut down the trees. Rains washed away the topsoil. In time, the hills turned brown and dry. The lands became desert in many places. Visitors in the land of Israel saw these sad sights.

SHOW YOUR KNOWLEDGE

1. Visitors to Palestine saw that:
    a. _____ had been cut from hillsides.
    b. Rains had washed _____ away.
    c. Water turned farmland into _____ .
    d. Some farmland had become _____ .
2. God's law commanded the Jews to let their land rest one year out of every _____ years.
3. When the nation of Israel became sinful, they disobeyed God and stopped _____ .
4. How long were the Jews away from their land the first time God scattered them?
5. God used the _____ to punish the Jews when they did not believe on Jesus.
6. What do the letters *A. D.* mean?

SHARE YOUR KNOWLEDGE

1. When the land rested, what were the people to do with fruit and grain that grew without being planted?
2. Study Leviticus 25:20, 21. How did the Jews have enough food to eat when the land rested?

CLP Staff Photo

A NATION BEGINS ANEW

On May 14, 1948, newspapers printed an exciting story. The land of Israel had been given back to the Jews.

Jews were moving to Israel from countries all over the world. In some of these countries, they had been treated unkindly. For many Jews, moving to Israel was a happy dream come true. The people who live in Israel today are called **Israelis** (is rā´ lēz).

Photos: Israel National Museum

Some of the Dead Sea Scrolls were found in this cave.

Workers carefully unrolled the Dead Sea Scrolls. Then they placed the old Hebrew writings in a museum for visitors to see.

Photo: David Wagler

241

Many signs in Israel have both Hebrew and English words on them.

A DEAD LANGUAGE BECOMES ALIVE

One day almost 50 years ago, an Arab boy was rounding up his goats near the Dead Sea. One goat hid in a hole among the rocks. The boy threw a stone in to bring it out.

Crash! Something inside broke. It sounded like a jar. The next day, the boy crawled into the hole to explore. He found himself in a cave. And sure enough, around him stood tall clay jars.

Each jar held a roll of leather, a scroll. The scrolls had old Hebrew writing on them. Scholars studied the writings. They turned out to be the Book of Isaiah, an Old Testament book.

Men searched and found other caves and more scrolls with

Hebrew writings. Today these scrolls are called the **Dead Sea Scrolls**.

The Dead Sea Scrolls are 2,000 years old. The dry climate around the Dead Sea kept them all these years from rotting away.

The Hebrew language on the Dead Sea Scrolls looks strange to us. But the Jews spoke this language long ago. Mothers spoke Hebrew to their babies. Buyers shouted Hebrew in the marketplace. Hebrew was a **living language**.

After God scattered the Jews, they had to learn the languages of other countries. Jews in Germany learned the German language. Jews coming to North America learned English.

Hebrew soon became a **dead language**. This means people forgot how to speak it. For years, the Jews only used Hebrew when they read from the old Hebrew Scriptures, prayed, and worshiped God.

When Jews began coming to the new nation of Israel, they spoke many different languages. The new nation needed one language everybody could understand.

Most Israelis knew some Hebrew from hearing the Hebrew Scriptures. They began to learn the Hebrew language again.

Making an old language work in our day was not an easy job. The Israelis had no words for many new things.

The Israelis had to find new Hebrew words for *car, telephone, plastic, electricity,* and thousands of other modern things. They put parts of old Hebrew words together to make new words. They used some words from other languages.

Today Hebrew is a living language again. A living language grows by adding new words. The Hebrew language had to grow fast to catch up.

Now the people in Israel read Hebrew newspapers. Modern signs are written in Hebrew. Children and adults study Hebrew in schools. The Hebrew language helps to build the new nation.

The Israelis must work hard to make homes in the new country. In this chapter, you will learn about how they are using natural resources in Israel.

SHOW YOUR KNOWLEDGE

1. Today Israel belongs to the (Jews, Romans, Arabs).
2. How did the Dead Sea Scrolls stay in such good shape for 2,000 years?
3. When the Jews moved to other lands and learned the languages there, Hebrew became a (living, dead) language.
4. The Israelis started using the Hebrew language again because:
    a. this was a lost language that was found again when an Arab boy found the Dead Sea Scrolls.
    b. Jewish mothers taught Hebrew to their babies.
    c. the new nation needed one language which Jews coming from many countries could understand.
5. A living language grows because:
    a. boys and girls learn the language in schools.
    b. people need new words for new things.
    c. modern signs have the language on them.

"And God said unto them [man and woman], . . . multiply, and replenish the earth, and subdue [rule over] it" (Genesis 1:28b).

Using Natural Resources In Israel

Israel is one of the smallest countries in the world. For many years people thought this country did not have many natural resources.

When the scattered Jews began coming to Israel, they found no large forests, no oil wells, and no coal mines.

Israel did have good soil. But much of the land in the south was very dry.

The Dead Sea is in the south. But the salty water from this sea could not be used to irrigate desert farmlands.

The northern part of Israel had some good farmland. But many people were coming to live in Israel.

These people would all need food, clothing, and homes. How could all these people live in such a small country with few natural resources?

The Israelis knew that food brought from other nations would cost more than food grown in Israel. They wanted to supply most of their needs from their own land.

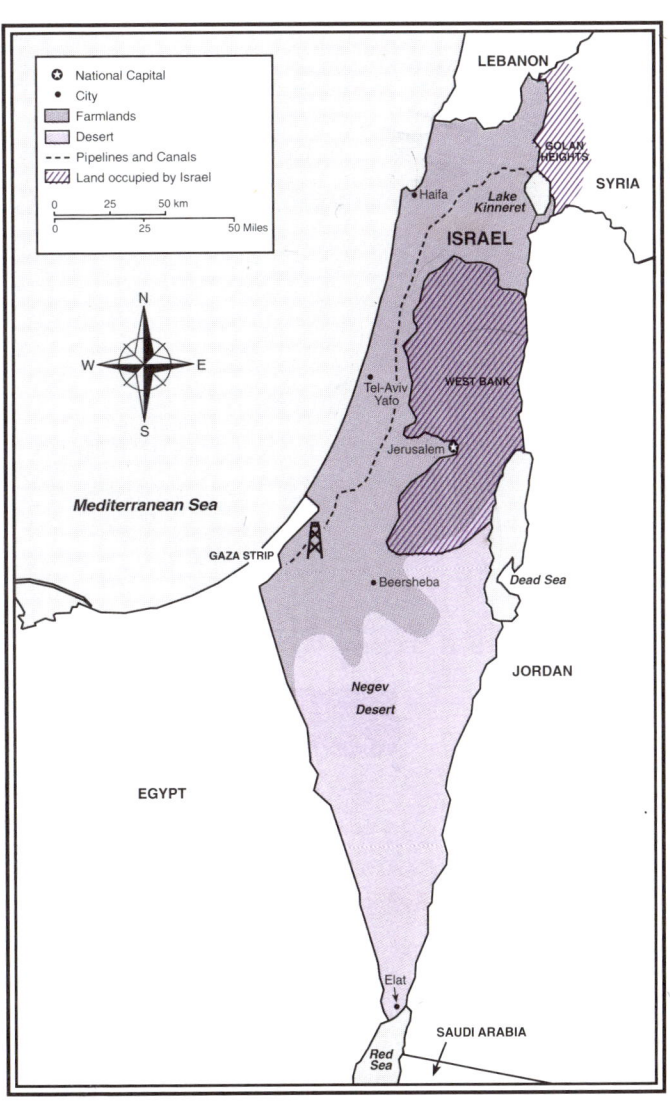

245

These farmlands in the Hula Basin were part of a wasted swamp. The Israelis drained the swamp. They now grow crops in the soil.

People coming to Israel knew the land was small and wasted. But these people were willing to work hard to grow crops for food.

The people coming to Israel had been doctors, scientists, merchants, and workers in many different jobs.

Most of these people had never milked a cow or plowed a field. But they wanted to be farmers in the new country.

In the lands where they had lived, most of the Jews were not able to own farms. In Israel they wanted to work the land like the Jews who lived there in Bible times.

The Israelis carefully used every resource and searched for more. Every Israeli wanted to help build up the wasted land of Israel.

REBUILDING FARMLAND IN THE NORTH

In Bible times, the northern part of Israel had many farms. This part gets enough rain for growing crops. It has wide valleys and streams of water from the hills.

Long ago, God told the Israelites about this good farmland. He said it did not need to be irrigated like the farms of Egypt.

Deuteronomy 11:10,11

"For the land . . . is not as the land of Egypt . . . where thou sowedst thy seed, and wateredst it with thy foot . . . but . . . is a land of hills and valleys, and drinketh water of the rain of heaven."

This northern part of Israel still gets plenty of rain. But much of the good farmland was in bad shape when the first

Jews came to Israel.

Find Lake Kinneret (kin ə ret´) on the map on page 245. Another name for this lake is the Sea of Galilee.

The Jordan River flows into Lake Kinneret from the north. Years ago, the Jordan River became clogged. Water overflowed and spread out over the land.

Good farmland turned into soggy **marshes** thick with papyrus plants and water lilies. In the middle of the marshes stood swampy Lake Hula (hū´ lə).

The Israelis decided to drain the Hula **Basin**. They used large earth-moving machines to dig out a deep ditch where the river could flow.

Workers dug up large patches of papyrus. They made canals to drain the water from the marshes into the river.

Some Israelis knew about a kind of tree that could help dry up the marshes. These trees, called **eucalyptus** (yü kə lip´ təs), grow very fast. Their roots soak up lots of water.

Eucalyptus trees could not be found in Israel. The Israelis brought small eucalyptus trees from Australia. They planted thousands of eucalyptus trees in the wet Hula Basin. The eucalyptus trees helped dry up the soggy soil.

Draining the Hula Basin took seven years of hard work. At first, mosquitoes bothered the workers. These insects carried a dreadful disease called malaria (mə ler´ ē ə). At places, large signs said, "Keep out! Malaria!"

Mosquitoes hatch their eggs in marsh waters. Many workers in the marshes got malaria and became very sick. Some died.

After the marshes were drained, the land

Photo: Robert Maust/Photo Agora

Eucalyptus trees grow fast and become very large. These trees use lots of water. The Israelis planted many eucalyptus trees to dry up swampy land in Israel. The wood from these trees can be made into lumber. The sap can be used to make medicines and other manufactured products.

dried off. The mosquitoes disappeared.

The swamp had made the soil very rich over the years. In new fields farmers planted corn, cotton, melons, flower bulbs, and vegetables. The first crops were twice as large as the crops in other parts of Israel.

SHOW YOUR KNOWLEDGE

1. Israel had good soil, but much of the land in the south was too _____ to grow crops.
2. Why can't water from the Dead Sea be used for irrigating?
3. Why did the Israelis want to supply most of their needs from their own land?
4. In Israel, rain falls mostly in the (north, south, east, west).
5. What is another name for Lake Kinneret?
6. How did the Hula Basin become a marsh?
7. The Israelis dried up the Hula Basin by:
    a. digging a _____ where the Jordan River could flow.
    b. making _____ to drain the water into the river.
    c. planting many _____ trees.
8. The workers were bothered by _____ which carried a disease called _____ .
9. Why were the first crops in the Hula Basin larger than crops in other parts of Israel?

SHARE YOUR KNOWLEDGE

1. Study Deuteronomy 11:10-12. In Bible times, how was farming in the land of Israel different from farming in Egypt?
2. Study Joshua 11:5. In this verse, the "waters of _____" are what we call Lake Hula today.
3. In Judges 18, some men from the tribe of Dan were hunting a better place for the tribe to settle. They passed through the Hula Basin. Study Judges 18:9,10 and answer these questions.
    a. List two things these men said about this land.
    b. What changes took place years after these men saw this land?

WATER FOR THE DESERT

The farmland in the north supplied some of the Israelis' needs. But more farmland was needed.

A large piece of land in the south was not being used. But this land was a hot, dry desert called the Negev (ne´ gev). For many years people said no large group of people could make a living there.

Israeli leaders studied what the Bible had to say about this land.

The Bible told about a king named Uzziah who "built towers in the desert, and digged many wells."

II Chronicles 26:10a

Find Beersheba on the map on page 245. Beersheba is a town in the Negev. The Bible told about people living "at Beersheba, and in the villages thereof."

Nehemiah 11:27b

To the Israeli leaders, it seemed that in Bible times many people had lived in some parts of the Negev. They wanted to know how these people long ago made a living there.

The Israelis studied the desert. They found the farms of some people who lived in the Negev in Bible times.

These farmers knew how to save the little bit of rain that falls in the Negev.

Many years ago these dry lands on the Negev were farmed by people called Nabateans (nab´ ə tē ənz). The Nabateans made ways to catch water the few times it rained in this part of Israel. They drained water from many hillsides and saved it to water their fields.

Today this pipeline helps to carry water all the way from Lake Kinneret to thirsty farms and towns in the Negev. It is part of the National Water Carrier.

Photo: Israel Office of Information

In the Negev, heavy rains sometimes fall during a few days or weeks in the spring each year. Then floodwaters gush down through dry riverbeds.

The sun soon dries up the water from these spring rains. For the rest of the year, the desert is scorched and dry.

The Israelis found **reservoirs** (re´ zə vwȯrz) in the Negev where farmers long ago stored water from the spring rains.

This plant at Elat takes salt from sea water. It produces fresh water for the people in this port city. The Israelis keep looking for a cheaper way to make fresh water from salt water. Why do they work so hard at this job?

Photo: Israel Office of Information

These farmers had ditches to bring water from the hillsides to their reservoirs. In the dry season they used water from the reservoirs to irrigate fields of crops.

Today some Israelis are trying out these old ways of farming the Negev. Other farmers in the desert are using new ways to get water.

The Israelis decided to bring water down to the Negev from the north. They laid pipelines from the Yarkon River to farms and towns in the Negev.

Still, the Negev did not have all the water it needed. The Israelis used a plan to get more water from Lake Kinneret.

Workers dug canals and laid more pipelines to carry the water from Lake Kinneret to the pipelines at Yarkon River. At some places along the way, large pumps must force the water up mountainsides.

Now water can flow all the way to the Negev from Lake Kinneret.

The Israelis use Lake Kinneret as a reservoir to store up water during the rainy season. Then during the long hot summer, this stored-up water flows south to thirsty places in the Negev.

The canals and pipelines carrying water to the northern part of the Negev are called the National Water Carrier.

In the south, Israelis have dug wells to find a water supply. But the water from many of these wells is salty and not fit for crops.

The Israelis have found some crops can be grown with salt water if it is not too salty.

Some farmers mix salty water from their wells with fresh water from other places. They use this mixture to grow certain kinds of crops.

On the map on page 245 find three salty seas around the Negev. The desert could have plenty of water if the Israelis could find a way to change sea water to fresh water.

Israeli scientists are looking for a way to take salt out of sea water. Different ways have been found. But all of these ways cost more than people want to pay.

On the map on page 245, find Elat (ē´ lat), Israel's port city on the Red Sea. The people at Elat had to use water from the sea. They built a plant to change sea water to fresh water.

The plant at Elat changes enough water for all the people who live there. But the Israelis still want to find a better way to do the job.

If the Israelis can find a cheap way to get fresh water from the sea, many more farms will be formed in the Negev.

SHOW YOUR KNOWLEDGE

1. When Israeli leaders studied the _____ they learned that people had lived in some parts of the Negev.
2. Long ago, farmers had stored water from the spring rains in _____ .
3. The National Water Carrier brings water from _____ _____ to the _____ .
4. How can farmers use salty well water?
5. Look at the map on page 245. Name three salty seas near the Negev.
6. Israelis do not change more sea water to fresh water because:
    a. they would have too much water.
    b. it costs too much money.
    c. they are not willing to work so hard.

SHARE YOUR KNOWLEDGE

1. From these verses, find the names of Bible people who came to the desert town of Beersheba.
    a. Genesis 26:19, 23
    b. Genesis 28:10
    c. 1 Kings 19:1-3
    d. Joshua 19:1, 2 tells us this city was given to the tribe of _____ .

The Israelis grow flowers to sell in Europe during winter months. During these months the people of Europe have very cold weather. But in Israel some places are warm enough for growing crops and flowers.

Photo: J. Otis Yoder

GROWING CROPS IN ISRAEL

The winter **climate** of many countries is too cold for growing crops. People in these countries cannot raise fresh fruits and vegetables during the winter months.

In many parts of Israel, the climate is warm during the winter. Crops can grow all year long. Farmers in some parts of Israel grow four crops a year.

During the warm winters in Israel, farmers can grow crops to sell in countries where winters are cold.

The warmest part of Israel during the winter is the Negev. One hot valley in the Negev is called the Araba (ar´ ə bə).

The soil in the Araba was salty when the first farmers went there.

The Israeli farmers set up sprinklers. These sprinklers watered the salty soil with fresh water for several months.

The fresh water washed the salt deep into the ground. Then the topsoil was free from salt and ready for crops.

First, the farmers planted different kinds of grass. They cut the first two grass crops and plowed them back into the soil. This helped to make the soil richer.

At last the soil was ready for vegetables and melons. First the farmers laid plastic hoses in long ditches and covered them with soil. Then they planted their crops.

The farmers irrigated their crops by running water through the plastic hoses. The water seeped through holes in

The Israeli farmers grow tomatoes under these plastic tunnels on a farm near the Dead Sea.

Photo: Abner Stoltzfus

the hoses and soaked the plant roots.

This kind of irrigation keeps most of the water under the ground where the sun cannot dry it up. In the desert, every drop of water must be saved.

The cost of raising crops in the desert is high. But the Israelis fly their crops to countries having cold winters where they bring high prices.

The northern parts of Israel are not as warm as the Negev during the winter. Farmers in the north often grow winter crops and flowers under long plastic tunnels. These winter crops are shipped to countries in Europe.

The Israelis also grow summer crops. They plant and harvest the summer crops by the seasons in Israel. These seasons have not changed since Bible times.

The country of Israel has a rainy season and a dry season. The rainy season begins in the month of November. It ends in April.

The dry season is from May to the end of October. Rain almost never falls during these dry season months.

Song of Solomon 2:11b The Bible tells it this way. "The winter is past, the rain is over and gone."

Israeli farmers plow their fields after the first rains in November have made the ground soft. These first rains are called the "former rains" in the Bible.

The farmers plant their crops between January and

These oranges will be exported from Israel to a country with a cooler climate.

Photo: Israel National Museum

February. By April the crops are reaching the time of harvest. The last rains of the season are needed to keep the crops growing until they ripen.

The Bible calls these last rains the "latter rains." Without the latter rains, the crops would die and the harvest would fail.

God said to the Israelites years ago, "Ask ye of the LORD rain in the time of the latter rain; so the LORD shall make bright clouds, and give them showers of rain, to every one grass in the field."

Zechariah 10:1

The seasons in Israel have not changed in the many years since Bible times. The Israeli farmers still look for the "former" and "latter" rains.

But today Israeli farmers irrigate if the rains do not fall at just the right time. Irrigating gives the Israelis crops that would have been lost in Bible times.

The Israeli farmers now grow much of the food their country needs. They export winter crops and some summer crops.

An important export crop from Israel is **citrus fruit.** Citrus fruits are fruits such as oranges, grapefruit, and lemons. Israel exports citrus fruits to countries all over the world.

Citrus fruits grow well in the sunny climate of Israel. They grow well at some places in the Negev. Peach trees also grow well in the Negev.

More and more trees are being planted in Israel. Trees keep the wind from carrying off soil in the desert. Trees help stop water erosion on the hillsides in the north.

Genesis 21:33a

The Israelis wanted to plant trees at Beersheba. The Bible says, "Abraham planted a grove in Beersheba." The word *grove* in this verse means a **tamarisk** (tam´ ə risk) tree.

The Israelis tried to grow tamarisk trees at Beersheba. They found that tamarisk trees grow better there than any other trees.

The Israelis want to replant the trees that disappeared from their land over the years. School children, grown-ups, and visitors have helped to plant trees in many parts of Israel.

SHOW YOUR KNOWLEDGE

1. Crops can grow all year long in some parts of Israel because the winter climate is _____ .
2. How did farmers get the salt out of the topsoil in the Araba?
3. Why do some Israeli farmers use hoses under the ground for irrigation?
4. The Israelis can get high prices for their crops from countries that have _____ winters.
5. Northern Israel has a (warmer, cooler) climate than southern Israel.
6. How do the farmers in northern Israel grow winter crops?
7. The months from November to April are (rainy, dry) season months.
8. Why are the "latter rains" important?
9. Why are the Israelis planting so many trees in their country?

SHARE YOUR KNOWLEDGE

1. Study Deuteronomy 11:12, 14. Who sets the times for the "former" and "latter" rains?
2. Study James 5:7b. A *husbandman* is a farmer. After a farmer has planted and irrigated his crops, he still must _____ for the fruit of the earth. Why?

In 1951 the land around the old town of Beersheba looked barren and dry. Ten years later, in 1961, this same town had beautiful green grass and many trees. Water made the difference. How did the Israelis bring water to this city in the Negev?

Photo: Abner Stoltzfus

Photo: Abner Stoltzfus

The workers on a kibbutz eat together in a large dining room.

FARM COMMUNITIES

In the year of 1910, a small group of young people came to Israel. They wanted to be farmers.

These young people were given a piece of land just south of Lake Kinneret.

The young farmers wanted to work together in one group.

These children live in a special house for them on a kibbutz. Each evening they go to visit their parents. But they eat their meals and sleep in a home with children from many other families. The teachers and other workers care for the children on a kibbutz.

They wanted to share everything together as one big family.

The new kind of farm was called a **kibbutz** (kib bŭts´). *Kibbutz* is a Hebrew word that means "group." Today, Israel has many farm groups or kibbutz farms.

On a kibbutz, the land, the buildings, and other goods all belong to the whole group. No person in a kibbutz owns anything all by himself.

The people in a kibbutz have many jobs to do. The workers divide the jobs between themselves.

Some work in the fields with the crops. Some work around the farm buildings with the farm animals.

Others do the washing and cooking for the rest of the workers. At mealtime all the workers eat together in one big dining hall.

No one in a kibbutz gets pay for his work. When crops are sold, the money is used to buy farm machines, seeds, and food and clothing for everyone.

Today, the kibbutz groups in Israel do not all have farms. Some kibbutz groups have factories. A kibbutz in Israel today may run a hotel for visitors or a printing shop.

On a kibbutz, the children do not live in the houses of their parents.

The children all live together in houses. While their

parents are at work on the farm during the day, the children work, play, and study together. Kibbutz teachers and workers look after them.

In a kibbutz school, Israeli children learn to read and do arithmetic problems just as children do in your school. Israeli children also learn to read and write the Hebrew language.

Israeli children study the Bible in every grade in school. From the Bible, they learn many things about their nation's past.

The Bible tells about Israel's natural resources and old ways of farming the land. The Bible also helps teach good ways of using the land of Israel.

The Israeli children study mostly from the Old Testament of the Bible. Most Israeli people still do not believe that Jesus is the Messiah. They do not believe the Gospel story of the New Testament.

But there are some Christian Jews in Israel today. These Christians are witnessing to their own people about Jesus.

The children on a kibbutz go to visit their parents for a short time at the end of each day.

After the visit, the boys and girls go back to their houses to eat and sleep.

Years ago, the Valley of Jezreel was too dry in many places for crops to grow. The Israelis piped water to this valley. Today it is covered with rich farmlands.

Some people did not like everything about the kibbutz way of life. These people wanted to spend more time with their children. They wanted to farm pieces of land they could call their own. But these people wanted to keep the kibbutz way of doing many things together as one big family.

A few families left kibbutz groups to begin a new kind of farm called a **moshav** (mō shäv´).

The families set up the first moshav in the Jezreel Valley. Together the moshav workers drained the swampy land. Then they marked off a piece of land for each family.

Together the families worked to build the houses in the new moshav. Each family was given its own house where parents could live with their children.

The families on a moshav all share the farm machines together. They work together in selling their crops and buying supplies.

But on a moshav, families farm their own fields. They may decide what crops to grow. Each family plans its own work.

The children help their parents on the land they have to farm. The parents living on a moshav have more time to spend with their children than parents living in a kibbutz do.

Many Israeli farmers like the way a moshav is set up. Israel today has more moshav farms than kibbutz farms.

SHOW YOUR KNOWLEDGE

1. On a kibbutz, who owns the land, the buildings, and the other goods?
2. What happens to the money a kibbutz gets when crops are sold?
3. In Israel, schoolchildren learn a lot about using their land from _____.
4. Families farm their own fields and plan their own work on a (kibbutz, moshav).
5. Parents can spend more time with their children on a (kibbutz, moshav).

SHARE YOUR KNOWLEDGE

1. List the ways an Israeli school is like your school. List the ways it is different.
2. Study Deuteronomy 6:7. How would parents be able to obey this command better on a moshav than on a kibbutz?
3. Find the Valley of Jezreel on the map on page 100. This large valley is also called the Plain of _____ .

FINDING MINERALS TO USE

The people in Israel use many manufactured goods such as clothes, dishes, tools, and farm machines.

At first, the Israelis bought many manufactured goods from other countries. But the Israelis wanted to do their own manufacturing. Israel could save money that way.

To do manufacturing, a country must have the right kind of natural resources. The Israelis began looking for oil, metals, and other **minerals** in their country.

The Israelis studied the reports of other people who had looked for minerals in Israel.

These reports said the country of Israel had no oil and hardly any metals. But the Israelis knew the Bible gave a different report.

The Bible said Israel was "a land whose stones are iron [iron ore], and out of whose hills thou mayest dig brass [copper]."

Deuteronomy 8:9b

The Israelis knew King Solomon once had copper mines somewhere in Israel. They finally found the ruins of these mines far to the south at Timna near Elat.

Nearby, the Israelis found copper ore under the ground.

Copper can be used to make electric wires, pans, coins, and many other things people use every day. Today Israel mines enough copper for export and trade.

The Israelis drilled into the ground to find oil. They struck an oil well about 25 miles north of Beersheba. Soon other oil wells were dug in the same area.

The oil is pumped through a pipeline to the city of Haifa

261

(hī´ fə) in northern Israel.

At Haifa, the oil is manufactured into fuel to run trucks and machines in Israel's factories. Gasoline is also manufactured from oil at Haifa.

The oil wells in Israel do not give enough oil for the country's needs. Oil is brought from other countries by ship to the port at Elat.

At Elat, the oil is pumped into a long pipeline that goes all the way to Haifa.

An important natural resource in Israel comes from the Dead Sea. The Dead Sea is so full of salts that a person can float in its water and not sink.

The sun is very hot around the Dead Sea. At the southern end of the Dead Sea the salty water is placed in large shallow pools. The hot sun quickly dries up the water and leaves the salts.

From the salts of the Dead Sea, the Israelis make **potash.** Potash is used in making soap, glass, and many other products. The Israelis also use potash for **fertilizer** to build up soil for better crops.

A mineral called phosphate (fäs´ fāt) is also needed for

Today the Israelis get copper from the earth at Timna near the place where King Solomon's workers mined copper in Bible times. The Bible helped them find the old copper mines.

Photo: J. Otis Yoder

It is thought the Dead Sea has enough salts to supply the whole world with potash for many years.

Photo: J. Otis Yoder

manufacturing fertilizer.

The Israelis found phosphate about 25 miles southwest of the Dead Sea. Israel is one of the few places in the world where potash and phosphate are found so close together.

Big trucks haul fertilizer from factories near the Dead Sea to Elat. There it is exported to countries all over the world.

Some people say the Dead Sea has enough salts to make fertilizer for the whole world for many years.

Near Elat, sand for making glass has been found. Now glass factories at Haifa no longer need to import sand from faraway countries.

Men have found marble rocks for buildings in Israel. They have discovered clays for making cement, washbasins, bricks, and many other things.

Some iron ore was discovered in the Negev and the northern part of Israel. But factories in Israel must still import most of the iron ore they need.

The Israelis are always looking for more minerals in their small country. Every mineral they find cuts down the amount Israel needs to import.

Now the Israelis know their country has many minerals just as the Bible said many years ago.

The natural resources in Israel were there all the time. "The earth is full of thy riches."

Psalm 104:24b

SHOW YOUR KNOWLEDGE

1. Why did the Israelis want to do their own manufacturing?
2. To do manufacturing, a country must have:
    a. natural resources.
    b. large rivers.
    c. a modern language.
3. Even though reports said Israel had hardly any metals, the Israelis kept looking because _____ .
4. How is copper used?
5. What happens to the oil at Haifa?
6. Potash is made from the salts of the _____.
7. Other natural resources found in Israel are:
    a. _____ for making glass   sand potash
    b. _____ rocks for buildings   marble
    c. _____ for making cement and bricks   clays
8. Why do the Israelis keep looking for more and more minerals?

SHARE YOUR KNOWLEDGE

1. Study 1 Chronicles 29:11,12.
    a. The earth's riches belong to _____ .
    b. Men are (owners, stewards) of these riches.
2. How do you feel when you see someone carefully using a gift you have given them? How do you think God feels when He sees people using His gifts wisely?

The city of Haifa stands on the slope of Mount Carmel where the Prophet Elijah built his altar to the true God. The port of Haifa is Israel's main seaport.

THREE CITIES

Find the city of Haifa on the map on page 245. Haifa is located on the slope of Mount Carmel beside the sea.

In Bible times, God gave the land around Mount Carmel to the tribe of Zebulun. There is a lovely bay at the foot of Mount Carmel.

The Bible says, "They shall suck of the abundance of the seas."

Deuteronomy 33:19b

Today Haifa is Israel's main seaport. Most of the people coming to live in Israel arrive at this port.

Haifa has three parts above each other up the side of Mount Carmel. That is why the Israelis call Haifa "a cake of three layers."

The first layer is at the foot of the mountain beside the

bay. This part of the city has many factories where oil, cement, and metal products are manufactured. Haifa is an important manufacturing city.

The second layer of the city is the **business district**. This part of the city has many stores for shopping.

The most beautiful layer is at the top of the mountain. Most of the people live in this new part of the city. Here they have a beautiful view from the mountaintop.

Haifa is one of the greenest cities in Israel with its parks and gardens. Most of its people work in factories or in the shipyards. Haifa is often called the "workers' town" in Israel.

Find the city of Tel Aviv (tel ə vēv´) on the map on page 245. Some years ago, there was no city where Tel Aviv is today. This place was only an area of sand dunes beside the small city of Yafo (yä´ fə). Yafo is the new name for the old Bible city of Joppa.

Jonah 1:3a You remember how "Jonah rose up to flee . . . from the presence of the LORD, and went down to Joppa; and he found a ship going to Tarshish."

This happened at Yafo, the city called Joppa long ago. Joppa was Israel's most important seaport in Bible times.

While the Jews were scattered, the people living in Yafo were mostly Arabs. Only a few Jews lived in this old city.

These Jews wanted a place for their own people. They bought a plot of sand dunes outside Yafo and began building a **suburb** for Jews. The Jews called the new suburb Tel Aviv, a

This is the only wall left of the temple. The Israelis call it the Western Wall. Day and night, Israeli people come to visit this wall and think about the great nation of Israel many years ago.

Photo: J. Otis Yoder

Jerusalem is the capital of Israel today. The city of Jerusalem is over 3,000 years old. Find the large building with a dome on top. In Bible times, the temple stood at this spot.

Photo: Israel National Museum

name that means the "Hill of Spring."

When Jews began coming to Israel, many of them came to live at Tel Aviv. The suburb grew. Soon it was larger than its mother city, Yafo.

Suburbs grew up around Tel Aviv and it became a **metropolitan city**.

Tel Aviv is a modern city with wide streets. But many visitors still like to visit the narrow streets of Yafo, the old city that has become a suburb of Tel Aviv.

Jerusalem is one of the oldest cities in Israel. Today it is the capital of the country.

For a while, Jerusalem was a divided city. The Arab people living in Israel would not give up the city when the country was given back to the Israelis.

The Arabs and Israelis were bitter enemies. The Arabs kept the old part of the city. This part has the place where the temple stood and other important places of Bible times.

The Israelis had only the new part of Jerusalem. Ugly walls and rolls of barbed wire divided the two parts of Jerusalem.

During a war in 1967, the Israelis took over the old part of Jerusalem. In two days, the Israelis had pushed down the dividing walls. Today the whole city belongs to the Israelis.

Many Israelis still follow Old Testament laws. The Israelis rest on the Sabbath day or Saturday rather than Sunday. Many of the people in Jerusalem obey the Israeli laws against working on the Sabbath.

To the Israelis, the most important reminder of Bible times in Jerusalem is the place where the temple stood before the Romans destroyed it in 70 A.D. Years later, a Turkish leader set up a building for heathen worship at this spot.

But one wall of the Jewish temple still stands.

Day and night, Israeli people come to this wall to pray and worship. This old temple wall was called the "Wailing Wall," because for many years Jews came there to weep about the loss of their temple. Now it is called the Western Wall.

Many Israelis worshiping at the Western Wall do not believe their Messiah has come yet.

The Israelis need to be told that Jesus Christ, the Messiah, did come to save them from their sins. They must accept Jesus before they can be saved.

Acts 4:12b "There is none other name under heaven given among men, whereby we must be saved."

The Israelis are wisely using the land where Jesus lived. But many do not yet believe on Jesus as their Saviour.

There are Christians in Israel telling the Gospel story. Some of these are Christian Jews who are witnessing to their own people. Many more are needed for this work.

SHOW YOUR KNOWLEDGE

1. Write the name of the city for each clue.
    a. the capital of Israel
    b. "a cake of three layers"
    c. Israel's most important seaport in Bible times
    d. started outside Yafo as a suburb for Jews
    e. Israel's main seaport and an important manufacturing city
    f. a suburb of Tel Aviv
2. Why was the Western Wall called the "Wailing Wall"?

SHARE YOUR KNOWLEDGE

1. The name "Salem" comes from a Hebrew word "Shalom" that means "peace." The name "Jerusalem" must mean "the city of _____."
2. Why did the Israelis want the old part of Jerusalem so badly?
3. Study II Chronicles 2:16 and look for the places in this verse on the map on page 245. The wood for Solomon's temple was cut in the country of _____ and floated down to _____ on the _____ Sea. From there it was carried across the land to _____.

GLOSSARY

The next 11 pages are a special dictionary called a glossary. This glossary will help you understand what some of the words in this book mean. It will also help you spell the words you want to write.

The words in this glossary are listed as they are in large dictionaries. Words that begin with "a" are first. Those that begin with "b" are next, and so on through the alphabet. We say that words listed like this are in alphabetical order.

Suppose you find the word *canal* while you are reading in this book. If you do not understand what it means, turn to the glossary. Find the words which begin with "C." Then look for the word *canal*. What does the glossary say it means? Turn back to the page where you were reading about canals. Find the sentence with the word *canal* in it. Now do you understand better what the sentence says?

You won't find all the words in this book in the glossary. But you will find many of the harder ones. The page number after each definition tells where the word was used first in this book.

Whenever you have trouble with a word, see if you can find it in the glossary. Use your glossary often. It will become easier and easier for you to find words.

Pronunciation Key: cat, bāke, fäther, /â/ for care, /au̇/ for out; pet, easy, trip, life, flow, order, oil, pu̇t, rüle; /ə/ for alert, taken, pencil, lemon, under; /ər/ for herd, bird, fur; child; long; thin; /th/ for these; /hw/ for which; /yü/ for use; /yu̇/ for furious; /zh/ for measure; /sh/ for shy, mission, machine.

A

acropolis (ə krä′ pə ləs) – A high hill of a Greek city used for protection and idol worship. *Page 151.*

adultery (ə dəl′ tə rē) – Married people leaving their husbands and wives to live with others the way married people do. Adultery is a terrible sin. *Page 152.*

agora (a′ gə rə) – The marketplace in Greece long ago. The agora was the place where the Greek people also had important meetings. *Page 149.*

almshouse – A home for people who do not have enough money to live on. *Page 232.*

Amalekites (a′ mə lə kīts) – People that fought the Hebrews when they traveled from Egypt to Canaan. God promised to someday destroy them completely. Page 91.

Anabaptist (a nə bap′ tist) – A person who believes Christians should be baptized only after they believe on Jesus. *Page 186.*

assembly – A group of men chosen by the people to help make laws. *Page 227.*

B

bargain – To try to agree on the price of something being sold. *Page 113.*

barge – A boat with a large, flat bottom for carrying cargo on a river. *Page 64 and 169.*

bar mitzvah (bär mits′ və) – A special service where a thirteen-year-old Jewish boy promises to obey the Law of Moses. *Page 118.*

barter – Buying and selling by trading rather than with money. *Page 115.*

basin – All the land and streams that drain into one river. *Page 247.*

battlement – A wall built around the top of a building for protection. *Page 122.*

bay – A part of a sea or lake reaching into the land. *Page 157.*

bema – (bē′ mə) A place in old Greece where people were brought to be judged. *Page 128.*

booth – A small temporary shelter for protection from the weather. *Page 112.*

brave – An American Indian fighter. *Page 205.*

Brethren – A group of Christians who believed and lived much like the Mennonites did at Germantown. *Page 225.*

bronze – A hard metal made of copper and tin or copper and other soft metals. *Page 114.*

bulrushes – Large, tall plants that grow in wet places. Bulrushes may have been the name for papyrus plants in Bible times. *Page 57.*

business district – The part of a city with many stores where people shop. *Page 266.*

C

canal (kə nal′) – A ditch dug for water to flow through. Small canals are made for irrigating crops. Large canals are made for ships to go through. *Page 55 and 142.*

capital – A city where government leaders meet to make laws. *Page 41.*

caravan – (kar′ ə van) – A group of traders traveling together with their animals. *Page 111.*

cargo – Load of goods carried by a ship. *Page 142.*

Cenchrea (sen krē′ ə) – The port 8½ miles to the east of Corinth. *Page 136.*

chaff – Stiff, straw-like bits that cover grains of wheat, rye, barley, or oats. *Page 60.*

charter – A written agreement between government leaders and their people. *Pages 180 and 204.*

Christians – Persons who believe on Jesus to save them from their sins and then follow Jesus' commandments. *Page 157.*

church – A group of Christians who believe on Jesus and follow His commands. *Page 158.*

citrus fruits – Fruits that usually grow in warm climates such as, lemons, oranges, limes and grapefuit. *Page 225.*

city block – A square space between streets in a city. *Page 212.*

city parks – Places in a city with trees, bushes, and flowers for everybody to enjoy. *Page 234.*

clay – A sticky kind of earth that hardens when it is baked. *Page 146.*

clean animals – The kinds of animals God said the Hebrews could eat. A clean animal chewed its cud and had split hoofs. *Page 86.*

climate – denarius

climate (klī′ mət) – The kind of weather a place has most of the time. *Page 28.*

cloak – A loose outer coat the Jews wore when the weather was cool. Jewish men often used their cloaks for covers at night. *Page 124.*

coast (kōst) – Land along the sea where the water and land meet. *Page 42.*

colony (kä′ lə nē) – A settlement made by a group of people who leave their own home to live in another place. *Page 209.*

community (kə myü′ nə tē) – A group of people living together. *Page 18.*

construction (kən strək′ shən) – The making of new roads and buildings. *Page 35.*

continents (kän tən ənts) – The largest bodies of land on God's earth. God's earth has seven continents. *Page 7.*

cooperate (kō ä′ pa rāt) – To work together and help each other. *Page 33.*

Corinthians (kə rin′ thē ənz) – The people who lived at Corinth in the time of Paul. *Page 137.*

corruptible (kə rəp′ tə bəl) – Something that will decay and go back to the earth. *Page 154.*

council – A group of men chosen by the people to suggest laws to be made. *Page 128.*

country. (kən′ trē) – The land belonging to a nation. *Page 37.*

courts – Places where people are brought to be judged for their actions. *Page 93.*

courtyard – An open space with walls or houses built around it. *Page 122.*

covenant (kə′ və nənt) – An agreement between two people or two groups of people. *Page 90.*

covet (kə′ vət) – To want something one should not have. To want something that belongs to another person. *Page 94.*

craftsmen – Skillful workmen. *Page 179.*

crier – A person who shouts important news for others to hear. *Page 110.*

curds – Thick lumps of sour milk. *Page 85.*

current – The flow of water or air in a certain direction. *Page 53.*

customs (kəs′ təmz) – The usual ways people in a community do things. *Page 28.*

D

dairy (der′ē) – Farm where cows are kept for their milk, or the place where milk is made into cheese and butter to be sold. *Page 194.*

dairy farmer – A man who keeps cows for their milk. *Page 33.*

dam – A wall built to hold back the water of a stream or river. *Page 46.*

dead language – A language people no longer speak. *Page 242.*

Dead Sea Scrolls – Parts of the Old Testament and some other writings in the Hebrew language copied on scrolls almost 2000 years ago. These scrolls were found in a cave in 1947. *Page 242.*

debts (dets′) – Something a person owes someone else. *Page 127.*

delta (del′ tə) – A piece of land formed at the mouth of a river where the water drops its silt. A river delta usually has three sides and looks much like a triangle. *Page 46.*

denarius (di nar′ ē əs) A small coin used by the Romans and the nations they ruled. In the Bible a

desert – Feast

denarius is called a penny. A denarius was pay for a day of work. *Page 149.*

desert (de′ zərt) – A place that is too dry or too cold for growing crops. *Page 8.*

diet (dī′ ət) – The usual food for a person or a group of people. *Page 29.*

dike – A wall of earth or a dam to keep back the water of a river or a sea. *Page 166.*

direction finder – A small drawing that looks like a star on many maps. The points of the star show the directions: North, South, East, and West. *Page 39.*

discus (dis′kəs) – A round plate of stone or metal for throwing. *Page 154.*

E

Eastern Hemisphere – The half of the world with all the continents but North America and South America. *Page 37.*

elders – 1. Men who are the leaders in a group or tribe of people. 2. Older persons. *Page 88.*

elect – To choose by voting. Page 180

embalm – (im bäm) – To work on a dead body to keep it from decay. *Page 63.*

emperor (em′ pər ər) – A ruler over a group of countries. *Page 149.*

ephah (e′ fə) – A measure of a little over half a bushel. An ephah was a measure used in Bible times. *Page 113.*

equator (ē′ kwā tər) – A circle around the earth half-way between the North Pole and the South Pole. *Page 38.*

erosion (i ro′ zhən) – The carrying of soil away by wind or water. *Page 11.*

eucalyptus (yü kə lip′ təs) **tree** – A fast-growing tree from Australia. Eucalyptus trees use lots of water and grow very tall. *Page 247.*

evaporate (i va′ pə rāt) – To turn from water or other liquid into vapor. *Page 106.*

exodus (ek ′sə dəs) – A going away from a place. *Page 72.*

exports – The goods sent out of a country to be sold in another country. *Page 145.*

F

factory (fak′ tə rē) – A place where workers make clothes, cars, furniture, and other things to supply community needs. *Page 33.*

family – A father and mother with their children. God made the family to be the smallest community in the world. *Page 15.*

family worship – A family meeting to honor God by singing, Bible reading and praying together. *Page 15.*

famine (fa′ mən) – A time of starving because food is scarce. *Pages 47.*

fashions (fa′ shənz) – Customs and styles that come from the world or the unsaved community. *Page 208.*

Feast of Booths – A feast of the Jews held after the last fruit of the season had been gathered in. This feast was also called the Feast of Ingathering or the Feast of Tabernacles. At this feast the Jews celebrated and lived for 7 days in booths made from sticks and branches. The booths reminded them of the time when the Hebrew nomads had lived in tents. *Page 130.*

Feast of Ingathering – *Page 130.* See Feast of Booths.

Feast of Pentecost (pen′ ti käst) –

Feast – herring

A feast of the Jews held 50 days after their Passover Feast to celebrate the end of the wheat harvest. *Page 130.*

Feast of Tabernacles – *Page 130.* See Feast of Booths.

Feast of Unleavened Bread – *Page 130 See Passover.*

Feast of Weeks – *Page 130.* See Feast of Pentecost.

fertilize (fər′ təl īz) – Adding manure or other materials to the soil to make it richer. *Page 171.*

fertilizer (fər′ təl ī zər) – Manure or other materials added to the soil to make it richer. *Page 262.*

fiber – Thread-like strings of any material. The stems of many plants have fibers. *Page 60.*

fine – Money paid by a person as punishment for doing the wrong thing. *Page 228.*

flails (flālz′) – Tools used to beat the grains from stalks of wheat, barley, and other grains. *Page 60.*

flax – A thin plant used to make linen cloth. Linseed oil is made from flax seeds. *Page 60.*

flint – A very hard stone that makes a spark when it is struck against a piece of steel. *Page 203.*

fresh water – Water that is not salty. *Pages 9 and 103.*

frontier (frən tir′) – The area of the settled part of a country that lies next to an unsettled part. *Page 232.*

G

Gentile (jen′ tīl) – A person who is not a Jew. *Page 156.*

gird – To tuck part of the tunic-coat up under the girdle to make running or working easier. *Page 124.*

girdle – A leather or linen belt used to hold the tunic coat when a person was running or working. *Page 124.*

globe – A small model of our sphere, the earth. *Page 6.*

government (gə′ vərn mənt) – The job of ruling a community or nation; a government must have leaders and laws. *Pages 24 and 58.*

governor – The person at the head of the government in each state of the United States. *Page 217.*

Great Treaty – The agreement between William Penn and the Indians who lived in Pennsylvania. *Page 217.*

gristmill – A mill for grinding grain. *Page 220.*

gulf – A large bay. *Page 136.*

H

handmills – Mills used to grind grain into flour by hand. *Page 128.*

hardware – Goods made from metal. Locks, nails, screws, and knives are hardware. *Page 229.*

hearth (härth′) – The floor of a place where fires are built. *Page 83.*

heathen (hē′ th ən) – People who do not believe in the true God. *Page 65.*

Hebrews (hē′ brüz) – The people who came from the twelve tribes of Jacob. *Page 51.*

hemisphere (he′ mə sfir) – 1. Half of a ball or sphere. 2. Any of the halves into which the earth's surface is divided in geography. *Page 37.*

herb (ərb′) – A plant with a soft stem which dies down after the growing season. *Page 130.*

herd – A group of larger animals living together. *Page 33.*

herring – A fish used for food found in the northern part of the Atlantic Ocean. *Page 178.*

holy – longhouse

holy – To be without sin; perfect; pure. *Page 151.*

humus (hyü′ məs) – A part of the soil that comes from dead plants and animals. *Page 10.*

I

image (i′ mij) – The likeness of a person made of stone, wood, or some other material. God commands us not to worship any images. *Page 66.*

immoral (i′ mȯr′ əl) – Anything that breaks or goes against a moral law. Immoral actions are sins. *Page 152.*

imports – Goods brought into a country from another country. *Page 145.*

incinerator (in si′ nə rā tər) – A place for burning things. *Page 234.*

income – The money a person gets paid for the work he does. *Page 33.*

Indians (in′ dē əns) – The copper colored people who lived in America before the white people came. These Indians are known as the American Indians. *Page 201.*

irrigation (ir ə gā′ shən) – To water dry land by means of canals, ditches, or pipes. *Page 55.*

islands (ī′ ləndz) – Small bodies of land with water all around them; God's earth has many islands. *Page 7.*

Israeli (iz rā′ lē) – A person who makes his home in the land of Israel today. *Page 241.*

Isthmian (is′ mē ən) **Games** – A festival held every two years on the isthmus of Corinth long ago. Games were played at this festival. *Page 125.*

isthmus (is′ məs) – A narrow strip of land joining two larger bodies of land. An isthmus has water on both sides. *Page 136.*

J

jerky – Dried strips of meat. *Page 220.*

judge – One who decides when a person has done wrong and needs to be punished. A judge also decides when a person should not be blamed for doing wrong. *Pages 89 and 110.*

K

kibbutz (ki bu̇ts′) – A farm group that owns everything together. No one in a kibbutz owns anything all by himself. *Page 258.*

L

Latin (la′ tən) – The language spoken by the Romans long ago. *Page 184.*

laws – Rules for people in a community to obey. *Page 24.*

leben (lā′ bən) – A kind of food made from sour milk curds. *Page 85.*

Lechaeum (le kī′ əm) – The port 1½ miles to the west of Corinth. *Page 136.*

leeks – Plants much like onions. *Page 56.*

linen – Cloth, thread, or yarn made from the fibers of flax plants. *Page 61.*

linsey-woolsey – A strong, coarse cloth made from linen and woolen threads. *Page 220.*

living language – A language spoken by people today. *Page 242.*

locust – A kind of grasshopper. *Page 71.*

longhouse – A kind of house built by the Delaware Indians large enough for more than one family. *Page 204.*

loom – natural resources

loom – A machine for weaving cloth. *Page 220.*

Lord – A person who has the right to rule the lives of others. Christians must let Jesus be their Lord. *Page 157: secular, 175.*

M

magistrate (ma′ jə strāt) – A ruler or leader of the government who has power to carry out laws. *Page 34.*

manufacturing (man yə fak′ chər ing)– Making useful goods from raw materials. *Page 144.*

map – A drawing of the earth or a part of the earth. *Page 37.*

map legend (le′ jənd) – A key on a map that tells what map symbols mean. *Page 41.*

marketplace – A place where goods are bought and sold. *Page 112.*

marsh – Soft, wet, swampy land. *Page 247.*

martyr (mär′ tər) – A person who is put to death for his beliefs. *Page 186.*

Mennonites (me′ nə nīts) – A group of Christians who seek to follow the teachings of the New Testament in everyday living. The Mennonites get their name from a Dutch Anabaptist leader whose name was Menno Simons. *Page 223.*

merchant – A person who trades or buys and sells. *Page 178.*

metal (me′ təl) – A material such as iron, gold, silver, copper, lead, and tin. *Pages 13 and 203.*

metropolitan (me trə pä′ lə tən) **city** – A city made up of a number of towns. *Page 267.*

Midian (mi′ de ən) A region in the southeastern part of the land of Sinai. *Page 69.*

mine – A large hole dug in the earth to get out coal and other natural resources. *Page 13.*

minerals – Materials such as coal and iron ore, dug from the earth. *Page 261.*

moat – A deep, wide ditch dug around a castle to protect it from enemies. Moats were often filled with water. *Page 175.*

mold – A hollow form used to shape something from a wet material such as clay. *Page 67.*

moneychanger – A person who changes the coins people have for a different kind of coins they need. *Page 129.*

moral laws – Laws that show the difference between right and wrong ways of living. *Page 94.*

mortar (mȯr′ tər) – A very hard stone or wooden bowl where materials are to be pounded into powder. *Page 81.*

moshav – (mō shäv′) – A farm group that shares farm machines and goes together to sell farm crops. In a moshav each family farms its own fields. *Page 260.*

mouth [of a river] – The end of a river where it enters a larger body of water. *Page 46.*

mummy – A dead body kept from decay for many years. *Page 63.*

N

nation (nā′ shən) – A group of people living in the same country under the same government. The people in a nation usually speak the same language. *Page 51.*

native (nā′ tiv) – A person born in the country where he lives is a native of that country. *Page 203.*

natural resources (na′ chə rəl re′ sȯr səz) – Supplies God placed on His earth for our needs. Water, soil, and ores are natural resources. *Page 8.*

New World – poles

New World – The lands of the Western Hemisphere. *Page 9.*

nomad (nō′ mad) – A person in a tribe that moves from place to place finding food for herds of cattle. *Page 77.*

nonresistant (nän ri zis′ tənt) **people** – People who love their enemies will not do anything to harm them. *Page 181.*

Northern Hemisphere – The half of the earth from the North Pole to the equator. *Page 38.*

North Pole – The point farther north than any other place on God's earth. *Page 6.*

O

oasis (ō ā səs) – A place in a desert with water and good soil. *Page 55.*

oceans (ō′ shənz) – The largest bodies of water on God's earth. Some divide the earth's oceans into the Atlantic, Pacific, Indian, Arctic and Antarctic Oceans. Others include the Antarctic Ocean as parts of the Atlantic, Pacific and Indian Oceans. *Page 6.*

omer (ō′ mər) – A measure of about two quarts. The omer was a measure used in Bible times. *Page 84.*

ordinance (ȯrd′ nəns) – An order given by someone who has a right to set up laws. *Page 25.*

ores (ōrs′) – Rocks, sand, or dirt that have some metals in them. *Page 13.*

P

palace (pa′ ləs) – A grand house where a king or queen lives. *Page 58.*

palisade (pa lə sād′) – A fence made of stakes placed in the ground side by side. *Page 205.*

papyrus (pə pī′ rəs) – 1. A tall water plant that grew along the Nile River in Egypt. 2. The material made from this plant that was used for writing on. *Page 54.*

Passover – A feast of the Jews held every year to help them remember the night God saved their oldest sons from the plague of death in Egypt. *Pages 72 and 130.*

peninsula (pə nin′ sə lə) – A body of land with water almost all around it. *Pages 76 and 135.*

persecute (pər′ si kyüt) – To make others suffer for their beliefs. *Page 202.*

pestle (pe′ səl) – A tool for pounding materials in a mortar. *Page 81.*

pharaoh (fā′ ro) – A name given to the Kings of Egypt long ago. *Page 51.*

phylactery (fə lak′ tə rē) – A small box a Jew tied to his arm or to his forehead. The Jews place parts of the Law inside each phylactery. *Page 120.*

piles – Heavy beams driven into the ground or the bed of a river to make a solid place for building. *Page 175.*

pioneers (pī ə nirs′) – The first people to settle in a part of a country. *Page 211.*

pitch – A black sticky material used to cover roofs and ships and to make roads. *Page 54.*

plague (plāg′) – Something that makes a group of people suffer. *Page 70.*

plain – Large, flat stretch of land. *Page 46.*

polder – A low piece of land claimed back from the sea. *Page 169.*

poles – Two points God's earth turns around. *Page 6.*

policeman – sap

policeman (pə lēs′ mən) – A man in the government wo makes sure people obey the laws. *Page 25.*

pomegranate (pä′ mə gra nət) – A reddish fruit with many seeds and a sweet red juice. *Page 86.*

population (pä pyə lā′ shən) – The number of people in a community or place. *Page 35.*

port – 1. A good place along a sea for ships to stop. 2. A town or city at the place where ships often stop. *Page 133.*

potash – A material used to make fertilizer, soap, and many other things. *Page 262.*

pottery – Pots, dishes, and vases, made from clay and baked hard. *Page 81.*

priest (prēst′) – A special servant of God in Old Testament times. A priest talked to God for the people and offered sacrifices for their sins. *Pages 97 and 183.*

profit (prä fət) – The money a person gains from the things he sells after the expenses are taken off. *Page 145.*

publican (pə′ bli kən) – A tax collector for the Roman rulers. *Page 117.*

public square – An open space in a city with trees, bushes, and flowers for everyone to enjoy. *Page 213.*

pure – Without any sin. *Page 160.*

pyramid (pir′ ə mid) – A building with a pointed top and four sides each in the shape of a triangle. *Page 63.*

Q

Quakers (kwā′ kərz) – A religious group of people who dressed in plain clothes and would not fight. Many Quakers settled in Pennsylvania. *Page 207.*

quarry (kwȯr′ ē) – A place where stone is dug out for use in building things. *Page 64.*

R

rabbi (ra′ bī) – A Jewish teacher. *Page 116.*

race – People in a group who have the same color of skin and look much alike in other ways. *Page 30.*

raisin (rā′ zən) – A sweet dried grape. *Page 132.*

raw material – A natural resource or other material used for manufacturing. *Page 144.*

record (re′ kərd) – Anything written down and kept for the future. *Page 62.*

rent – The pay a person must give for using something belonging to another person. *Page 175.*

reservoir (re′ zə vwȯr) A place where water is stored for later use. *Page 250.*

respect (ri spekt′) – 1. Honor and obedience to someone who has the right to rule. 2. To be kind and courteous to others. *Page 25.*

rural (rür əl) **community** – A community where people do not usually live very close together: communities out in the country are rural communities. *Page 22.*

S

sackcloth – A coarse cloth usually made from goat's hair in Bible times. *Page 80.*

sacrifice (sa′ krə fīs) – An offering made to God. *Page 97.*

Sahara (sə har′ə) – A large desert in North Africa. The Sahara is the largest desert in the world. *Page 45.*

sandal – A kind of shoe made by tying a sole onto the foot with straps. *Page 123.*

sap – A sticky juice from trees.

Rubber, tar, and paint are some of the things made from sap. *Page 15.*

scale of miles – A line on most maps that helps a person find the number of miles between places. *Page 42.*

scribe – A person who spends his time copying writings. *Page 119.*

scrip – A skin bag where a shepherd carried his food. *Page 132.*

scrolls – Rolls of papyrus, animal skins, or other material which used to be used for writing on. *Page 119.*

sea breezes – Breezes blowing from the sea to the land. *Page 135.*

sea level – The level of the earth's oceans and largest seas. *Page 105.*

seas – Small bodies of water on God's earth; God's earth has many seas. *Page 6.*

shadoof (shə düf´) – A lever and bucket device used to lift water up into irrigation ditches. *Page 55.*

Shema (shə mä´) – A part from the Law of Moses that begins with, "Hear O Israel; the LORD our God is one LORD." The whole Shema had these verses: Deuteronomy 6:4-9; 11:12-21; Numbers 15:37-41. The Shema gives the most important beliefs of the Jews. *Pages 119.*

silt – Small pieces of soil or sand carried by moving water. *Page 46.*

Sinai (sī´ nī) – A piece of desert land north of the Red Sea and east of Egypt. *Page 69.*

slave – A person belonging to someone else. A slave is forced to obey his owner. *Page 51.*

slum – A crowded, dirty part of a city where the poorest people live. *Page 234.*

source (sōrs) – The beginning of a stream or river. *Pages 45 and 102.*

Southern Hemisphere – The half of the earth from the South Pole to the equator. *Page 38.*

South Pole – The point farther south than any other place on God's earth. *Page 6.*

sphere (sfir´) – Something in the shape of a ball. *Page 5.*

sphinx (sfingks´) – An image with the head of a man and the body of a lion. *Page 66.*

spices – Seasonings for food such as pepper, cinnamon, cloves, ginger, and nutmeg. *Page 200.*

squaw – An American Indian woman or wife. *Page 205.*

stadium (stā´ de əm) – A special place where games are played for people to watch. *Page 153.*

stake – A stick or small post pointed at one end for driving into the ground. *Page 80.*

staves – Narrow strips of wood or iron placed side by side to make a barrel or vessel. *Page 229.*

steel – A strong metal made from iron. *Page 13.*

steward (stü´ ərd) – A person who takes care of things that belong to another person. *Page 15.*

stewardship (stü´ ərd ship) – The care a steward gives to the things he is keeping for another person. *Page 15.*

suburb – A small community that grows up beside a city. *Page 266.*

succotash (sə´ kə tash) – Corn and lima beans cooked together. *Page 216.*

sugar cane – A tall plant with flat leaves. Sugar is made from sugar cane. *Page 230.*

Supreme Court (sə prēm´ kȯrt) – Court where the hardest problems in our country are judged. *Page 93.*

survey (sər vā´) – To measure off pieces of land and mark the borders. *Page 212.*

symbol – vineyard

symbol (sim′ bəl) – A mark or drawing that stands for some real thing. *Page 41.*

synagogue (si′ nə gäg) – A place used by the Jews for worship on Sabbath days and for a school on other days. *Page 118.*

swab – A large piece of cloth used to fight fires. *Page 231.*

T

tabernacle (ta′ bər na kəl) – A special tent the Hebrews built exactly like God told them to make it and where God met with them. *Page 97.*

tamarisk (ta′ mə risk) **tree** – A kind of tree that usually grows in desert soil. *Page 256.*

taskmaster – A person who forces others to do hard work. *Page 51.*

tax – The money people must pay to help run the government. *Pages 34 and 59.*

temple – A stone building where the Jews went to make sacrifices and worship God. The temple took the place of the tabernacle tent after the Jews settled in the land of Palestine. *Page 129.*

terrace (ter′ əs) – A strip of level land formed on a hillside to keep erosion from taking place. *Page 132.*

the world – See world, the. *Page 208.*

tithe (tīth) – One part out of ten parts of everything a person owns. *Page 129.*

toll – Money paid for the use of something. *Page 142.*

top soil – The top layer of soil where most plants grow. *Page 11.*

torture (tȯr chər) – To cause a person to suffer great pain. *Page 188.*

tram – A streetcar. *Page 194.*

tramway – A track for moving things. *Page 141.*

transportation (trans pər tā′ shən) – Ways of carrying people and things from one place to another. *Page 30.*

treaty – An agreement between two different governments. *Page 217.*

triangle of trade – The triangle-shaped path of the merchant ships from Philadelphia to the West Indies, to England and back to Philadelphia. *Page 230.*

tunic (tü nik) – A piece of clothing much like a shirt without sleeves. A tunic the Jews wore usually came a little below the knees. *Page 124.*

tunic-coat – A coat with long sleeves that a Jew wore over top of his sleeveless tunic. The tunic-coat the Jews wore usually reached to the ankles. *Page 124.*

turban (tər′ bən) – A piece of cloth tied around the head. Jewish men wore turbans. *Page 124.*

U–V

unclean animals – The kinds of animals God told the Hebrews not to eat. *Page 86.*

unleavened (ən le′ vənd) **bread** – Flat loaves of bread made without any yeast. *Page 130.*

urban (ər′ bən) **community** – A community where people live closely together; towns and cities are urban communities. *Page 22.*

valley – A flat plain between hills. *Page 104.*

vat – A large tank for oil or other liquids. *Page 132.*

veil (vāl) – A flowing piece of cloth worn by Jewish women to cover their heads. *Page 104.*

venison (ve′ nə sən) – Deer meat. *Page 216.*

vineyard (vin′ yərd) – A place planted with grape-vines. *Page 132.*

W

wampum (wäm′ pəm) – Beads made from seashells used by the American Indians. *Page 217.*

warehouse – Place where goods are stored. *Page 179.*

wares – Goods to be sold. *Page 111.*

wave offering – A kind of sacrifice where the offering was waved over the altar. *Page 130.*

Western Hemisphere – A half of the earth with the continents of North America and South America. *Page 37.*

whiskey (hwis′ kē) – A strong drink made from grain or potatoes. Whiskey can make a person become drunk. *Page 232.*

wick – A piece of twisted thread placed into the oil of a lamp for lighting. *Page 81.*

winnow (wi′ nō) – To remove the chaff from the grain by blowing the chaff away. *Page 60.*

witness – A person who tells others what he knows to be true. *Page 27.*

world – The community of unsaved people where Christians often live. Christians witness to the world and do not copy worldly customs. *Page 208.*

Index

The index is on the next 6 pages. It helps you to find the pages in your textbook that tell about people, places, and things. These subjects are in alphabetical order, just as they were in the glossary.

Sometimes you will want to find out about certain things. Suppose you want to learn about a *bema*? Find the letter "B" in the index. Find the word *bema* among the "B" words. On what page in your book can you read about a *bema*?

In the index, the last name of a person is always listed first. If you want to find out about William Penn, look for the name *Penn* under "P." Where can you read about him? What name will you look for to find the place to read about Ellert Jans?

Suppose you want to read about a place called Philadelphia. Turn to the index and find the "P" words. Find Philadelphia. Where in your book can you read about Philadelphia?

As you study *Living Together on God's Earth*, you may want to find out all you can about a certain subject. Or maybe your teacher will ask you to make a report on a subject. This index will be a big help in finding the pages with the information you want.

A

acropolis, 151, 152 *(picture)*
Adam and Eve, 18
Adriatic Sea, 161 *(map)*
Aegean Sea, 134 *(map)*, 135-136
Africa, 44 *(map)*, 74-75
agora, 149 *(picture)*
Alkmaar, 194, 195 *(picture)*
almshouses, 232
Amalekites, 91
Amstel River, 173-175, 178 *(picture)*
Amsterdam, 164 *(map)*, 171, 173-198
Anabaptists, 186-192, 223

Aphrodite, 151-152
Araba, 253
Arabs, 266-267
Asia, 74-75
Asia Minor, 161 *(map)*
Athens, 136 *(picture)*, 137

B

baptism, 182-183, 185-187
bar mitzvah, 118-119
Beersheba, 249, 257 *(picture)*, 261
bema, 156, 157 *(picture)*
Bering Strait, 203 *(map)*
Bible printing and translation,

184, 185 *(picture)*, 226
Brethren Christians, 225-226

C

Canaan, 76, 89 *(map)*, 98-99, 100 *(map)*, 101-102 *(see* Palestine)
canals, 55, 142-143, 170-171, 173 *(picture)*, 179, 193, 196
caravan, 111
charter, 180-181, 209
Christian communities, 157-158
citrus fruits, 255-256
city gates, 110 *(picture)*, 111
city government, 24-25, 180-182
clean and unclean animals, 86, 129
climate, 28-30, 135, 253-255
clothing in Palestine, 124
Columbus, Christopher, 199, 200-202
construction, 35
copper, 14, 261
Corinth, 136-137, 139-162
customs, 28-33, 66, 72, 198

D

dairy farmers, 33
dead language, 243
Dead Sea, 104-106, 108, 245, 262
Dead Sea Scrolls, 241 *(picture)*, 242-243
Delaware Bay, 211 *(map)*
Delaware Indians, 203-205, 215-217
Delaware River 203, 211 *(map)*, 212
delta, 46, 165-166

dikes, 166, 167-168 *(pictures)*, 169-170, 196
direction finder, 39
Dock, Christopher, 226 *(picture)*, 227

E

East Indies, 199-200
Eastern Hemisphere, 37, 38 *(map)*, 74
Egypt, 44-78, 247
Elat, 245 *(map)*, 250 *(map)*, 151-252, 261-262
England, 207-209, 229-230
Ephesus, 161
equator, 38
erosion, 11, 132, 237-238, 256
eucalyptus trees, 246 *(picture)*, 247
Europe, 164 *(map)*, 165, 199, 202, 223

F

factories, 33, 197, 262-263
family, 18-21
family worship, 18
famines, 47-49
Fayum, 55, 59
Feasts of Israel, 130-131
flat maps, 38-39
flax, 60-61
flower bulbs, 194-195, 248
former rains, 254-255

G

Galilee, 105 *(map)*, 106, 131
Gentiles, 156-157
Germantown, 223-226, 234
Giza, 48 *(map)*, 63

globe, 6, 37-38
Greece, 134 *(map)*, 135-163
Greek language, 156
Greenland, 7
gristmill, 221
Gutenberg, Johannes, 185

H

Haifa, 245 *(map)*, 261-263, 265 *(picture)*, 266
Harvesting, 59
Hebrew language, 242-243, 259
Herod, 129
Hezekiah, 116
hieroglyphics, 62 *(picture)*
Hula Basin, 246 *(picture)*, 248
humus, 10
Holland, 165, *(see* Netherlands*)*

I

Ijsselmeer, 169 *(see* Lake Ijssel*)*
Indians, 201, 203-205, 215-217
Ionian Sea, 134 *(map)*, 135
irrigation, 55-56, 245, 253-255
Isthmian Games, 153-154, 160-161
isthmus, 136, 140-142
Israel, 237-268, *(See* Palestine*)*

J

Jacob, 47-48, 63
Jans, Ellert, 186 *(picture)*, 187-191
Jerusalem, 109-133, 240, 267-268
Jesus Christ, 100, 106, 120, 155-157, 173, 181, 183, 190, 227, 240 *(see* Messiah*)*

Jethro, 92
Jezreel, 259 *(picture)*
Joppa, 266 *(see* Yafo*)*
Jordan River, 102 *(picture)*, 103-106, 131, 247
Joseph, 47-49, 63
Judea, 105 *(map)*, 106
Judah, *(see* Judea*)*
judges, 89, 92-93, 97, 110-111

K

kibbutz, 257-260
klompen, 176 *(picture)*

L

Lake Hula, 102, 247
Lake Ijssel, 164 *(map)*, 168-169
Lake Kinneret, 247, 251, 257 *(see* Sea of Galilee*)*
Lake Victoria, 44 *(map)*, 45
large communities, 21-27
latchstring, 219-220
Latin language, 184-185
latter rains, 254-255
leben, 85
linen, 61, 220, 224
linsey-woolsey, 220
living language, 243

M

magistrates, 34
malaria, 247-248
manna, 84
manufacturing, 144-146, 197
map legend, 41
marketplaces, 112-115, 149, 243
marriage, 19
martyrs, 186-187, 198
Mediterranean Sea, 7, 45,

74 *(map)*, 106, 134-136
Menno Simons, 223 *(picture)*
Mennonites, 223-226
Messiah, 133, 155-156, 240, 268
mezuzah, 120-121
Midian, 48 *(map)*, 69
minerals, 261-263
mines, 14
moat, 176 *(picture)*
moneychangers, 129
Moses, 68-72, 76, 80, 94, 97
moshav, 260
mosquitoes, 247-248
Mount Carmel, 265
Mount Hermon, 101-103
mummies, 63, 64 *(picture)*

N

Nabateans, 249
National Water Carrier, 250 *(picture)*, 251
natural resources, 9-15, 245-263
Negev, 249 *(picture)*, 250-254, 263
Netherlands, 164 *(map)*, 165-198, 199, 223
New World, 200 *(map)*, 201
Nile River, 44 *(map)*, 45-46, 50-58, 65, 70-71
Noah, 36
nomads, 77-78, 80-91, 131, 203
nonresistant Christians, 181, 215, 223, 228, 232
North America *(map)*, 43
North Pole, 6, 7, 38
North Sea, 164-165, 169
North Sea Canal, 164 *(map)*, 196
Northern Hemisphere, 38 *(map)*

O

oasis, 55, 79-80, 84
obedience to governments, 24-25, 34
oil, oil wells, 12 *(picture)*, 261-262
olives, olive oil, 106, 132
Old World, 200 *(map)*, 201

P

Palestine, 100 *(map)*, 101-133
palisades, 204 *(picture)*, 205
paper making in America, 224-225
papyrus, 54 *(picture)*, 62
Passover, 72, 130
Pastorius, Francis, 224
Paul, 155-162
peninsula, 76, 135
Penn, William, 207-209, 212, 214, 217
Pennsylvania, 209, 227-228, 229
pharoah, 51, 58. 62-64, 65-66
Philadelphia, 207-235
Philistines, 77, 101
phosphate, 262-263
phylactory, 120 *(picture)*
pipelines, 250-251
Pithom, 67
polders, 169, 170 *(picture)*, 171
policemen, 25
Pool of Siloam, 116
population, 35
Poseidon, 153-154
potash, 262-263
priests, 97, 130, 183, 188
punishments for lawbreaking, 96-97
pyramids, 63 *(picture)*, 64

Q

Quakers, 207-232
quarry, 12 *(picture)*, 64

R

Ra (Egyptian sun-god), 65
race, 30, 32
Red Sea, 76-77, 251
Rephidim, 79-80
reservoirs, 250-251
Rhine River, 196
Rittenhouse, William, 224-225
roads, 147, 148 *(picture)*, 149, 221 *(picture)*
Rome, 140, 149
Roman Catholic Church, 182-184, 186, 191-192
rural communities, 22, 33

S

Sabbath day, 123, 125-128, 155, 238-239, 268
sacrifices, 97
Sahara, 44 *(map)*, 45, 48
Samaria, 105 *(map)*, 106
Sauer, Christopher, 225-226
scale of miles, 42
Schuylkill River, 211 *(map)*, 212
sea breezes, 135
sea level, 104, 165-166, 173
Sea of Chinnereth, 102-103, *(see Sea of Galilee and Lake Kinneret)*
Sea of Galilee, 101-103
separation from evil, 34
shadoof, 55, 56 *(picture)*
Shema, 119-120
Sinai, 48 *(map)*, 69, 74-78, 93-94
Skippack River, 226

slaves, slavery, 51-52, 64, 127, 139-141
soil, 10, 46, 245, 248
Solomon, 261
South Pole, 6, 7, 38
Southern Hemisphere, 38 *(map)*
Spain, 200 *(map)*, 201
sphere, 5
sphinx, 66 *(picture)*, 68 *(picture)*
Spice Islands, 200
stadium, 153 *(picture)*
steel, 13
stewards, stewardship, 15
suburb, 266-267
Supreme Court, 92 *(picture)*, 93
synagogues, 118-120, 125-126

T

tabernacle, 97-99
tamarisk trees, 256
tax, 34, 59, 117, 180
tax collectors, 117
Tel Aviv, 266-267
Temple, 129-130
Ten commandments, 94-95
terpen, 174
terraces, 132, 238 *(picture)*
Thebes, 58
Timna, 261, 262 *(picture)*
tithes, 129
Titus, 239
tombs in Egypt, 63-64
topsoil, 11, 46, 237
Townsend, Richard, 221
transportation, 29-30
treaty, 217, 232
triangle of trade, 229 *(map)*, 230
tribes of Israel, 88, 89 *(map)*
Turks, 199-200

U
urban communities, 22

V
Vespucci, Amerigo, 201-202

W
wampum, 217 *(picture)*
West Indies, 200 *(map)*, 201
Western Hemisphere, 37 *(map)*, 38
Western Wall, 266 *(picture)*, 268
William of Orange, 192
windmills, 13 *(picture)*, 176, 177 *(picture)*
witnessing, 27, 198, 205, 235, 268

Y
Yafo, 266-267

Z
Zuider Zee, 168-169, 173-174, 178, 196

Scripture Index

Here is a list of all the Bible verses in this book. There are verses from most of the books of the Bible. The Bible books are listed below. Under the name of each book you will find a list of references used in this book. Beside each reference is the page where you can find it. Page numbers with a star (*) beside them mean that the verse is only mentioned in the "Show Your Knowledge" or "Share Your Knowledge" questions.

GENESIS
1:2a, p.6
1:9, p.6
1:11a, p.10
1:28b, p.245
2:18-20, p.17
2:21-24, p.18
2:24, pp.18, 19
3:17, 18, p.12*
12:10, p.49*
13:10, 11, p.104
17:8a, p.101
19:24, 25, p.36*
21:14, p.84*
21:33a, p.256
26:19, 23, p.252*
28:10, p.252*
41:48a, p.48
41:49, p.61*
45:5b, p.49
47:24b, p.58
48:1, p.92*
49:3-27, pp.91*, 92*
50:2, 3a, p.63
50:24b, 25b, 26, p.63

EXODUS
1:7, p.51
1:9, p.52*
1:11b, p.51
1:12, p.52*
1:14a, p.52
2:3, p.57*
3:8, p.87*
3:8b, pp.105, 238

12:12b, p.70
12:26, 27a, p.72
13:17b, p.77
14:21, 22a, p.76
15:22-25, 27, p.83*
16:15b, 16a, p.84
16:31b, p.84
18:17b, 18b, p.92
19:2, p.78*
20:3-17, p.94
20:14, p.152
22:26, 27, p.125*
23:2, p.33
23:10, 11, p.133*
25:8, 22a, p.97
31:15, p.123
35:3, p.126
40:38a, p.97

LEVITICUS
11:3, p.86
11:45b, p.66
19:36b, p.114
25:3-5, p.238
25:20, 21, p.240*
26:33b-34, p.239

NUMBERS
9:11b, p.130
9:17, p.98
10:12a, p.75
11:8a, p.84
26:55, p.88
34:5b, p.45

DEUTERONOMY
3:17b, p.101
5:7-21, p.94
6:4, 5, p.119
6:6, 7, pp.20, 23*, 261*
6:8, p.120
6:9, p.120
6:22a, p.50
8:7, 8, 9a, p.87*
8:7-9a, p.238
8:9b, p. 261
11:10, p.57*
11:10, 11, p.247
11:10-12, p.248*
11:12, p.238
11:12, 14, p.256*
11:26, 27a, 28a, p.126
15:7, 8a, p.221
15:12, p.127
15:12-14, p.222*
15:13, 14, p.129*
16:18a, p.110
20:19b, p.15
21:18-21, p.111*
22:5a, p.124
22:8, p.122
25:15b, p.114
33:19b, p.265

JOSHUA
11:5, p.248*
15:2, p.107*
15:12, p.8*, p.107*
19:1, 2, p.252*

288

JUDGES
18:9, 10, p.248*

2 SAMUEL
7:6b, p.98
7:23a, p.79

1 KINGS
19:1-3, p.252*

2 KINGS
3:11, p.91*
20:20b, p.116

1 CHRONICLES
29:11, 12, p.264

2 CHRONICLES
2:16, p.269*
26:10a, p.249
26:15a, p.110

EZRA
6:1, p.121*
7:6, p.121*

NEHEMIAH
3:1, 3, 28, p.115*
11:27b, p.249
13:19, p.125*

JOB
5:10, p.10
26:7, p.5
28:2, p.13
38:8a, 11, p.166

PSALMS
24:1a, p.15
37:3, p.216
50:10, p.16*
78:1-6, p.21
89:11, p.5
89:12, p.6
104:16a, p.15
104:24, p.14
104:24b, p.263
107:8, p.197
107:23, p.145
115:5-7, p.66
115:16, p.6
122:3, p.109

PROVERBS
3:33, p.210*
11:10a, p.207
11:11, pp.36, 95, 180
12:20, p.218*
16:7, p.215
22:7, 9, p.180*
25:25, p.199
28:21a, p.208

ECCLESIASTES
3:20, p.10
9:18b, p.27

SONG OF SOLOMON
2:11b, p.254

ISAIAH
30:24, p.61*
40:22, p.8*
42:10, p.165
42:15, p.237
43:21a, p.18
44:15, p.16*

JEREMIAH
5:22, p.168*
10:1-3, p.31*
10:12a, p.5
17:19b, 20a, p.110
36:2, p.121*
49:19a, p.106

EZEKIEL
39:21a, p.205

JONAH
1:3a, p.266

ZECHARIAH
10:1, p.255

MALACHI
3:10a, p.129

MATTHEW
5:13, p.27
5:16, p.235
5:41, p.133*
5:44, p.181
10:22, p.186
10:23a, p.202
20:2, p.149
22:35-40, p.96*

MARK
12:17, p.118*
16:16a, pp.182, 223

LUKE
5:1, p.104*
5:27, p.118*
6:31, p.26
6:38, p.115*
7:32, p.114
8:39, p.236*
10:35, p.150*
19:45, 46, p.131*
22:19b, p.223

JOHN
1:41, p.159*
2:13-16, p.131*
3:16 (Latin), p.184
4:4, 5, p.107*
4:25, 26, p.159*
12:3-5, p.150*

ACTS
4:12b, p.268
5:29b, p.25
7:22, p.69
8:1, 4, p.202*
14:17, p.12*
16:1, p.138*
17, p.137
17:26a, p.32
18:1-3, p.143*
18:4, p.150*
18:6b, p.156
18:8b, p.139
18:11b, p.160
18:13, 15b, p.157
20:2, p.135
22:3, p.121*
22:21, p.159

ROMANS
3:18b, p.232
3:23a, p.27
12:2a, p.208
12:18, p.17

12:18b, p.228
12:21, p.192
13:1b, p.24
13:2a, p.25
13:3, p.27*
13:4b, P.228
13:6, p.34
14;19b, p.232

1 CORINTHIANS
4:2, p.15
9:24b, p.154
9:25, p.155*
9:25b, p.161

2 CORINTHIANS
6:17a, p.34

EPHESIANS
4;28, p.198*

PHILIPPIANS
2:3, p.210*
3:14, p.161

COLOSSIANS
3:18-20, 19

1 TIMOTHY
2:1, 2, p.34
2:5, p.183
6:7, p.64*

2 TIMOTHY
3:12, pp.173, 193*

TITUS
3:1, p.34

HEBREWS
12:14, p.233*
12:14a, p.217
13:5b, p.199

JAMES
1:12, p.154
5:7b, p.256*

1 PETER
2:17, p.34

1 JOHN
2:3, P.227*
2:15, p.163*

REVELATION
21:25, p.112*

ACKNOWLEDGMENTS:

Artists: David Miller, Treda Beachy, Anna M. Pellman, and others.
Cover Designer: Elmore Byler.